DATE DUE	
JUN 2 1 2003	
MAR 0 8 2004	
4/8/04	
MAR 8 - 2006	
APR 2 1 2007	
MAR 2 4 2008	

DEMCO, INC. 38-2931

DOCUMENTARY HISTORY OF THE MODERN CIVIL RIGHTS MOVEMENT

DOCUMENTARY HISTORY OF THE MODERN CIVIL RIGHTS MOVEMENT

Edited by

PETER B. LEVY

GREENWOOD PRESS

New York • Westport, Connecticut • London

Library of Congress Cataloging-in-Publication Data

Documentary history of the modern civil rights movement / edited by
  Peter B. Levy.
    p. cm.
  Includes bibliographical references and index.
  ISBN 0-313-27233-6 (alk. paper)
    1. Afro-Americans—Civil rights—History—20th century—Sources.
  2. Civil rights movements—United States—History—20th century—
  Sources. 3. United States—Race relations—Sources.   I. Levy,
  Peter B.
  E185.61.D64   1992
  323.1'196073—dc20   91-27240

British Library Cataloguing in Publication Data is available.

A paperback text edition is available from the Praeger Publishers imprint
of Greenwood Publishing Group, Inc. under the title *Let Freedom Ring*
(ISBN 0-275-93434-9).

Library of Congress Catalog Card Number: 91-27240
ISBN: 0-313-27233-6

First published in 1992

Greenwood Press, 88 Post Road West, Westport, CT 06881
An imprint of Greenwood Publishing Group, Inc.

Printed in the United States of America

The paper used in this book complies with the
Permanent Paper Standard issued by the National
Information Standards Organization (Z39.48-1984).

10 9 8 7 6 5 4 3 2 1

COPYRIGHT ACKNOWLEDGMENTS

Southern Regional Council, "The Civil Rights Crisis: A Synopsis of Recent Developments, April 1963-June 29, 1963." Reprinted by permission of the Southern Regional Council.

"Letter to Dr. King," *New Leader*, Vol. XLVI, no. 13 (June 24, 1963), p. 5. Reprinted by permission of the publisher, the American Labor Conference on International Affairs, Inc.

John Lewis, "Address at the March on Washington" [draft], August 28, 1963. Reprinted by permission of the author.

Eugene Patterson, "A Flower for the Graves," *Atlanta Constitution*, September 16, 1963, p. 14. Reprinted by permission of the *Atlanta Constitution*.

Anne Moody, *Coming of Age in Mississippi*. Copyright © by Anne Moody. Used by permission of Doubleday, a division of Bantam Doubleday Dell Publishing Group, Inc.

E. W. Steptoe, "Affidavit"; Aaron Henry, "Affidavit"; and June Johnson, "Affidavit," in *Mississippi Black Paper*, compiled by COFO. Random House, 1965, pp. 3, 7, and 23-24. Reprinted by permission of Random House.

Sally Belfrage, *Freedom Summer*. Copyright © 1965. Reprinted by permission of the publisher, the University of Virginia Press and Curtis Brown, Ltd.

"Testimony of Fannie Lou Hamer Before the Credentials Committee of the Democratic National Convention," August 22, 1964, Atlantic City, New Jersey. Reprinted by permission of the Democratic National Committee.

Lawrence Guyot and Mike Thelwell, "Toward Independent Political Power," *Freedomways*, Vol. 6, no. 3 (Summer 1963), pp. 246-254. Reprinted by permission of Mike Thelwell.

Amelia Platts Boynton, *Bridge Across Jordan: The Story of the Civil Rights Struggle in Selma*. Carlton Press, 1979, pp. 138-140. Reprinted by permission of author.

"The Stench of Freedom" by Ralph Featherstone. Copyright © 1965. From *The Negro History Bulletin*, Vol. 28, no. 6 (March 1965), p. 130. Reprinted by permission of the publisher, the Association for the Study of Afro-American Life and History.

Sheyann Webb, *Selma, Lord, Selma: Girlhood Memories of the Civil Rights Days*. University of Alabama Press, 1980, pp. 92-99. Reprinted by permission of The University of Alabama Press.

Daniel Berrigan, "Selma and Sharpeville," *Commonweal* ©, April 9, 1965, pp. 71-75. Reprinted by permission of Commonweal.

Bayard Rustin, "From Protest to Politics," *Commentary*, Vol. XXXIX, no. 2 (February 1965), pp. 21-23. Reprinted by permission of Walter Naegle, Executor, Estate of Bayard Rustin.

Staughton Lynd, "Coalition Politics or Nonviolent Revolution?" *Liberation*, Vol. X, no. 4, pp. 18-21. Reprinted by permission of the author.

James Farmer, *Freedom When?* Random House, 1965, pp. 25-27, 42-47, and 49. Reprinted by permission of Random House.

Malcolm X, "Address to a Meeting in New York, 1964." Reprinted by permission of Pathfinder Press. Copyright © 1965 by Betty Shabazz and Merit Publishers.

Julius Lester, "The Angry Children of Malcolm X," *Sing Out*, Vol. 17 (Oct.-Nov. 1966), pp. 20-25. Reprinted by permission of Julius Lester.

Stokely Carmichael (Kwame Ture), "What We Want," from *New York Review of Books*, September 26, 1966. Reprinted by permission of the author.

"State/Meant," from *Home: Social Essays* by LeRoi Jones (Amiri Baraka). Copyright © 1965, 1966 by the author. Reprinted by permission of William Morrow & Co. and by Sterling Lord Literistic, Inc.

In memory of my mother, Phyllis Kulick Levy
and to my father, Allan Levy

CONTENTS

Civil Rights Act
of 1964

ACKNOWLEDGMENTS

This book bears only my name on the title page. Yet, it is truly the result of a collective effort, having benefited enormously from the constructive criticism and moral and logistical support of many people and institutions. By encouraging me to develop a course on the modern civil rights movement, Jan Lewis and Clement Price of Rutgers University–Newark, provided the foundation out of which this book grew in the first place. Simply by using many of the documents that I had compiled, Clem, in particular, without even knowing it, motivated me to transform some sloppy xeroxes, bunched together in the reserve reading room of the library, into a publishable manuscript. By sharing their insights on the civil rights movement during a "Retrospective" at Rutgers–Newark and/or at a panel discussion on ways to teach the history of the movement at the 1989 conference of the Organization of American Historians, David Garrow, Clayborne Carson, J. Mills Thornton, Don Miller, Dorothy Cotton, Cheryl Greenberg, and Martha Norman sharpened my understanding of the movement and encouraged me to push on with my book. My friends and colleagues at Columbia University, Rutgers University–Newark, and York College helped me in innumerable ways, but most importantly through hallway and luncheon chats that kept my spirits up. In particular let me thank Tim Gilfoyle, Myra Sletson, Richard Giardano, Mary Curtin, Barbara Tischler, Tim Coogen, Colin Davis, Abigail Mellen, Roger Whitney, Phil Avillo, Mel Kublicki, and Chip Miller. Dean William

DeMeester and my students of the civil rights movement and race relations courses at Rutgers and York also deserve credit and thanks. The readers and editors at Greenwood Press have been extremely helpful and a delight to work with. Cynthia Harris has helped me craft a much better work than I otherwise would have done on my own ever since I approached her with my initial proposal. Maureen Melino aided me in the arduous task of obtaining copyright permissions. And Penny Sippel has given her all in the final stages of production. Let me also thank the New Jersey Department of Higher Education and York College for the financial support they have given, which allowed me to start and complete the book. Finally, let me thank my family: my children Jessica and Brian, for *not* spilling their juice on my computer discs or scattering my manuscript all over the floor, and my wife, Diane Krejsa, who helps put a roof over our heads, food on the table, and love in our family, and whose own drive and talents, as a mother and an attorney, serve as an inspiration to all who know her, especially me.

ABBREVIATIONS

ACMHR	Alabama Christian Movement for Human Rights
ADA	Americans for Democratic Action
AFL-CIO	American Federation of Labor and Congress of Industrial Organization
A&T	North Carolina Agricultural and Technical College (Greensboro)
CIO	Congress of Industrial Organizations
COFO	Council of Federated Organizations
CORE	Congress of Racial Equality
DRUM	Dodge Revolutionary Union Movement
FBI	Federal Bureau of Investigation
IWW	Industrial Workers of the World
KKK	Ku Klux Klan
MFDP	Mississippi Freedom Democratic Party
MIA	Montgomery Improvement Association
NAACP	National Association for the Advancement of Colored People
NAG	Nonviolent Action Group
PWA	Public Works Administration
SCLC	Southern Christian Leadership Conference

SDS	Students for a Democratic Society
SNCC	Student Nonviolent Coordinating Committee
UAW	United Automobile Workers
UPWA	United Packinghouse Workers Association
WPA	Work Projects Administration
WPC	Women's Political Council

INTRODUCTION

One day the South will recognize its real heroes. They will be the
James Merediths, courageously and with a majestic sense of purpose
facing jeering and hostile mobs . . . they will be old, oppressed,
battered Negro women, symbolized in a 72-year-old woman of
Montgomery, Alabama, who rose up with a sense of dignity and
with her people decided not to ride the segregated buses, and responded to one who inquired about the tiredness with ungrammatical
profundity: "My feet is tired, but my soul is rested." . . . One day
the South will know that . . . they were in reality standing up for the
best in the American dream and the most sacred values in our Judeo-
Christian heritage. . . .
> —Martin Luther King, Jr., "Letter from Birmingham Jail"

This book traces a heroic struggle for freedom in America, the modern
civil rights movement. It takes as its major premise Martin Luther King,
Jr.'s pronouncement that the movement had a vast array of heroes, men
and women, old and young, well-known and unknown, and that the words
of these individuals, even when ungrammatical, counted. This book also
seeks to display the veracity of King's argument that the modern civil
rights movement stood up for the American dream and the most sacred
values of western culture, that it sought to turn the ideals of the Declaration of Independence and Christian morality into a reality for all of

America's citizens. The book's format is drawn from the closing line of King's "I Have a Dream" speech. By highlighting the writings and speeches of the civil rights activists themselves, with only a minimum of editorial commentary, I seek to vividly convey the sounds or music of a people in the process of defining the meaning of freedom. In other words, I hope to "Let Freedom Ring," from cover to cover of this book. Words were not immaterial to the movement; the pieces that follow were not the mere meditations of lonely intellectuals. Rather they were the products of men and women in the midst of a struggle for justice and equality. Indeed, I am convinced that the reader will develop a fuller understanding and appreciation for the modern civil rights movement, in particular, and the universal struggle for freedom, in general, by examining the words of civil rights activists, themselves, than they could hope to achieve by reading some of the leading secondary studies of the movement.

While we owe a great debt to the many recent studies of the civil rights movement, they cannot serve as a substitute for direct contact with the historical actors. By their very nature, secondary works turn the subjects of history into objects. Active men and women become passive entities; poignant speeches and writings are transformed into illustrations of "deeper" interpretations. Many recent studies even undercut their own argument that ordinary folk were not being acted upon by the traditional subjects of history, rather, that they were the "movers and shakers." They weaken the claim that the James Merediths and Fannie Lou Hamers of America were the real freedom fighters of the period and that America's leaders, from Eisenhower to Kennedy, reacted to their lead, not the other way around.

This is not to devalue the worth of many of the fine studies of the civil rights years. My selection of documents and contextual remarks draw heavily on a growing body of literature written by academics and independent scholars. My views of Martin Luther King, Jr., have been greatly influenced by the research and writings of David Garrow and Taylor Branch. My sense of the battle to desegregate southern schools has benefited from my reading of Richard Kluger's *Simple Justice.* Although this work can be read on its own, as an account of the civil rights movement, it is hoped that it will be used in conjunction with secondary sources and additional primary sources.

Besides allowing the subjects of history to speak for themselves, this book serves another purpose. I hope to encourage readers to interpret the past through their own eyes, to begin to play the role of historians themselves. I seek to prompt readers to inquire as to the meaning of the civil rights movement and to draw their own conclusions and ask their own set of questions. What were its goals? Was it an attempt to prod the country to live up to its ideals? Was it a struggle for power between an emergent group and others who had already "made it"? Was the movement merely the product of outside agitators who disrupted previously calm and tranquil locales, as white Southerners often claimed? And what lessons did the movement leave behind?

I also hope that this book coaxes those who are well read on the civil rights movement to re-examine it afresh, to go back to some of the classic and not-so-classic documents with an eye toward testing the standard interpretations of the movement, including those that have become part of American mythology. For instance, it is common to treat Martin Luther King, Jr., as a moderate figure, to emphasize his peaceful method and dream of a color-blind society. This view of King is prominent among those who compare him to the Student Nonviolent Coordinating Committee (SNCC) and Malcolm X. Yet, a re-reading of King's "Letter from Birmingham Jail," "Beyond Vietnam," and "Where Do We Go from Here?" may produce a different interpretation, one that emphasizes his commitment to direct action and belief that American society needed to be radically altered if his dream was to come true.

This documentary collection, like others before it, most of which are now out of print, contains many of the classical speeches and writings of the era, such as Martin Luther King, Jr.'s "I Have a Dream" speech. It also samples lesser-known pieces that grew out of campaigns for equality which took place in small towns scattered throughout the South, such as "Terrible" Terrell County (Georgia), Fayette County (Tennessee), and McComb (Mississippi).

Whereas women are invisible in many descriptions of the civil rights movement, this book places them on equal footing with men. Women were not incidental to the fight for equality. In spite of the fact that few received lasting public acclaim, from the moment that Rosa Parks refused to give up her seat on a Montgomery bus, they played a seminal role. They served as catalysts for change (such as Parks and Barbara Johns), as grass-roots organizers (such as Jo Ann Robinson and Amelia Platts Boynton), as front-line freedom fighters (such as Diane Nash and Fannie Lou Hamer), and as elder stateswomen (such as Ella Baker and Septima Clark).

Just as the movement operated within a certain context, so does this book. Like others, I have been constrained by space and time. Many more documents would have been included if possible. An early version of this work had twice as many selections and was nearly three times as long. In finalizing my selections I tried to follow several broad guidelines. First, since the movement was not a monolith, a variety of perspectives and participants have been included, from those of long-established organizations to those of unaffiliated individuals. Martin Luther King, Jr.'s words appear more often than any other individual, because I believe that he was the most prominent leader of the movement. Yet, overall, only about 5 percent of all the words are King's; the Student Nonviolent Coordinating Committee is the single most represented organization in the collection. Second, I sought to use pieces that were written by civil rights activists, themselves, rather than by reporters, and to use as many contemporary documents as possible, or, when I saw fit, recollections of those events. Third, I attempted to include documents that come from sources which are available at public libraries (at least research facilities). This allows the readings, themselves, to act as a rough reference guide. Last, I sought to use a mix of readings that would display the movement's quiet or introspective side and its militant or extroverted side. For example, Chapter Three, on the Montgomery bus boycott, contains an interview with Rosa Parks, which puts the reader back on the streets and an excerpt from Jo Ann Gibson Robinson's autobiography, which places the reader behind the scenes.

Above all else, I hope this book fills a void that I discovered when I first undertook to teach a course on the civil rights movement. Documentary readers exist, but they are out-of-date, out-of-print, and/or uneven. Many fine synthetic works are available, but they tend to be either too long and/or overly anaytical. In addition, they tend to lose some of the drama of the era. A handful of primary works are still in print, such as Martin Luther King, Jr.'s *Stride Toward Freedom* and James Forman's *The Making of Black Revolutionaries*. Yet they tend to be narrow in their focus and lack historical perspective. Hence, I set out to write an up-to-date, concise, reasonably comprehensive and vivid portrayal of the civil rights movement.

The following brief survey of the history of African-Americans is intended to provide a context for the documents that follow. A much fuller context can be gained by reading one of many general histories, some of which are listed in the bibliography.

In almost every way that the status of African-Americans can be measured, they were second-class citizens on the eve of the modern civil rights movement. At roughly mid-century, blacks had half the average annual income and twice as high an unemployment and poverty rate as whites. While U.S. scientific technology, consumer goods, colleges and universities, and suburban homes were the envy of the world, millions of African-Americans continued to battle the age-old problem of inadequate health care, education, and housing. (See Exhibits VI-XIII in the Appendix.) Even blacks who were not poor faced legal and extralegal barriers to full citizenship. In the South blacks faced a rigid set of Jim Crow laws that limited where they could go to school, eat, recreate, and much more. Only a minority of black Southerners enjoyed the right to vote and rarely were allowed to exercise it in cases that could affect policy. While blacks who migrated to the North or West, as blacks did in extraordinary numbers in the middle of the twentieth century (Exhibits III and IV in the Appendix), left behind Jim Crow laws and a society that openly espoused its belief in white supremacy, they found themselves living in segregated neighborhoods and limited by customs and codes in terms of employment and their public lives. Moreover, though African-Americans in the North could vote, and on occasion elected blacks to office, only rarely did whites face the prospect of having African-Americans set the laws and policies for majority white communities. In sum, in the midst of the Cold War, as American leaders touted the freedom of the West versus the tyranny of the East, African-Americans were not a free people. As President John F. Kennedy rhetorically observed in a nationally televised address in June 1963: ''Who among us [meaning whites] would be content to have the color of his skin changed and stand in his [meaning blacks] place?''

The modern civil rights movement clearly sought a revolution in race relations in America. It sought to dramatically alter the answer to President Kennedy's question, so that whites would be content to have their color changed and blacks would not feel that white skin color meant superiority. While blacks differed over the best way to achieve equality, and disagreed over the extent to which the American system would have to be changed in the process, they had relatively few differences over the ultimate goal.

Yet to define the goal of the civil rights movement somewhat begs the central historical question, which is: Why did the civil rights movement take place when it did and take the shape which it took? In other words, African-American inequality was not new in the 1950s, but the intensity of the movement to gain freedom was. How come?

The modern civil rights movement did not emerge out of thin air. Rather, it was built on a long history of struggle and sacrifice. More so than any other group of Americans, African-Americans have shared a history of struggle for freedom and human dignity, partly because, right from the start, white Americans sought to deny them from achieving either. Unlike all other migrants to North America, Africans did not come of their own free will. They were forcibly imported in order to meet the demand for cheap labor. As slaves, African-Americans faced physical cruelty and economic exploitation. They were inhumanly stripped of the profits of their toil and they were consciously dehumanized by their masters and the American system of law that defined them as property. True, the vast majority of whites both in the South and the North never owned slaves. Yet, except for a radical minority, most whites championed their constitution as a perfect document, despite the fact that it sanctioned slavery. Indeed, until the middle of the Civil War, even Abraham Lincoln felt more bound by the constitution's promise to protect property (in other words slaves) than he did by his ethics which told him that slavery was immoral.

Despite the inhumanity of the system of slavery, however, African-Americans managed to maintain some degree of freedom and human dignity. From the dreaded middle passage, from Africa to North America, to the years that followed emancipation, during which most blacks became sharecroppers, when a different kind of servitude emerged, African-Americans resisted virtually all attempts to dehumanize them. As Lawrence Levine has aptly written in *Black Culture and Consciousness* (New York: Oxford, 1977):

> Upon the hard rock of racial, social and economic exploitation and injustice black Americans forged and nurtured a culture and they formed and maintained kin networks, made love, raised and socialized children, built a religion and created a rich and expressive culture, in which they articulated their feelings and hopes and dreams. (xi)

While it is incorrect to argue that African-Americans simply got tired of being treated as second-class citizens, which is another way of saying that the civil rights movement was inevitable, it is equally incorrect to ignore the accumulated effect of years of struggle and sacrifice. Like bars of steel, African-Americans were tempered and hardened by their experiences. Black women, for instance, built up personal and collective reservoirs of strength upon which they could and did draw in the 1950s and 1960s.

Just as important, in the years that preceded the modern civil rights movement, African-Americans developed several prominent institutions which provided resources and an organizational foundation for the movement's rapid growth in the mid-1950s. The most important institution or group of institutions was the black church. Among other things, the church served as a training ground for charismatic leaders, enlisted a mass and decentralized membership, accumulated a reservoir of money and fund-raising experiences, and preached a doctrine or ideology that at its core contradicted the ideology of white supremacy. Other important institutions that blacks established included civil or human rights organizations, most notably the National Association for the Advancement of Colored People (NAACP), black colleges and universities, and the black press. Blacks also joined multiracial organizations, such as Congress of Industrial Organizations (CIO) unions, which in their own way aided the civil rights movement in the 1960s.

Moreover, in the years before the modern civil rights movement erupted on the streets, several structural or impersonal changes took place that set the stage for its emergence. First, millions of blacks moved from the rural South to the North, West, and urban South. In doing so they gained a degree of political power, or the space to join and form interracial organizations, and a greater access to the media than ever before. Second, the outbreak of the Cold War and the simultaneous decolonization of the Third World (most of which was nonwhite), opened up new opportunities to those who sought to challenge white supremacy. The latter inspired African-Americans to engage in their own struggle for freedom; the former prompted American leaders to support race reforms, so as to fend off the Soviet Union's charge that the United States was not really a land of freedom and equality. Third, the general affluence of the postwar years provided a hospitable climate for the civil rights movement. Whites and blacks had more money at hand with which to support various civil rights organizations. Affluence augmented the power of the mass media and increased the size of the college population (black and white). More subtly, the dynamism of capitalism in the decades that followed World War II, both the fluidity of people and capital, ran against the grain of traditional race relations, in which blacks had a very proscribed station in life.

Of course, many more structural factors could be mentioned and those that I have referred to above could easily be expanded. Yet to do so would distract the reader from the main focus of this book: the individuals who made the movement. Structural changes and the long-term development of civil rights organizations and allies certainly set the stage for the emergence of the modern civil rights movement. Yet, ultimately the movement depended on the actions of individuals who chose to make the most of the favorable conditions. Thousands of men and women like Rosa Parks, James Meredith, Elizabeth Eckford, and Robert Moses had to make the personal decision to risk their well-being, to initiate the struggle for equality. Civil rights leaders like Martin Luther King, Jr., had to ignore the counsel of many who told him that conditions, though improved, were not ripe enough for mass demonstrations in the streets. Indeed, one of the central legacies of the modern civil rights movement is that it reminded people of their own power to make history. They learned that freedom does not grow like a leaf on a tree but that it is the product of struggle. And even though the movement fell short of the ultimate goal of freedom for all, it left thousands of individuals with a newfound sense of their own power, of their ability to challenge things that had historically terrified them or stopped them from demanding their freedom in the past, and it left a record of this lesson, part of which follows.

Chapter One

ANTICIPATING THE MOVEMENT

The eight selections in this chapter present a sense of the mood of America on the eve of the modern civil rights movement. Taken together, they suggest that the nation was on the verge of a major shift in race relations. Even the pieces by Paul and Eslanda Robeson and W.E.B. DuBois, which implicitly reveal the damage that the onset of the Cold War did to the cause of civil rights, are optimistic in their tone. The essays and speeches also anticipate many of the central issues and debates of the civil rights movement.

1.1 Gunnar Myrdal's An American Dilemma, *published in 1944, is a case in point. Commissioned by the Russell Sage Foundation, Myrdal, a Swedish sociologist, produced one of the most comprehensive studies on race relations in America ever written. The book, and the wide praise and attention that it received, exhibited the intellectual receptivity toward reform in America which existed at the time. Myrdal's thesis, that the "Negro problem" in America was largely a moral one, that pitted the reality of racial discrimination against the American creed of equality for all, and that whites, not blacks, were at the center of this problem, would be repeated by many liberals, black and white, in the ensuing years. While nearly all blacks appreciated the sentiment of Myrdal's book, not all agreed with his thesis. A. Philip Randolph and John Henrik Clarke, as we will see, did not see the Negro problem in moral terms nor did they propose that reform depended on whites taking the lead.*

1.1 Gunnar Myrdal, *An American Dilemma: The Negro Problem and Modern Democracy* (New York: Harper & Row, 1944), pp. lxix-lxxv.

There is a "Negro problem" in the United States and most Americans are aware of it, although it assumes varying forms and intensity in different regions of the country and among diverse groups of the American people. Americans have to react to it, politically as citizens and, where there are Negroes present in the community, privately as neighbors.

To the great majority of white Americans the Negro problem has distinctly negative connotations. It suggests something difficult to settle and equally difficult to leave alone. It is embarrassing. It makes for moral uneasiness. The very presence of the Negro in America, his fate in this country through slavery, Civil War and Reconstruction, his recent career and his present status, his accommodation, his protest and his aspiration, in fact his entire biological, historical and social existence as a participant American represent to the ordinary white man in the North as well as in the South an anomaly in the very structure of American society. To many, this takes on the proportion of a menace—biological, economic, social, cultural, and, at times political. This anxiety may be mingled with a feeling of individual and collective guilt. A few see the problem as a challenge to statesmanship. To all it is a trouble.

These and many other mutually inconsistent attitudes are blended into none too logical a scheme which, in turn, may be quite inconsistent with the wider personal, moral, religious, and civic sentiments and ideas of the Americans. Now and then, even the least sophisticated individual becomes aware of his own confusion and the contradiction in his attitudes. . . . But most people, most of the time, suppress such threats to their moral integrity together with all of the confusion, the ambiguity, and inconsistency which lurks in the basement of man's soul. This, however, is rarely accomplished without mental strain. . . .

The strain is increased in democratic America by the freedom left open—even in the South, to a considerble extent—for the advocates of the Negro, his rights and welfare. All "pro-Negro" forces in American society, whether organized or not, and irrespective of their wide differences in both strategy and tactics, sense that this is the situation. They all work on the national conscience. They all seek to fix everybody's attention on the suppressed moral conflict. No wonder that they are often regarded as public nuisances. . . .

The American Negro problem is a problem in the heart of the American. It is there that the interracial tension has its focus. It is there that the decisive struggle goes on. This is the central view point of this treatise. Though our study includes economic, social, and political race relations, at bottom our problem is the moral dilemma of the American—the conflict between his moral valuations on various levels of consciousness and generality. The "American Dilemma," referred to in the title of this book, is the ever-raging conflict between, on the one hand, the valuations preserved on the general plane which we shall call the "American Creed," where the American thinks, talks, and acts under the influence of high national and Christian precepts, and, on the other hand, the valuations on specific planes of individual and group living, where personal and local interests; economic, social and sexual jealousies; considerations of community prestige and conformity; group prejudice against particular persons or types of people; and all sorts of miscellaneous wants, impulses, and habits dominate his outlook. . . .

The Negro problem in America would be of a different nature, and, indeed, would be simpler to handle scientifically, if the moral conflict raged only between valuations held by different persons and groups of persons. The essence of the moral situation is, however, that the conflicting valuations are also held by the same person. The moral struggle goes on within people and not only between them. . . . The unity of a culture consists in the fact that all valuations are mutually shared in some degree. We shall find that even a poor and uneducated white person in some isolated and backward rural region in the Deep South, who is violently prejudiced against the Negro and intent upon depriving him of civic rights and human independence, has also a whole compartment in his valuation sphere housing the entire American creed of liberty, equality, justice, and fair opportunity for everybody. He is actually also a good Christian and honestly devoted to the ideals of human brotherhood and the Golden Rule. And these more general valuations—more general in the sense that they refer to all human beings—are, to some extent, effective in shaping his behavior. Indeed, it would be impossible to understand why the Negro does not fare worse in some regions of America if it were not constantly kept in mind that behavior is the outcome of a compromise between valuations, among which the equalitarian ideal is one. At the other end, there are few liberals, even in New England, who have not a well-furnished compartment of race prejudice, even if it is usually suppressed from conscious attention. Even the American Negroes share in this community of valuations: they have eagerly imbibed the American Creed and the revolutionary Christian teaching of common brotherhood; under closer study, they usually reveal also that they hold something of the majority prejudice against their own characteristics. . . .

Although the Negro problem is a moral issue both to Negroes and to whites, we shall in this book have to give primary attention to what goes on in the minds of white Americans. To explain this direction of our interest a general conclusion from our study needs to be stated at this point. When the present investigator started his inquiry, his preconception was that it had to be focused on the Negro people and their peculiarities. This is understandable since, from a superficial view, Negro Americans, not only in physical appearance, but also in thoughts, feelings, and in manner of life, seemed stranger to him than did white Americans. Furthermore, most of the literature on the Negro problem dealt with the Negroes: their racial and cultural characteristics, their living standards. . . . But as he proceeded in his studies into the Negro problem, it became increasingly evident that little, if anything, could be scientifically explained in terms of the peculiarities of the Negroes themselves. As a matter of fact, in their basic human traits the Negroes are inherently not much different from other people. Neither are, incidentally, the white Americans. But Negroes and whites in the United States live in singular human relations with each other. All the circumstances of life—the "environmental" conditions in the broadest meaning of that term—diverge more from the "normal" for the Negroes than for the whites, if only because of the statistical fact that the Negroes are the smaller group. The average Negro must experience many times more of the "abnormal" interracial relations than the average white man in America. The more important fact, however, is that practically all the economic, social, and political power is held by whites. The Negroes do not by far have anything approaching a tenth of the things worth having in America.

It is thus the white majority group that naturally determines the Negro's "place." All our attempts to reach scientific explanations of why the Negroes are what they are and why they live as they do have regularly led to determinants on the white side of the race line. In the practical and political struggles of effecting changes, the views and attitudes of the white Americans are likewise strategic. The Negro's entire life, and consequently, also his opinions on the Negro problem, are, in the main, to be considered as secondary reactions to more primary pressures from the side of the dominant white majority.

1.2 A. Philip Randolph's address to the March on Washington Movement, like Myrdal's An American Dilemma, *reflected the optimistic mood that many civil rights advocates shared during World War II. As president of the Brotherhood of Sleeping Car Porters and one of the most prominent blacks of the first half of the century, Randolph organized the March on Washington Movement in 1941 to pressure President Franklin Delano Roosevelt to desegregate the armed forces and defense industry. Randolph threatened the president with a mass march in Washington, D.C., if the movement's demands were not met. Rather than risk such a challenge, Roosevelt issued an executive order that prohibited racial discrimination in the defense industry, which in turn allowed for the entrance of millions of blacks in America's plants and factories for the first time in the nation's history. (Roosevelt did not desegregate the military.)*

But Randolph's concerns went well beyond those tied directly to the war effort. He anticipated the goals and methods of the modern civil rights movement with remarkable clarity. Unlike Myrdal, Randolph announced that blacks would be in the forefront of the struggle to revolutionize race relations, that reforms would not be handed to them. The March on Washington Movement was an all-black organization, which accepted the support of whites but which was led by and for black Americans. It was also an organization that took the black struggle into the streets. Furthermore, as Randolph's remarks made clear, the "Negro dilemma" was not just a moral one. More than men's souls would have to be changed if blacks were to attain equality.

1.2 A. Philip Randolph, "Keynote Address to the March on Washington Movement," September 26, 1942.

Fellow Marchers and delegates to the Policy Conference of the March on Washington Movement and Friends:

We have met at an hour when the sinister shadows of war are lengthening and becoming more threatening. As one of the sections of the oppressed darker races, and representing a part of the exploited millions of the workers of the world, we are deeply concerned that the totalitarian legions of Hitler, Hirohito, and Mussolini do not batter the last bastions of democracy. We know that our fate is tied with the fate of the democratic way of life. And so, out of the depth of our hearts, a cry goes up for the triumph of the United Nations. But we would not be honest with ourselves were we to stop with a call for a victory of arms alone. We know this is not enough. We fight that the democratic faiths, values, heritages and ideals may prevail.

Unless this war sounds the death knell to the old Anglo-American empire systems, the hapless story of which is one of exploitation for the profit and power of monopoly capitalist economy, it will have been fought in vain. Out aim then must not only be to defeat nazism, fascism, and militarism on the battlefield but to win the peace, for democracy, for freedom and the Brotherhood of Man without regard to his pigmentation, land of his birth or the God of his fathers. . . .

Thus our feet are set in the path toward equality—economic, political and social and racial. . . . Equality is the heart and essence of democracy, freedom and justice. Without equality of opportunity in industry, in labor unions, schools and colleges, government, politics and before the law, without equality in social relations and in all phases of human endeavor, the Negro is certain to be consigned to an inferior status. There must be no dual standards of justice, no dual rights privileges, duties or responsibilities of citizenship. No dual forms of freedom. . . .

Our nearer goals include the abolition of discrimination, segregation, and jim-crow in the Government, the Army, Navy, Air Corps, U.S. Marine . . . and defense industries; the elimination of discrimination in hotels, restaurants, on public transportation conveyances, in educational, recreational, cultural, and amusement and entertainment places such as theaters, beaches and so forth.

We want the full works of citizenship with no reservations. We will accept nothing less.

But goals must be achieved. They are not secured because it is just and right that they be possessed by Negro or white people. Slavery was not abolished because it was bad and unjust. It was abolished because men fought, bled and died on the battlefield. . . . They must win them and to win them they must fight, sacrifice, suffer, go to jail and, if need be, die for them. These rights will not be given. They must be taken.

Democracy was fought for and taken from political royalists—the kings. Industrial democracy, the rights of the workers to organize and designate the representative of their own choosing to bargain collectively is being won and taken from the economic royalists—big business. . . .

As to the composition of our movement. Our policy is that it be all-Negro, and pro-Negro but not anti-white, or anti-semitic or anti-labor, or anti-Catholic. The reason for this policy is that all oppressed people must assume the responsibility and take the initiative to free themselves. . . .

This does not mean . . . that our movement should not call for the collaboration of Jews, Catholics, Trade unions and white liberals. . . . No, not at all. . . .

The essential value of an all-Negro movement such as the March on Washington is that it helps to create faith by Negroes in Negroes. It develops a sense of self-reliance with Negroes depending on Negroes in vital matters. It helps to break down the slave psychology and inferiority-complex in Negroes which comes and is nourished with Negroes relying on white people for direction and support. . . .

Now, let us be unafraid. We are fighting for big stakes. Our stakes are liberty, justice, and democracy. Every Negro should hang his head in shame who fails to do his part now for freedom. This is the hour of the Negro. It is the hour of the common man. May we rise to the challenge to struggle for our rights. Come what will or may, let us not falter.

1.3 Most studies of the civil rights movement downplay the period 1945 to 1955. While minor reforms took place during these years, from the desegregation of the armed forces to the breaking of the color line in professional baseball, significant change and mass protest did not occur until a decade after World War II ended. Why? Largely because the Cold War at home and abroad dampened the reform spirit in general and left civil rights groups in particular groping to maintain some of the momentum that they had built up during the New Deal and World War II. Rather than pushing forward the cause of equality, liberal groups became consumed with fighting communism within their own ranks and defending American foreign policy abroad. At the same time, radical organizations, which had pushed for civil rights for years, were ravaged.

The experience of W.E.B. DuBois and Paul and Eslanda Robeson provide evidence of this. All three faced extraordinary persecution due to the anti-communist hysteria of the post-war years. These heretofore giants of the black world were virtually silenced because of their criticism of American foreign policy and alleged ties to the Communist party. DuBois, for instance, was arguably the most important black man of the first half of the twentieth century. A co-founder of the NAACP, a renowned scholar and the father of pan-Africanism, he still led a very active life when World War II came to a close. Yet, by 1952, DuBois' life lay shattered and not because of poor health. The NAACP forced him to resign his post and the federal government turned him into a persona non grata, *even stripping him of his passport. In the piece that follows, delivered to the Southern Negro Youth Congress, a radical black organization, in the fall of 1946, DuBois urged black youths to remain in the South and to dedicate themselves to toppling Jim Crow. His vision of young educated blacks protesting against the "southern way of life" prefigured the emergence of a powerful student-led civil rights movement in the early 1960s.*

1.3 W.E.B. DuBois, "Behold the Land," reprinted in *Freedomways* (First Quarter 1964), pp. 8-15.

The future of American Negroes is in the South. Here three hundred and twenty-seven years ago, they began to enter what is now the United States of America; here they have made their greatest contribution to American culture; and here they have suffered the damnation of slavery, the frustration of reconstruction and the lynching of emancipation. I trust, then, that an organization like yours is going to regard the South as the battleground of a great crusade. Here is the magnificent climate; here is the fruitful earth under the beauty of the Southern sun; and here, if anywhere on earth is the need of the thinker, the worker and the dreamer. This is the firing line not simply for the emancipation of the American Negro, but for the emancipation of the African Negro and the Negroes of the West Indies; for the emancipation of the colored races; and for the emancipation of the white slaves of modern capitalist monopoly.

If, now, you young people, instead of running away from the battle here in Carolina, Georgia, Alabama, Louisiana and Mississippi, instead of seeking freedom and opportunity in Chicago and New York—which do spell opportunity—nevertheless grit your teeth and make up your minds to fight it out right here if it takes every day of your lives and the lives of your children's children; if you do this, you must in meetings like this ask yourselves what does the fight mean? How can it be carried on? What are the best tools, arms and methods? And where does it lead?

I should be the last to insist that the uplift of mankind never calls for force and death. There are times, as both you and I know, when:

> Tho' love repine and reason chafe,
> There came a voice without reply,
> "Tis man's perdition to be safe
> When for truth he ought to die."

At the same time and even more clearly in a day like this, after millions of mass murders that have been done in the world since 1914, we ought to be the last to believe that force is ever the final word. We cannot escape the clear fact that what is going to win in this world is reason if this ever becomes a reasonable world. The careful reasoning of the human mind backed by the facts of science is the one salvation of man. The world, if it resumes its march toward civilization, cannot ignore reason. This has been the tragedy of the South in the past; it is still its awful and unforgivable sin that it has set its face against reason and against the fact. It tried to build slavery upon freedom; it tried to build tyranny upon democracy; it tried to build mob violence on law and law on lynching. . . .

Nevertheless, reason can and will prevail; but of course it can only prevail with publicity—pitiless, blatant publicity. You have got to make the people of the United States and of the world know what is going on in the South. You have got to use every field of publicity to force the truth into their ears, and before their eyes. You have got to make it impossible for any human being to live in the South and not realize the barbarities that prevail here. You may be condemned for flamboyant methods; for calling a congress like this; for waving your grievances under the noses and in the faces of men. That makes no difference; it is your duty to do it. It is your duty to do more of this sort of thing than you have done in the past. As a result of this you are going to be called to sacrifice. It is no easy thing for a young black man or a young black woman to live in the South today and to plan to continue to live here; to marry and raise children; to establish a home. They are in the midst of legal caste and customary insults; they are in continuous danger of mob violence; they are mistreated by the officers of the law and they have no hearing before the courts and the churches and public opinion commensurate with the attention which they ought to receive. But that sacrifice is only the beginning of a battle; you must rebuild this South. . . .

Here in this South is the gateway to the colored millions of the West Indies, Central and South America. Here is the straight path to Africa, the

Indies, China and the South Seas. Here is the path to the greater, freer, truer world. It would be shame and cowardice to surrender this glorious land and its opportunities for civilization and humanity to the thugs and lynchers, the mobs and the profiteers, the monopolists and gamblers who today choke its soul and steal its resources. The oil and sulphur; the coal and iron; the cotton and corn; the lumber and cattle belong to you, the workers, black and white, and not to the thieves who hold them and use them to enslave you. They can be rescued and restored to the people if you have the guts to strive for the real right to vote, the right to real education, the right to happiness and health, and the total abolition of the father of these scourges of mankind, *poverty.*

"Behold the beautiful land which the Lord thy God hath given thee." Behold the land, the rich and resourceful land, from which for a hundred years its best elements have been running away, its youth and hope, black and white, scurrying North because they are afraid of each other, and dare not face a future of equal, independent, upstanding human beings, in a real and not a sham democracy.

To rescue this land, in this way, calls for the *Great Sacrifice.* This is the thing that you are called upon to do because it is the right thing to do. Because you are embarked upon a great and holy crusade, the emancipation of mankind, black and white; the upbuilding of democracy; the breaking-down, particularly here in the South, of forces of evil represented by race prejudice in South Carolina, by lynching in Georgia, by disenfranchisement in Mississippi, by ignorance in Louisiana, and by all these and monopoly of wealth in the whole South.

There could be no more splendid vocation beckoning to the youth of the twentieth century, after the flat failures of white civilization, after the flamboyant establishment of an industrial system which creates poverty and the children of poverty which are ignorance and disease and crime; after the crazy boasting of a white culture that finally ended in years which ruined civilization in the whole world; in the midst of allied peoples who have yelled about democracy and never practiced it either in the British Empire or in South Carolina.

Here is the chance for young women and young men of devotion to lift again the banner of humanity and to walk toward a civilization which will be free and intelligent, which will be healthy and unafraid, and build in the world a culture led by black folk and joined by peoples of all colors and all races—without poverty, ignorance and disease!

1.4 Paul Robeson, a star on the silver screen and stage and a world famous singer, was at the pinnacle of his career when World War II ended. In 1942 and

1943 he received universal praise for his performance in Othello *on Broadway, and in 1945 he was bestowed with the NAACP's and Howard University's highest honors, the Spingarn medal and an honorary Ph.D., respectively. By the early 1950s, however, like DuBois, Robeson's views and alleged ties to the Communist party earned him the wrath of government, business, the press, and even the very black organizations that had honored him during World War II. In the following speech, which he delivered to the Conference for Equal Rights for Negroes in the Arts, Sciences, and Professions, in December 1951, Robeson focused on one of his life-long concerns: the role and importance of African-American culture. Robeson was convinced that cultural liberation was key to the emancipation of blacks. Blacks would have to celebrate their heritage and demand recognition of their contributions to American and world civilization if they were to become free.*

1.4 Paul Robeson, "Address to the Conference for Equal Rights for Negroes in the Arts, Sciences, and Professions," reprinted in *Masses and Mainstream* (January 1952), pp. 7-14.

We are here today to work out ways and means of finding jobs for colored actors and colored musicians, to see that the pictures and statues made by colored painters and sculptors are sold, to see that the creation of Negro writers are made available to the vast American public. We are here to see that colored scientists and professionals are placed in leading schools and universities, to open opportunities for Negro technicians, to see that the way is open for colored lawyers to advance to judgeships—yes, to the Supreme Court of the United States, if you please.

It is not just a question of jobs, of positions, of commercial sales. No—the questions at hand cannot be resolved without the resolution of deeper problems involved here. We are dealing with the position in this society of a great people—of fifteen million closely bound human beings, of whom ten millions in the cotton and agricultural belt of the South form a kind of nation based upon common oppression, upon a magnificent common heritage, upon unified aspirations for full freedom and full equality in the larger democratic society. . . .

Yes, we are dealing with a great people. Their mere survival testifies to that. One hundred millions sacrificed and wasted in slave ships, on the cotton plantations, in order that there might be built the basic wealth of this great land. It must have been a tremendously strong people, a people of tremendous stamina, of the finest character, merely to have survived. Not only have the Negro people survived in this America, they have given to these United States almost a new language, given it ways of speech, given it perhaps its only indigenous music.

One great creation, modern popular music—whether it be in theater, film, radio, records; wherever it may be—is almost completely based upon the Negro idiom. . . . There is no leading American singer, performer of popular songs, whether it be a Crosby, a Sinatra, a Shore, a Judy Garland . . . who has not listened (and learned) by the hour to Holiday, Waters, Florence Mills, to Bert Williams, to Fitzgerald, and to the greatest of all, Bessie Smith. Without these models, who would ever have heard of a Tucker, a Jolson, a Cantor?

Go into the field of dance. Where could there have come an Astaire, an Eleanor Powell and a James Barton without a Bill Robinson, a Bert Williams. . . . How could Artie Shaw and Benny Goodman have appeared but for a Teddy Wilson, Turner Latan. . . ? Whence stems even Gershwin? From the music of Negro Americans joined with the ancient Hebrew idiom. Go and listen to some of the great melodies. Here again is a great American composer, deeply rooted, whether he knew it or not, in an African tradition, a tradition very close to his own heritage.

I speak very particularly of this popular form. This is very important to the Negro artists, because literally billions of dollars, have been earned, are being earned from their creation, and the Negro people have received almost nothing. . . . The fruits have been taken from us. Think of Handy, one of the creators of the blues; think of Count Basie, playing to half-filled houses at the Apollo; colored arrangers receiving a pittance while white bands reap harvests. What a heartbreak for every Negro composer! Publishing houses taking his songs for nothing and making fortunes. Theaters in the heart of the Negro communities dictating to Negro performers what they shall act . . . arrogantly telling Negro audiences what they shall see. . . .

Why this discrimination? Well, these mass media are based on advertising, commercialism at its worst, and the final answer is very simple. It goes to the root of all that has been said. The final answer is: ''The South won't take it.'' . . .

The final problem concerns new ways, new opportunities based upon a deep sense of responsibility in approaching the problem of the Negro people in its totality. . . . Somewhere, with the impetus coming from the arts, science and professions, there are literally millions of people in America who could come to hear us, the Negro artists. . . .

But, the final point. This cannot be done unless we as artists have the deepest respect for these people. When we say that we are artists, we must mean that. I mean it very deeply. . . . So, in the end, the culture with which we deal comes from the people. We have an obligation to take it back to the people, to make them understand that in fighting for their own cultural heritage they fight for peace. They fight for their own rights, for the rights of the Negro people, for the rights of all in this great land.

1.5 Eslanda Robeson, like her husband, was persecuted because of her out-spoken views. In the address that follows, which was delivered in New York City, in October 1951, to a mass meeting for the victims of the Smith Act (the anti-Communist law under which numerous individuals were imprisoned, including a sizeable number of blacks), she appealed for unity in the fight for equality and human dignity. This type of plea, which had struck a responsive chord in the thir-ties and World War II, fell on deaf ears in the 1950s. Liberals refused to cooper-ate with Communists and their allies (fellow travelers). Labor Unions, political organizations, and civil rights groups purged Communists and cooperated with the government's persecution of "reds." Not until the early 1960s, with the emergence of the new left, would such exclusionary practices be rejected.

1.5 Eslanda Robeson, "The Freedom Family," reprinted in *Freedomways* (Fall 1966), pp. 343-345.

Many years ago I was born into the Cardozo-Goode family, in Washington, D.C., and spent my very early childhood there among my many blood relations. My father died when I was six, and my mother brought our small immediate family—my two brothers and myself—to New York, where she could better earn a living and educate us in nonsegregated schools.

In New York, in Harlem, I found that I belonged to a much larger family—the Negro family—and that I had 15 million Negro relations.

In the public schools of New York I learned that I belonged to a still larger family, the American family, and that I had 150 million American relations. (This proved to be a mixed blessing, however, because some of the mean, white, arrogant members of this family kept trying to exclude, abuse, persecute and even kill Negro members, and treated us like black sheep and poor relations.)

When I was confirmed in the Episcopal Church, I joined the Christian family, and found that I had millions of Christian relations all over the world. (But this, too, proved to be a mixed blessing. I joined the Church because I believe in the ideas and the ideals of the Christian religion—especially in the Brotherhood of Man, the do unto others . . . only to find that many of my Christian relations also keep trying to exclude Negro members, treat us like black sheep and poor relations, and if they believe in their ideas and ideals, they certainly do not practice them.) . . .

Then I took a most important step in my life. I married into the Robeson family, thereby acquiring a super-duper husband, later a wonderful son, and now a dear and lovely daughter-in-law and a grandson who are out-of-this-world. . . . Later on when I travelled through Africa, I discovered that I belonged to the African family, with 150 million African relations, with an ancient and honorable historical and cultural background. With more travelling, experience, and study I learned that I also belonged to the family of colored peoples, a family so numerous and widespread that four out of every five people in the world are my Colored relations.

Some years ago when I began to write professionally, I joined another kind of family, a working family, the Union family (The Family of Organized Labor), when I became a member of the Authors' League and the Playwrights Guild.

When I began to feel that I must take some direct and active part in the political life of my country, I joined a Political family (The Progressive Party), and with my Progressive relations of all colors, religious backgrounds, work for a truly democratic, healthy, honest, peaceful administration of our country.

When threat of a Third World War loomed up on the horizon I joined still another kind of family, the family of Women (The American Women for Peace), and together with my Sisters work in every way I can for Peace-in-our-time. This family is of course related to Women and Peace Fighters everywhere.

And now, as I look back and look forward, I find that I belong to the most important family of all—the Freedom family—which is made up of people of all ages, colors, nationalities, and religions who yearn and fight and work for Freedom for themselves and for everyone all over the world. It is a wonderful thing to belong to this Freedom family. It is a family you join by choice, not by accident of birth. The only way you can join is by working and fighting actively for Freedom for yourself and for your fellow human beings. The only way you can remain in the Freedom family is by continuing to work and fight. When you feel the going is too tough, or you are too tired, or you are too busy with other matters, then you automatically retire from this Freedom family. When you say or do anything against Freedom, you automatically divorce yourself from this family and throw yourself out. You, yourself, do this. Members join this Freedom family and remain in it because they want to, because they have important common ideas, ideals, interests, and very important goals.

It is a warm and wonderful experience to be greeted by a complete stranger in a strange place, only to find that he or she is not a stranger at all, but a relation in our Freedom family. The members of our Freedom family take great pride in their membership, which is varied and widely scattered throughout the fabric of North and South America, Eastern and Western Europe, Asia and Africa. Our numbers, strength, prestige and morale are increasing steadily and rapidly. There is no doubt in my mind that the Freedom Family will be the Ruling family in the world in this era.

1.6 Though the Cold War initially stultified the civil rights movement, in the long run it also contributed to the federal government's support for race reforms. Race was America's "Achilles heel," declared Henry Cabot Lodge, the U.S. Ambassador to the United Nations. The persistence of racial inequality hindered America's efforts to win the support of Third World nations (many of them newly independent) and provided a constant source of propaganda for the Soviet Union. As blacks became increasingly cognizant of America's concern over its image abroad, they learned to turn the Cold War to their own advantage. For example, in the following speech, delivered at a meeting of the Catholic Interracial Council of New York in October 1956, John Hope Franklin, an eminent black historian, carefully outlined the connection between the Cold War and America's race problem. Franklin artfully reminded his committed cold warrior audience of the damage that America's "Negro problem" was doing to American foreign policy. Perhaps not so coincidentally, Presidents Truman, Eisenhower, and Kennedy consistently justified reforms on the grounds that racial inequality at home was threatening the success of America's crusade against communism abroad.

1.6 John Hope Franklin, "America's Window to the World: Her Race Problem," reprinted in *Rhetoric of Racial Revolt*, ed. by Roy L. Hill (Denver: Golden Bell Press, 1964), pp. 202-210.

There was a time when we in the United States could make a sharp distinction between those problems and policies having to do with our foreign relations and those having to do with our domestic relations. That distinction was always more apparent than real. Now it can hardly be said to exist at all. The contraction of the world that has come with the transportation and communication revolution and the worldwide drive toward political, social and economic democracy have certainly reduced any apparent distinctions between foreign and domestic problems. I believe, too, that there has been an increasing recognition on the part of the countries of the world of the ramifications and implications of the most intimate domestic problems and their inevitable involvement, under certain conditions, with the most delicate and difficult problems in foreign affairs. Thus, an American delegate to the current General Assembly to the United Nations can argue before an Assembly Committee that when any nation violates the human-rights pledges of the Charter its violation is "a matter of concern to all of us."

This comment was in connection with the question of whether or not apartheid in South Africa was the business of the United Nations or any of its members other than the Union of South Africa. Twelve years ago, when a group of American Negroes called the attention of the United Nations to some of the more sordid aspects of the American race problem in a document called "An Appeal to the World," the effort was almost universally condemned here as a deliberate attempt to embarrass the United States by holding up to ridicule a problem that was peculiarly domestic. [Editor's note: this document was co-authored by W.E.B. DuBois.] It may be seriously do ibted that the people of the United States would relish such a discussion of the American race problem any more today than they did twelve years ago. . . .

Whether we like it or not, many peoples of the world study race relations in the United States not merely because of their interests in the advancement of interracial justice but also to discover, if they can, the good faith or lack of it on the part of the United States in its relations with other countries. They are convinced that they can get a better understanding of the position of the United States on a vital matter by examining the status of race relations than by reading a lengthy and learned pronouncement. While they are not altogether correct in this conviction it is nevertheless a firm one with many peoples in other parts of the world. Thus they continue to peer through the window of race relations that gives a remarkable picture of American life to the world. . . .

These peoples are constantly asking themselves if the United States can be trusted to lead the world toward greater freedom for all and toward a greater recognition of the dignity of the individual. They are convinced that the answer is not to be found in the amount of military, financial and material aid given so generously by this country to the less fortunate. Rather the answer is to be found in the manner in which this country seeks to protect the rights of human beings in the area of equality, freedom and justice. . . .

When one calls our attention to the fact that the inability of the people of the United States to extend equality and justice to all its citizens is loosing friends for the United States throughout the world, we frequently shout that this is a Communist line. People who have cautioned this country that its relations were hurting an effective and constructive foreign policy have frequently been criticized as having fallen under some foreign un-American spell. But outrage or disgust with the criticism cannot wash it away. Nor can the sins of this country be expiated by the search, in which so many have indulged in recent years, for racial discrimination in the

Soviet Union. It should be of no consolation to any American to learn that there is racial discrimination in the Soviet Union, if such exists. It would seem quite irrelevant to any discussion of America's position, anyway.

In the first place, we, not the Russians, have been proclaiming to the world for more than a century and a half that we subscribe to the doctrine of equality of all men. We have, therefore, set ourselves a goal that we have not attained and which a considerable number of Americans actively oppose. And this the entire world knows. . . .

We are extremely vulnerable not merely because we have our deficiencies but also because we do have our strengths, one of which is our willingness to let the world know what goes on here. . . .

In so many respects, then, race relations is our big window, our picture window, to the world. What would we like for those who gaze in upon us to see? We would, of course, like to have our observers see us as a people who not only subscribe to the principles of equality but who put these principles into practice in every conceivable way. We would want them to see us making no discrimination or segregation among peoples on the highly questionable grounds of race or creed. We would want them to see us extending to every person in the United States the rights and privileges to which we as a nation are committed: the right to equality of opportunity to make of oneself what one can, to security of one's person, to be free of the indignities that degrade human beings, to move freely among one's fellows, and to exercise all the responsibilities and privileges of citizenship. If they could look in on us and see these practices, they would then have more confidence in our preachments and would attach more importance and meaning to them. They would also have infinitely more confidence in our seriousness of purpose as we set up goals of equality and freedom for peoples in other parts of the world. . . .

Perhaps there are those among us who do not care what others think of us. We have all seen the shrug of the shoulder of some of our fellows when it was suggested that the esteem in which we were held abroad was low because of our inhumanity to each other. If enough of us shrug our shoulders and assume an attitude of indifference in this matter we shall speed the process of disrespect of other peoples for us and add to the lack of confidence they have in us. In less time than we can imagine we shall have lost our position as a moral leader in the world and when that is gone our military and economic leadership will have little value. If people begin to regard us as fundamentally incapable of achieving interracial justice at home, they will begin to turn their faces from us. It will then be too late to make explanations based on legalisms and the splitting of hairs. . . .

1.7 and 1.8 Even in the midst of the Cold War, as the following documents demonstrate, black activists in the South and North were busy preparing the ground for the civil rights protests that would erupt in the latter half of the 1950s and early 1960s. In the South, Septima Clark tirelessly worked to develop grass-roots leaders and local freedom movements. Clark had been deeply influenced by the Highlander Folk School, an untraditional educational institution, established by Myles Horton in the 1930s. Originally established to train labor activists, in the 1950s, Highlander turned its attention to the nascent civil rights movement. Highlander sponsored interracial conferences and organized leadership training sessions, where Horton recruited a core of exceptional activists. Septima Clark, for instance, first attended a Highlander meeting in 1954, began working for it in 1955, and shortly thereafter became its director of education. Though Highlander, itself, became a victim of the "red scare," the Citizenship schools lived on, under the direction of the Southern Christian Leadership Conference (SCLC). From these schools emerged community leaders, many of whom played a prominent role in the civil rights movement, such as Bernice Robinson and Hosea Williams.

In the North, the Nation of Islam played a somewhat similar role. Led by Elijah Muhammad, the "Black Muslims," as they were often called, promoted black pride and self-sufficiency. Although the Nation's method and message differed from Highlander's, it too recruited and trained black community leaders. The Nation's most famous convert was Malcolm X, who spoke out militantly against whites and in favor of black nationalism. In this chapter's final piece John Henrik Clarke sketches out the Black Muslim's message and appeal. Though Clarke himself was not a member of the Nation of Islam, he was one of the first to note that it was striking a responsive chord among poor urban blacks, and he correctly predicted its rapid growth.

1.7 Septima P. Clark, *Echo in My Soul* (New York: E. P. Dutton, 1962), pp. 131-133 and 187-189.

The teacher wrote "Citizen" on the blackboard. Then she wrote "Constitution" and "Amendment." Then she turned to her class of 30 adult students.

"What do these mean, students?" She received a variety of answers, and when the discussion died down, the teacher was able to make a generalization.

"This is the reason we know we are citizens: Because it's written in an amendment to the Constitution."

An elderly Negro minister from Arkansas took notes on a yellow legal pad. A machine operator from Atlanta raised his hand to ask another question.

This was an opening session in an unusual citizenship education program that is held once each month at Dorchester Center, McIntosh, Georgia for the purpose of helping adults educate themselves. . . .

The program now being sponsored by the Southern Christian Leadership Conference has resulted in the training of more than eight hundred persons in the best methods to stimulate voter registration back in their home towns. Their home towns comprising eleven southern states from eastern Texas to northern Virginia. The program was transferred to SCLC from the Highlander Folk School in Monteagle, Tennessee.

I learned of Highlander in 1952 but attended my first workshop in 1954. In 1955 I directed my first workshop and did door to door recruiting for the school. . . . Highlander had always believed in people and the people trusted its judgment and accepted its leadership. It was accepted by Negroes and whites of all religious faiths because it had always accepted them and made them feel at home. The staff at Highlander knew that the great need of the South was to develop more people to take leadership and responsibility for the causes in which they believed. . . .

Legal and administrative barriers have forced the Negroes, especially, to realize their lack of educational opportunities. Former Highlander students have started an adult school on Johns Island (S.C.), and many members of that community learned to read and write, thus being enabled to pass the reading and writing tests for voter registration. Then leaders from neighboring islands came to Highlander to learn how they could establish adult schools.

So it was with all the workshops. They came with many problems. They carried most of them back home but they became eager to work on them and had many new ideas, as well as the example of encouragement of others to help them.

The basic purpose of the citizenship schools is discovering and developing local community leaders. One of the unique practical features of the concept is the ability to adapt at once to specific situations and stay in the local picture only long enough to help in the development of local leaders. These are trained to carry on an ever growing program of community development. The secret stems from the emphasis and the reliance on local leadership. It is my belief that creative leadership is present in any community and only awaits discovery and development.

1.8 John Henrik Clarke, "The New Afro-American Nationalism," *Freedomways* (Summer 1961), pp. 285-295.

Of all the nationalist groups in the United States, the Nation of Islam, called the Black Muslims, are the most written about and the most misunderstood. The interpreters of this group have not been able to decide whether the movement is religious or political. In a recent interview with Malcolm X, he said to me: "Our religion is mainly trying to find a way for the black man to get some heaven while he is down on earth."

To accomplish the above-mentioned objective, the Black Muslim movement will have to be both religious and political. It will have to be a spiritual, political and economic force.

A recent convert to the Black Muslim Movement, explaining why he joined the movement, and the basis of its appeal to an increasing number of Afro-Americans, said: "I am a man of forty years of age. I fought against people who were supposed to be this country's enemies in the Second World War, and my father fought in the First World War. I have been a patriotic citizen and I have always obeyed this country's laws. Yet, I have never been able to feel like a citizen or a man. I was a 33rd degree Mason and I have been a deacon in two different churches. I am a first class cabinet maker and I've had my own shop for nearly ten years. In spite of this, white people still treated me as if I was a boy. The Muslims have taught me that I am a man—a black man—and that's something I can feel proud of."

This convert has stated the case for the Black Muslims, in capsule. The drama of this search for dignity, definition and direction is old, the cast of characters is new. To some extent the Black Muslims are a latter-day version of the Garvey Movement, with a new sounding dogma which is basically the same as Marcus Garvey's.

To the Black Muslims the American promise and the American dream have grown sour without fulfillment. They have lost faith in the United States as a democratic nation.

The Black Muslims in the United States have created what is essentially a proletarian movement. This is the largest movement of this nature to emerge among Afro-Americans since the heyday of Marcus Garvey and the collapse of his "back to Africa" dream.

In the following quote from Eric Lincoln's book, *The Black Muslims in America*, he explains why the Black Bourgeoisie "leaders" had been a complete failure with the Afro-Americans who make up the growing Black Muslim Movement.

Organizations such as the NAACP and the National Urban League, for all their virtues, have not caught the imagination and adherence of the Negro masses. Their membership tend to comprise middle- and upper-class Negroes and whites, in each case the least disprivileged of their race. The Black Muslims, by contrast, are undeniably a mass movement. From their present base of more than 100,000 members, they are reaching for the support of the entire Negro lower class—and ultimately, of all other black Americans.

. . . The new Afro-American nationalists, with all their awkwardness and inadequacy, have learned a lesson and discovered a great truth that still eludes the "Negro leadership class" referred to here. They have learned the value of history and culture as an instrument in stimulating the spiritual rebirth of a people.

The cultural heritage of a people is directly related to their history. There can be no true understanding of the people of African origin in the United States until there is a better understanding, and more respect for, their African background. The culture of a people is the fuel that feeds the fires of their ambition, pride and self-esteem. There can be no meaningful advancement without this stimulation. A people must take pride in their history and love their memories in order to fulfill themselves. This is the lesson, I believe, the new Afro-American nationalists are trying to learn and teach. . . .

Chapter Two

DESEGREGATING THE SCHOOLS

In 1954, in Brown v. the Board of Education of Topeka, *the Supreme Court unanimously declared that segregation in public education was unconstitutional. Ever since* Plessy v. Ferguson *(1896), segregation had been legally part of American life. Now, because of the courts' decision, it was not. Yet, is it correct to claim that* Brown *unleashed the civil rights movement, as many studies do? And did the decision show that the federal government was on the civil rights movement's side? Or was* Brown *itself the product of a barely visible movement with deep roots in the African-American community, including NAACP lawyers who devised a strategy for attacking Jim Crow, social scientists who demonstrated the harm that segregation did to minorities, and school children, their parents, and communities, who as plaintiffs and support networks risked their well-being in order to topple the southern way of life? The following documents favor the latter perspective. Moreover, the selections suggest that as pivotal as the court's decision was, actual desegregation did not occur because the law changed. Rather, de facto desegregation depended on the emergence of a mass movement, which would demand that all Americans obey the law of the land (Fig. 2.1).*

2.1 The first document in this chapter, an article by Charles Houston, Dean of the School of Law at Howard University and Special Counsel to the NAACP, which appeared in Crisis, *the NAACP's magazine, displays the roots of the* Brown *case. Houston mapped out a complex plan for attacking segregation twenty years before the court made its decision. This included using Howard law school as a laboratory to test and improve legal arguments and developing a cadre of highly trained and dedicated attorneys, the most famous being Thur-*

Figure 2.1
School Segregation–Desegration, June 1961 (in Percent)

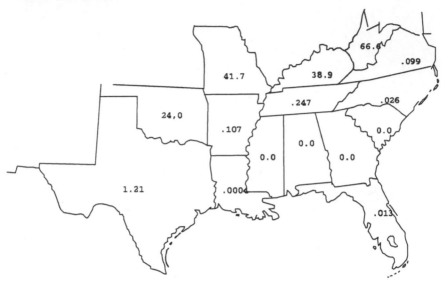

good Marshall, who would represent the plaintiffs in their legal battle and steer the challenge through the courts.

2.1 Charles Houston, "Educational Inequalities Must Go!" *Crisis* (October 1935), pp. 300-301.

The National Association for the Advancement of Colored People is launching an active campaign against race discrimination in public education. The campaign will reach all levels of public education from the nursery school through the university. The ultimate objective of the association is the abolition of all forms of segregation in public education, whether in the admission of activities of students, the appointment or advancement of teachers, or administrative control. The association will resist any attempt to extend segregated schools. Where possible it will attack segregation in schools. Where segregation is so firmly entrenched by law that a frontal attack cannot be made, the association will throw its immediate force toward bringing Negro schools up to an absolute equality with white schools. If the white South insists upon its separate schools, it must not squeeze the Negro schools to pay for them.

It is not the purpose or the function of the national office of the N.A.A.C.P. to force a school fight upon any community. Its function is primarily to expose the rotten conditions of segregation to point out the evil consequences of discrimination and injustice to both Negroes and whites, and to map out ways and means by which these evils may be corrected. The decision for action rests with the local community itself. If the local community decides to act and asks the N.A.A.C.P. for aid the N.A.A.C.P. stands ready with advice and assistance.

The N.A.A.C.P. proposes to use every legitimate means at its disposal to accomplish actual equality of educational opportunity for Negroes. A legislative program is being formulated. Court action has already begun in Maryland to compel the University of Maryland to admit a qualified Negro boy to the law school of the university. Court action is imminent in Virginia to compel the University of Virginia to admit a qualified Negro girl in the graduate department of that university. Activity in politics will be fostered due to the political set-up of and control over public school systems. The press and the public forum will be enlisted to explain to the public the issues involved and to make both whites and Negroes realize the blight which inferior education throws over them, their children and their communities.

The campaign for equality of educational opportunity is indissolubly linked with all the other major activities of the association. . . . The N.A.A.C.P. recognizes the fact that the discrimination which the Negro suffers in education are merely part of the general pattern of race prejudice in American life, and it knows that no attack on discrimination in education can have any far reaching effect unless it is bound to a general attack on discrimination and segregation in all phases of American life. . . .

2.2 *As Houston noted, the success of the NAACP's strategy depended on the generation of cases from the grass roots up. Black pupils would have to step forward as plaintiffs and ordinary individuals would have to bear the costs of challenging Jim Crow. A brief examination of one of the* Brown *cases,* Davis v. County School Board of Prince Edward County, Virginia, *provides some insight into this process. (*Brown *actually consolidated five separate suits.) The* Davis *suit was initiated by a student, Barbara Johns. In the spring of 1951 she prompted her fellow students to protest against the deplorable education that she and other blacks faced in the South. Implicitly, Johns challenged the South's claim that schools were separate* but *equal. Shortly after she organized the protest, she shrewdly convinced the NAACP that the teachers and principal had done so and that they needed the NAACP's help. In fact the teachers and principal had not taken part in the action nor called for outside support. Before the*

NAACP realized that students, not adults, had initiated the action, it had agreed to join the Prince Edward County case to suits against Topeka, Kansas, and Clarendon County, South Carolina.

In the sermon below, Reverend L. Griffin, a minister, urged the local black community to rally around the Prince Edward County students. Unlike the NAACP's lawyers, Griffin focused on the immorality of segregation, not its illegality. He assumed that the black community shared his religious zealousness and that if they believed that God opposed Jim Crow, they would join the crusade to abolish it.

Griffin's solidarity with the students symbolized an important development, the politicization of the black church. All across America, but especially in the South, black ministers began to play a leading role in the civil rights movement. By the early 1960s, hundreds of ministers had identified themselves with the freedom crusade. Many joined the Southern Christian Leadership Conference; others belonged to the NAACP and the Student Nonviolent Coordinating Committee.

2.2 Reverend L. Griffin, "The Prophesy of Equalization," *Afro-American* (Richmond edition) (July 1951).

"Every valley shall be exalted, and every mountain and hill shall be made low; and the crooked shall be made straight and the rough places plain; and the Glory of the Lord shall be revealed, and all flesh shall see it together; for the mouth of the Lord hath spoke it."—Isaiah 40:4-5.

One of the greatest evidences of our ignorance is our attempt to separate human races, according to pigmentation of skin, shape of skull and the subsequent theory of the superiority of one people over another.

Despite the findings of science and the self-evident facts concerning man's biological, physiological and psychological background, we tenaciously hold that races are unequal. No greater misstatement of fact has appeared in history. It is in conflict with the universal will of God. Yet we fail to realize that individual freedom is inextricably bound up with the freedom of all other human beings. Nonetheless, God is displeased over our action.

The great leveling process of which the prophet Isaiah writes in our morning text is evidence enough that Christianity could never support any "separate but equal" doctrine and be true to the light that has been revealed.

There can be no compromise with corrupt inclinations which tend to contradict righteousness. There can only be exalted valleys, leveled hills and straight places. When the Great Arbiter shall come, life must be on a level, races must dissolve; justice, liberty and human dignity must prevail. . . .

Recently, a mild atomic explosion took place among the other race; our own children resisted the silent oppression that has existed since slavery. [Editor's note: Griffin refers to the school strike sparked by Johns.] In doing this they acted in a manner more spiritual than most Chistians of long record, for the best definition of Spirituality is "the subordination of practical and material considerations to ideal ends." They weighed out their problems and faced them fearlessly.

The majority of us Christians believe in a safe Christianity that does not attack our status quo. No man can be a Christian who does not resist injustice regardless of the hazardous and dangerous risks involved. "For the cause," Jesus said, "came I into the world." Realizing the hazards involved in taking a stand against His contemporaries, Jesus nevertheless moved forward with faith because faith for Him was the courage that acts by understanding. . . .

Here we see the mission of the Christian Church revealed as plainly as is a direct command. If we are going to represent God, we must seek to aid in this divine purpose of bringing all men together. . . .

When is it that every Southern church and clergymen will proclaim the "accepted year of the Lord?" When shall men clamor for brotherhood and there shall be no man bound by the chains of circumstance? When can every citizen look to his leadership with veneration and respect? How long, Lord, how long? . . .

Of course, there are those who will cry that if you do not like the south, MOVE. How silly! There is no record which says you can solve a problem by running away from it. Furthermore, it is generally conceded that people desire the clime in which they were born, and as free moral agents they desire the privilege of going where they want, when they want, without interference. Still there are those who would sell their race in order to secure for themselves and families. . . .

To carry our point further, let us examine the case of the firing of our principal. Mr. Jones. Five hundred citizens, the very best of their race, the majority of whom had children in school, signed a petition expressing their desire to have Mr. Jones direct their children's education.

This petition was ignored in a democratic world.

You can have no say over who leads your child. . . . This decision is left to those who are unwilling to sit with you, eat with you, sleep with you, to die with you. . . .

No colored citizen is safe to live under such misused power, power that should only be in the hands of God. In order to be true to God and my fellowman, I must speak against such a miscarriage of justice. Such wanton disregard for human dignity.

If one does not build in opposition to such, our womanhood will remain unsafe, and our children will remain victims of a cruel system of philosophy for which they are not responsible.

Because I know that God does not desire segregation and desires equalization in its true sense—Because my heart is made sad when I think of cruelty heaped upon the colored man in slavery when white men raped their woman, harassed their children and brutalized the men, I must take a stand. When I think of the years of economical exploitation made on my people by the white race, and the hatred thrown against us, I must, in all sincerity, fight against such inhumanity to man with every ounce of energy given to me by God. I must resist with the ferocity of a prophet set on fire by the sights of injustice everywhere present. . . .

2.3 The following excerpt from the NAACP's legal brief to the Supreme Court reflects the contribution to the fight to desegregate schools made by social scientists. Written collectively by thirty-one experts, including Kenneth B. Clark, a black educator and psychologist with a Ph.D. from Columbia University, the brief moved the court to consider segregated schools, in and of themselves, discriminatory. This conclusion was based on a handful of studies, most importantly Clark's path-breaking "doll test" study, in which he and his wife, Mamie, argued that children learned racial prejudices at an early age and that education played a pivotal role in teaching prejudice. Some legal scholars and many laymen have argued that the court overstepped its traditional boundaries by using the studies of social scientists to justify its ruling. Yet others have countered that there was precedence to using "expert" testimony and that Clark's study played only a minor role in determining the court's decision.

2.3 "Appendix to Appellants' Brief," *Brown v. Board of Education, Topeka, Kansas*, September 1952.

The problem of segregation of racial and ethnic groups constitutes one of the major problems facing the American people today. It seems desirable, therefore, to summarize the contributions which contemporary social science can make toward its resolution. There are, of course, moral and legal issues involved with respect to which the signers of the present statement cannot speak with any special authority and which must be taken into account in the solution of the problem. There are, however, also factual issues involved with repect to which certain conclusions seem to be justified on the basis of the available scientific evidence. It is with these issues only that this paper is concerned. . . .

At the recent Mid-century White House Conference on Children and Youth, a fact-finding report on the effect of prejudice, discrimination and segregation on the personality of children was prepared as a basis for some of the deliberations. This report brought together the available social science and psychological studies which were related to the problem of how racial and religious prejudices influenced the development of a healthy personality. It highlighted the fact that segregation, prejudices and discriminations, and their social concomitants potentially damage the personality of all children—the children of the majority group in a somewhat different way than the more obviously damaged children of the minority group.[1]

The report indicates that as minority group children learn the inferior status to which they are assigned—as they observe the fact that they are almost always segregated and kept apart from others who are treated with more respect by the society as a whole—they often react with feelings of inferiority and a sense of personal humiliation. Many of them become confused about their own personal worth. On the one hand, like all other human beings they require a sense of personal dignity; on the other hand, almost nowhere in the larger society do they find their own dignity as human beings respected by others. Under these conditions, the minority group child is thrown into a conflict with regard to his feelings about himself and his group. He wonders whether his group and he himself are worthy of no more respect than they receive. This conflict leads to self-hatred and rejection of his own group. . . .

The report indicates that minority group children of all social and economic classes often react with a generally defeatist attitude and a lowering of personal ambitions. This, for example, is reflected in lower pupil morale and a depression of the educational aspiration level among minority group children in segregated schools. In producing such effects, segregated schools impair the ability of the child to profit from the educational opportunities provided him.

Many minority group children of all classes also tend to be hypersensitive and anxious about their relations with the larger society. They tend to see hostility and rejection even in those areas where these might not exist.

The report concludes that while the range of individual differences among members of a rejected minority group is as wide as among other peoples, the evidence suggests that all of these children are unnecessarily encumbered in some ways by segregation and its concomitants. . . .

Conclusions similar to those reached by the Mid-century White House Conference Report have been stated by other social scientists who have

[1]The most important presentation on this subject at the conference was, Kenneth B. Clark, "Effect of Prejudice and Discrimination on Personality Development." The report was explicitly cited by Warren in his written opinion on the *Brown* case.

concerned themselves with this problem. The following are some examples:

Segregation imposes upon individuals a distorted sense of social reality.

Segregation leads to a blockage in the communications and interactions between two groups. Such blockages tend to increase mutual suspicion, distrust and hostility.

Segregation not only perpetuates rigid stereotypes and reinforces negative attitudes toward members of the other group, but also leads to the development of a social climate within which violent outbreaks of racial tensions are likely to occur. . . .

In addition, enforced segregation gives official recognition and sanction to these other factors of the social complex, and thereby enhances the effects of the latter in creating the awareness of social status differences and feelings of inferiority. The child who, for example, is compelled to attend a segregated school may be able to cope with ordinary expressions of prejudice, regarding the prejudiced person as evil or misguided; but he cannot readily cope with symbols of authority, the full force of the authority of the State—the school or the school board, in this instance—in the same manner. Given both the ordinary expression of prejudice and the school's policy of segregation, the former takes on greater force and seemingly becomes an official expression of the latter. . . .

2.4 Supreme Court Chief Justice Earl Warren, a newcomer to the court, wrote the opinion to Brown. *In it he succinctly summarized the issues at hand, namely the legality of segregation in public education. As important as the logic of Warren's opinion was his ability to muster a 9–0 verdict. The court had first heard oral arguments on the case in December 1952, before Warren had been nominated to serve as chief justice. While the court might have sided with the plaintiffs, it was clearly divided. However, rather than making a decision, at the time, the court issued a list of questions to be answered by the two sides. Before reargument was heard, Chief Justice Vinson died unexpectedly. Warren took his place and mustered the entire court behind the decision to overturn* Plessy.

2.4 Supreme Court of the United States, *Brown v. Board of Education of Topeka*, 347 U.S. 483 (1954).[2]

(Opinion delivered by Chief Justice Earl Warren.)

The cases come to us from the States of Kansas, South Carolina, Virginia, and Delaware. They are premised on different facts and different

[2]The five cases consolidated under the *Brown* name were: *Brown v. Board of Education of Topeka, Kansas; Gebhart v. Belton* [Delaware]; *Bolling v. Sharpe* [District of Columbia]; *Briggs v. Elliot* [South Carolina]; and *Davis v. County School Board of Prince Edward County* [Virginia].

local conditions, but a common legal question justifies their consideration together in this consolidated opinion.

In each of the cases, minors of the Negro race, through their legal representatives, seek the aid of the courts in obtaining admission to the public schools of their community on a nonsegregated basis. In each instance, they have been denied admission to schools attended by white children under laws requiring or permitting segregation according to race. This segregation was alleged to deprive the plaintiffs of the equal protection of the laws under the Fourteenth Amendment. In each of the cases other than the Delaware case, a three-judge federal district court denied relief to the plaintiff on the so-called "separate by equal" doctrine announced by this court in *Plessy v. Ferguson*. . . . Under the doctrine, equality of treatment is accorded when the races are provided substantially equal facilities, even though these facilities be separate. In the Delaware case, the Supreme Court of Delaware adhered to that doctrine, but ordered that the plaintiffs be admitted to the white schools because of their superiority to the Negro schools.

The plaintiffs contend that segregated public schools are not "equal" and cannot be made "equal" and hence they are deprived of the equal protection of the laws. Because of the obvious importance of the question presented, the Court took jurisdiction. Argument was heard in the 1952 term, and reargument was heard this term on certain questions propounded by the Court.

Reargument was largely devoted to the circumstances surrounding the adoption of the Fourteenth Amendment in 1868. . . . This discussion and our own investigation convince us that . . . it is not enough to resolve the problem which we are faced. At best, they are inconclusive. . . .

An additional reason for the inconclusive nature of the Amendment's history, with respect to segregated schools, is the status of public education at the time. In the South, the movement toward free common schools, supported by general taxation, had not yet taken hold. . . .

In the first cases in this Court construing the Fourteenth Amendment, decided shortly after its adoption, the Court interpreted it as proscribing all state-imposed discriminations against the Negro race. The doctrine of "separate but equal" did not make its appearance in this Court until 1896 in the case of *Plessy v. Ferguson, supra*, involving not education but transportation. American courts have since labored with the doctrine for over half a century. In this Court, there have been six cases involving the "separate but equal" doctrine in the field of public education. . . . In more recent cases, all on the graduate school level, inequality was found in that specific benefits enjoyed by white students were denied to Negro students of the same educational qualifications. . . . In none of these cases was it necessary to re-examine the doctrine to grant relief to the Negro plaintiff. . . .

In the instant cases, the question is directly presented. Here . . . there are findings below that the Negro and white schools involved have been equalized, or are being equalized, with respect to buildings, curricula, qualifications and salaries of teachers. . . . Our decision, therefore, cannot turn on merely the comparison of these tangible factors in the Negro and white schools involved in each of the cases. We must look instead to the effect of segregation itself on public education.

In approaching this problem, we cannot turn the clock back to 1868 when the Amendment was adopted, or even to 1896 when *Plessy v. Ferguson* was written. We must consider public education in the light of its full development and its present place in American life throughout the Nation. Only in this way can it be determined if segregation in public schools deprives these plaintiffs of the equal protection of the laws.

Today, education is perhaps the most important function of state and local governments. Compulsory school attendance laws and the great expenditures for education both demonstrate our recognition of the importance of education to our democratic society. It is required in the performance of our most basic public responsibilities, even service in the armed forces. It is the very foundation of good citizenship. Today it is a principal instrument in awakening the child to cultural values, in preparing him for later professional training, and in helping him to adjust normally to his environment. In these days, it is doubtful that any child may reasonably be expected to succeed in life if he is denied the opportunity of an education. Such an opportunity, where the state has undertaken to provide it, is a right which must be made available to all on equal terms.

We come to the question presented: Does segregation of children in public schools solely on the basis of race, even though the physical facilities and other "tangible" factors may be equal, deprive the children of the minority group of equal education opportunities? We believe that it does.

In *Sweatt v. Painter, supra*, in finding that a segregated law school for Negroes, could not provide them equal educational opportunities, this Court relied in large part on "those qualities which are incapable of objective measurement but which make for greatness in a law school." In *McLaurin v. Oklahoma State Regents, supra*, the Court, in requiring that a Negro admitted to a white graduate school be treated like all other students, again resorted to intangible considerations: ". . . his ability to study, to engage in discussions and exchange views with other students, and, in general, to learn his profession." Such considerations apply with added force to children in grade and high schools. To separate them from others of similar age and qualifications solely because of their race generates a feeling of inferiority as to their status in the community that may affect their hearts and minds in a way unlikely to ever to be undone. . . . Whatever may have been the extent of psychological knowledge at the time of *Plessy v. Ferguson*, this finding is amply supported by modern authority. Any language in *Plessy v. Ferguson* contrary to this finding is rejected.

We conclude that in the field of public education the doctrine of "separate but equal" has no place. Therefore, we hold that the plaintiffs and others similarly situated for whom the actions have been brought are, by reason of the segregation complained of, deprived of equal protection of the laws guaranteed by the Fourteenth Amendment. This disposition makes unnecessary any discussion whether such segregation also violates the Due Process Clause of the Fourteenth Amendment.

Because these are class actions, because of the wide applicability of this decision, and because of the great variety of local conditions, the formulation of decrees in these cases presents problems of considerable complexity. On reargument, the consideration of appropriate relief was necessarily subordinated to the primary question—the constitutionality of segregation in public education. We have now announced that such segregation is a denial of the equal protection of the laws. In order that we may have the full assistance of the parties in formulating decrees, the cases will be restored to the docket, and the parties are requested to present further argument. . . . The Attorney General of the United States is again invited to participate. The Attorneys General of the states requiring or permitting segregation in public education will also be permitted to appear as *amici curiae* upon request to do so by September 15, 1954, and submission of briefs by October 1, 1954.

It is so ordered.

2.5 Warren hoped that the unanimity of the decision would preempt claims of regional or political bias. Moreover, since the court did not demand immediate relief, he hoped to work out a judicious method to actually desegregate schools. A year later, the court issued an "Enforcement Decree," which called for compliance with the decision with "all deliberate speed" and left the implementation or enforcement of the decree to lower (local) courts. Whether public schools would comply with this decree remained to be seen, though Chief Justice Warren found reason to be optimistic in the rapid desegregation of schools which was taking place in the District of Columbia and several border states.

2.5 *Brown v. Board of Education of Topeka*, Enforcement Decree, 349 U.S. 294 (1955).

(Opinion delivered by Chief Justice Earl Warren.)

The cases were decided on May 17, 1954. The opinions of the date declaring the fundamental principle that racial discrimination in public education is unconstitutional, are incorporated herein by reference. All provisions of federal, state, or local law requiring or permitting such discrimination must yield to this principle. There remains for consideration the manner in which relief is to be accorded.

Because these cases arose under different local conditions and their disposition will involve a variety of local problems, we requested further argument on the question of relief. . . . The parties, the United States, and the States of Florida, North Carolina, Arkansas, Oklahoma, Maryland, and Texas filed briefs and participated in the oral arguments.

The presentations were informative and helpful to the Court in its consideration of the complexities arising from the transition to a system of public education freed of racial discrimination. The presentations also demonstrated that substantial steps to eliminate racial discrimination in public schools have already been taken, not only in some of the communities in which the cases arose, but in some of the states appearing as *amici curiae*, and in other states as well. Substantial progress has been made in the District of Columbia and in the communities in Kansas and Delaware involved in this litigation. The defendants in the cases coming to us from South Carolina and Virginia are awaiting the decision of the Court concerning relief.

Full implementation of these constitutional principles may require solution of varied local school problems. School authorities have the primary responsibility for elucidating, assessing, and solving these problems; courts will have to consider whether the action of school authorities constitutes good faith implementation of the governing constitutional principles. Because of their proximity to local conditions and the possible need for further hearings, the courts which originally heard these cases can best perform this judicial appraisal. Accordingly, we believe it appropriate to remand the cases to those courts.

In fashioning and effectuating the decrees, the courts will be guided by equitable principles. Traditionally, equity has been characterized by a practical flexibility in shaping its remedies and by a facility for adjusting and reconciling public and private needs. These cases call for the exercise of these traditional attributes of equity power. At stake is personal interest of the plaintiffs in admission to public schools as soon as practicable on a nondiscriminatory basis. To effectuate this interest may call for elimination of a variety of obstacles in making the transition to school systems operated in accordance with the constitutional principles set forth in our May 17, 1954, decision. Courts of equity may properly take into account the public interest in the elimination of such obstacles in a systematic and effective manner. But it should go without saying that the vitality of these constitutional principles cannot be allowed to yield simply because of disagreement with them.

While giving weight to these public and private considerations, the courts will require that the defendants make a prompt and reasonable start toward compliance with our May 17, 1954 ruling. Once such a start has been made, the courts may find that additional time is necessary to carry out the ruling in an effective manner. The burden rests upon the defendants to establish that such time is necessary in the public interest and is consistent with good faith compliance at the earliest practicable date. To that end, the courts may consider problems related to administration, arising from the physical condition of the school plant, the school transportation system, personnel, revision of school districts and attendance areas into compact units to achieve a system of determining admission to the public schools on a nonracial basis, and revision of local laws and regulations which may be necessary in solving the foregoing problems. They will also consider the adequacy of any plans the defendants may propose to meet these problems and to effectuate a transition to a racially nondiscriminatory school system. During this period of transition, the courts will retain jurisdiction of these cases.

The judgments below, except that in the Delaware case, are accordingly reversed, and the cases are remanded to the District Courts to take such proceedings and enter such orders and decrees consistent with this opinion as are necessary and proper to admit to public schools on a racially nondiscriminatory basis with all deliberate speed the parties to these cases. . . .

It is so ordered.

2.6 In the following article Thurgood Marshall and Roy Wilkins, the NAACP's executive secretary, reviewed the long struggle to eradicate segregation. They heralded the court's decisions, emphasizing that it clearly established that the law was now on the NAACP's side. While the NAACP deserved to celebrate its victory, to an extent, Wilkins' and Marshall's words betrayed their naïveté. For decades, the legal arm of the NAACP assumed that the toppling of Plessy v. Ferguson *would produce desegregation. Compliance with the court's decision would come, "perhaps grudgingly," Wilkins and Marshall declared, but it would come nonetheless. And in areas where authorities refused to obey the law, Marshall and Wilkins asserted, the NAACP was determined to compel the courts to enforce the law. Yet, as we will see,* Brown *represented only the beginning of the battle and the law, even if a powerful weapon, was not the only one that blacks and their allies would have to employ to achieve their ends.*

2.6 Thurgood Marshall and Roy Wilkins, "Interpretation of Supreme Court Decision & the NAACP Program," *Crisis* (June 1955), pp. 329-334.

The May 31 decision [Enforcement Decree] combined with the May 17 decison of last year must be viewed as the latest in a series of steps toward full integration of the Negroes into American life. When the NAACP began this campaign it was met with state statutes requiring or permitting segregation in public education. These statutory provisions were a complete block to all voluntary efforts to end segregation.

The first cases destroyed the validity of out-of-state scholarships as an excuse for the exclusion of Negroes from professional schools. This was followed by the cases which declared unconstitutional provisions for jim-crow graduate and professional schools. And then the May 17, 1954 decision declared that segregation in public education was unconstitutional. This was followed by the May 31 decision that "all provisions of federal, state or local law requiring or permitting" segregation in public education "must yield to" the principle announced in the 1954 decision.

This determination by the Supreme Court clears the way for school boards to desegregate their systems voluntarily. This is being done in many parts of the South. The opinion also gives us the necessary legal weapons to bring about compliance in areas of the South which openly flout the mandate of the Supreme Court.

The question now before us is: under what conditions and with what directives were the school cases remanded to the lower courts: We know that the highest court did not (a) set a deadline date for either the beginning or the completion of desegregation in the public schools; and (b) outline a definite plan by which desegregation must proceed and by which lower courts might judge the efforts of local school boards toward compliance with the May 17 and May 31 rulings. Not having done this, what did the Court do? What language did it use?

May 17, 1954 decision re-affirmed. . . . All school segregation laws are invalid. . . . This means that all laws, local, state and federal, requiring or permitting racial segregation in the public schools are now null and void, and that no school or other public official body is bound by such laws. . . .

"Local school authorities responsible. . . ." This means just what it says. It means that it is right and proper for citizens and community groups to begin the campaign for desegregation with the local school authorities. "Good faith required." The Court is saying here that alleged good faith in carrying out the "governing" constitutional principle of non-segregation can be brought before a court for determination and need not rest upon mere assertion by school authorities or newspapers or politicians or others. . . . "Interest of the plaintiffs. . . ." Plaintiffs have a right . . . to admission to public schools on a non-discriminatory basis "as soon as practicable." The latter phrase must be taken to mean with only such delay as may be permitted by the lower courts in the context of language elsewhere in the May 31 opinion. . . .

"Obstacles to be eliminated. . . ." When the Court says, as it does here, that to protect the right of the plaintiffs "may call for the elimination of a variety of obstacles" it must be taken to mean that the Court in effect is ordering such obstacles be removed. By the strongest inference it means that pleas of the existence of such obstacles cannot be considered valid reasons for denying plaintiffs their rights. The defendants are duty bound, if such obstacles exist, to remove them, whatever their nature.

"Must start promptly. . . ." Here the Court says that even while the lower courts may give due weight to the public interest . . . and to private considerations . . . the courts "will require" a "prompt and reasonable start toward full compliance with our May 17, 1954 ruling." "Will require" is strong, definite, positive language in legal terms, a directive which no lawyer or judge misunderstands or underestimates. . . .

"Disagreement no basis for failure to comply. . . ." Very simply this means that just because individual citizens, officials, or groups do not like or do not agree with the May 17, 1954, opinion they may not ignore, evade or defy it. That is, they may not do so in court, in a final determination, no matter how much they talk or write about it in disagreement outside of a courtroom showdown.

"Burden upon the defendants. . . ." It should be noted that only *after* a start has been made will a request for additional time be considered. Here, as in other phases under the jurisdiction of the courts, we have the privilege of challenging such requests for time in the courts, forcing a hearing and a determination. We need not depend upon the mere assertion of a school official that more time is necessary. . . .

"Problems to be considered by courts . . . Non-Racial school districts . . . Revision of local laws. . . ." In all its pleading before the courts, the NAACP has granted that allowance should be made for the

solving of administrative problems, but it has insisted that diligent attention to solving these would not require a prolonged period. In its section
on administrative problems the Court enumerates those which the courts
may consider. The time alleged to be required is subject to the burden-of-
proof stipulation in the opinion. The nature of the solution of each problem is subject to the "good faith" and "constitutional principles" stipulation. All proposals are subject to challenges in the courts. . . .

In the overwhelming majority of instances it can be expected that compliance without legal action will be the rule, perhaps grudgingly and
reluctantly in some areas, but compliance, nevertheless. . . .

Armed with the powers embodied in the language of the Court's opinion,
we look confidently toward the future. We stand ready with qualified
experts in public education and community organizations to cooperate with
any and all school boards willing to work toward desegregation.

We always realized that there are those who would defy the ruling and
others who would drag their feet no matter what language the Supreme
Court used. We now have the weapons to make them accept the highest
court's affirmation of true American principles. . . .

2.7 Resistance to Brown *was widespread in the South. As of the beginning of
the 1957 school year only a small number of schools had complied with the
decision. Moreover, organized defiance, both through legal and extra-legal
channels, was on the rise (see chapter twelve). In Little Rock, Arkansas, however, there was reason to be optimistic. The school board had passed a plan for
gradually desegregating the schools, beginning with the admission of nine carefully selected students to Little Rock's Central High. Yet, shortly before the
school year commenced, opposition emerged. Most importantly, Governor
Orval Faubus, heretofore a moderate, voiced his opposition and white mobs
assembled in town to stop the plan from being implemented. The following piece,
an interview with Elizabeth Eckford, provides a vivid sense of the meaning of
those mobs.*

2.7 Elizabeth Eckford, "The First Day: Little Rock, 1957," in
Growing Up Southern: Southern Exposure Looks at Childhood, Then
***and Now*, ed. by Chris Mayfield (New York: Random House, 1981),
pp. 258-261.**

That night I was so excited I couldn't sleep. The next morning I was
about the first one up. While I was pressing my black-and-white dress—I
had made it to wear on the first day of school—my little brother turned on
the TV set. They started telling about a large crowd gathered at the

school. The man on TV said he wondered if we were going to show up that morning. . . .

Before I left home Mother called us into the living room. She said we should have a word of prayer. Then I caught the bus and got off a block from the school. I saw a large crowd of people standing across the street from the soldiers guarding Central. As I walked on, the crowd suddenly got very quiet. Superintendent Blossom told us to enter by the front door. I looked at all the people and thought, "Maybe I will be safer if I walk down the block to the front entrance behind the guards."

At the corner I tried to pass through the long line of guards around the school so as to enter the grounds behind them. One of the guards pointed across the street. So I pointed in the same direction and asked whether he meant for me to cross the street and walk down. He nodded "yes." So, I walked across the street conscious of the crowd that stood there, but they moved away from me.

For a moment all I could hear was the shuffling of their feet. Then someone shouted, "Here she comes, get ready!" I moved away from the crowd on the sidewalk and into the street. If the mob came at me I could then cross back over so the guards could protect me.

The crowd moved in closer and then began to follow me, calling me names. I still wasn't afraid. Just a little bit nervous. Then my knees started to shake all of a sudden and I wondered whether I could make it to the center entrance a block away. It was the longest block I ever walked in my whole life.

Even so, I still wasn't too scared because all the time I kept thinking that the guards would protect me.

When I got in front of the school, I went up to a guard again. But this time he just looked straight ahead and didn't move to let me pass him. I didn't know what to do. Then I looked and saw that the path leading to the front entrance was a little further ahead. So I walked until I was right in front of the path to the front door.

I stood looking at the school—it looked so big! Just then the guards let some white students through.

The crowd was quiet. I guess they were waiting to see what was going to happen. When I was able to steady my knees, I walked up to the guard who had let the white students in. He too didn't move. When I tried to squeeze past him, he raised his bayonet and then the other guards moved in and they raised their bayonets.

They glared at me with a mean look and I was very frightened and didn't know what to do. I turned around and the crowd came toward me.

They moved closer and closer. Somebody started yelling, "Lynch her! Lynch her!"

I tried to see a friendly face somewhere in the mob—someone who maybe would help. I looked into the face of an old woman and it seemed a kind face, but when I looked at her again she spat on me.

They came closer, shouting, "No nigger bitch is going to get in our school! Get out of here!"

I turned back to the guards but their faces told me I wouldn't get any help from them. Then I looked down the block and saw a bench at the bus stop. I thought, "If I can only get there I will be safe." I don't know why the bench seemed a safe place to me, but I started walking toward it. I tried to close my mind to what they were shouting, and kept saying to myself, "If I can only make it to the bench I will be safe."

When I finally got there, I don't think I could have gone another step. I sat down and the mob crowded up and began shouting all over again. Someone hollered, "Drag her over to this tree! Let's take care of that nigger." Just then a white man sat down beside me, put his arm around me and patted my shoulder. He raised my chin and said, "Don't let them see you cry."

2.8 Faubus' decision to defy Brown *placed President Dwight D. Eisenhower in a position he had sought to avoid through most of his tenure as president. Eisenhower had refrained from taking a public stance on* Brown *except to declare that it was the law of the land. He favored gradual rather than radical race reforms. Personally he felt segregation was wrong but he sympathized with Southerners who worried about the disorder that they believed would arise with desegregation. Faubus' decision to use state troops to block the admission of the Little Rock nine compelled Eisenhower to intervene. In an address to the American people, he explained his decision to send the National Guard to Little Rock. Eisenhower proclaimed that the legitimacy of the federal court and American system of law was at stake; he added that the incident was damaging America's reputation abroad.*

2.8 President Dwight D. Eisenhower, "Address on Little Rock," September 25, 1957.

My fellow citizens. . . . I must speak to you about the serious situation that has arisen in Little Rock. . . . In that city, under the leadership of demagogic extremists, disorderly mobs have deliberately prevented the carrying out of proper orders from a federal court. Local authorities have not eliminated that violent opposition and, under the law, I yesterday issued a proclamation calling upon the mob to disperse.

This morning the mob again gathered in front of the Central High School of Little Rock, obviously for the purpose of again preventing the carrying out of the court's order relating to the admission of Negro children to that school.

Whenever normal agencies prove inadequate to the task and it becomes necessary for the executive branch of the federal government to use its powers and authority to uphold federal courts, the President's responsibility is inescapable.

In accordance with that responsibility, I have today issued an Executive Order directing the use of troops under federal authority to aid in the execution of federal law at Little Rock, Arkansas. This became necessary when my Proclamation of yesterday was not observed, and the obstruction of justice still continues.

It is important that the reasons for my action be understood by all our citizens.

As you know, the Supreme Court of the United States has decided that separate public educational facilities for the races are inherently unequal and therefore compulsory school segregation laws are unconstitutional. . . .

During the past several years, many communities in our southern states have instituted public school plans for gradual progress in the enrollment and attendance of school children of all races in order to bring themselves into compliance with the law of the land.

They thus demonstrated to the world that we are a nation in which laws, not men, are supreme. . . .

Now let me make it very clear that federal troops are not being used to relieve local and state authorities of their primary duty to preserve the peace and order of the community. . . .

The proper use of the powers of the Executive Branch to enforce the orders of a federal court is limited to extraordinary and compelling circumstances. Manifestly, such an extreme situation has been created in Little Rock. This challenge must be met and with such measures as will preserve to the people as a whole their lawfully protected rights in a climate permitting their free and fair exercise.

The overwhelming majority of our people in every section of the country are united in their respect for observance of the law—even in those cases where they may disagree with that law. . . .

A foundation of our American way of life is our national respect for law.

In the South, as elsewhere, citizens are keenly aware of the tremendous disservice that has been done to the people of Arkansas in the eyes of the nation, and that has been done to the nation in the eyes of the world.

At a time when we face grave situations abroad because of the hatred that communism bears toward a system of government based on human rights, it would be difficult to exaggerate the harm that is being done to the prestige and influence, and indeed to the safety, of our nation and the world.

Our enemies are gloating over this incident and using it everywhere to misrepresent our whole nation. We are portrayed as a violator of those standards of conduct which the people of the world united to proclaim in the Charter of the United Nations. There they affirmed "faith in fundamental human rights" and "in the dignity and worth of the human person" and they did so "without distinction as to race, sex, language or religion."

And so, with deep confidence, I call upon the citizens of the State of Arkansas to assist in bringing an immediate end to all interference with the law and its processes. If resistance to the federal court orders ceases at once, the further presence of federal troops will be unnecessary and the City of Little Rock will return to its normal habits of peace and order and a blot upon the fair name and high honor of our nation in the world will be removed.

Thus will be restored the image of America and all its parts as one nation, indivisible, with liberty and justice for all.

2.9 The presence of federal troops in Little Rock allowed the students to attend Central High, although one of them, Minnie Jean Brown, was expelled after she threw a bowl of chili on a white boy, who along with other whites, had been harassing her. On the last day of the school year, Ernest Green, the only senior of the Little Rock Nine, became the first black student to graduate from Central High School, marking a victory for himself, the Little Rock Nine, and the NAACP. Yet the victory proved short-lived for blacks in Little Rock and nationwide. Rather than desegregate, Little Rock and other school districts, including Prince Edward County, Virginia, closed their schools.

Nonetheless, blacks refused to retreat. The NAACP continued to file one suit after another, at considerable expense. Black leaders and their allies, including liberal politicians from both political parties, such as Jacob Javits and Hubert Humphrey, demanded compliance with the law. More importantly, lesser-known individuals stepped forward to demand admittance to all-white institutions, knowing that they risked their lives in doing so. Among those to do so was James Meredith, a veteran of the Korean War and a native of the state of Mississippi.

When the University of Mississippi refused to admit Meredith, the NAACP took his case to court and, as in Little Rock, obtained a court order compelling the school to comply with Brown. Once again the governor of the state, this time Ross Barnett, defied the court's command, which in turn compelled a reluctant president, this time John F. Kennedy, to intervene. Throughout the ordeal, Meredith refused to withdraw his application, insisting that he had the same right as all other citizens to a college education.

2.9 James Meredith, "Statement," in *Three Years in Mississippi* (Bloomington: Indiana University Press, 1966), pp. 200-214.

In this time of crisis, I feel it appropriate for me to clarify my position as to my intention, my objectives, my hopes, and my desires.

For several months I have been involved in a struggle to gain admission to the University of Mississippi.

There are those in my state who oppose me in my efforts to obtain an education in the schools of my state. They do this because I am a Negro, and Negroes are not allowed to attend certain schools in my state. The schools that we are forbidden to attend are the only ones in the state that offer the training which I wish to receive. Consequently, those who oppose me are saying to me, we have given you what we want you to have and no more. And if you want more than we have given you, then you go to some other state or some other country and get your training.

What logic is it that concludes that a citizen of one state must be required to go to another state to receive the educational training that is normally and ordinarily offered and received by other citizens of that state? Further, what justification can there possibly be for one state to accept the responsibility for educating the citizens of another state when the training is offered to other citizens in the home state?

We have a dilemma. It is a fact that the Negroes of Mississippi are effectively not first-class citizens. I feel that every citizen should be a first-class citizen and should be allowed to develop his talents on a free, equal, and competitive basis. I think this is fair and that it infringes on the rights and privileges of no one. Certainly to be denied this opportunity is a violation of my rights as a citizen of the United States and the state of Mississippi.

The future of the United States of America, the future of the South, the future of Mississippi, and future of the Negro rests on the decision of whether or not the Negro citizen is to be allowed to receive an education in his own state. If a state is permitted to arbitrarily deny any right that is so basic to the American way of life to any citizen, then democracy is a failure.

I dream of a day when Negroes in Mississippi can live in decency and respect and do so without fear of intimidation and bodily harm, of receiving personal embarrassment, and with an assurance of equal justice under the law. . . .

Chapter Three

THE MONTGOMERY BUS BOYCOTT

On December 1, 1955, Rosa Parks boarded a bus in the downtown shopping district of Montgomery, Alabama, and sat down in an area open to blacks. In time, newcomers filled the empty seats until one white person was left standing. The bus driver, James Blake, requested that Parks and the other black passengers in the front give up their seats. All of them complied except for Parks. When the driver was unable to get Parks to obey the law, he notified the city police who placed her under arrest.

Parks' refusal to give up her seat sparked a mass bus boycott in Montgomery. For over a year blacks walked, car-pooled, and bicycled to work. Finally, following a Supreme Court decision which ruled that a local bus-segregation ordinance was unconstitutional, the buses were desegregated. In addition to displaying a new level of militancy, the boycott catapulted Martin Luther King, Jr.—prior to the protests an obscure minister—into the limelight. His philosophy of nonviolence struck a responsive chord among blacks and whites, and his charisma and oratorical skills fed and reinforced the determination of blacks, nationwide, to demand full equality.

3.1 In the first piece of this chapter, Parks, with simple eloquence, describes her refusal to give up her seat. While her decision was spontaneous, she had long been active in the local civil rights struggle. She had been a member of the NAACP and had attended human relations workshops conducted by the Highlander Folk School. She was close friends with several local activists, including E. D. Nixon and Clifford and Virginia Durr. These connections, along with her reputation in the black community, as a hard-working family woman, contributed to the success of the boycott. Earlier that same year, a young woman had been arrested for refusing to give up her seat, but a boycott was not tried, in part, because the arrestee was pregnant out-of-wedlock and black leaders feared her circumstances, not Jim Crow busing, would become the main issue.

3.1 Rosa L. Parks, "Recollections," in Howell Raines, *My Soul Is Rested* (New York: G. P. Putnam Sons, 1977), pp. 40-42.

I had left my work at the men's alteration shop, a tailor shop in the Montgomery Fair department store, and as I left work, I crossed the street to a drugstore to pick up a few items instead of trying to go directly to the bus stop. And when I finished this, I came across the street and looked for a Cleveland Avenue bus that apparently had some seats on it. At the time it was a little hard to get a seat on the bus. But when I did get to the entrance on the bus, I got in line with a number of other people who were getting on the same bus.

As I got up on the bus and walked to the seat I saw there was only one vacancy that was just back of where it was considered the white section. So this was the seat that I took, next to the aisle, and a man was sitting next to me. Across the aisle there were two women, and there were a few seats at this point in the very front of the bus that was called the white section. I went on to one stop and I didn't particularly notice who was getting on the bus, didn't particularly notice the other people getting on. And on the third stop there were some people getting on, and at this point all of the front seats were taken. Now in the beginning, at the very first stop I had got on the bus, the back of the bus was filled up with people standing in the aisle and I don't know why this one vacancy that I took was left, because there were quite a few people already standing toward the back of the bus. The third stop is when all the front seats were taken, and this one man was standing and when the driver looked around and saw he was standing, he asked the four of us, the man in the seat with me and the two women across the aisle, to let him have those front seats.

At his first request, didn't any of us move. Then he spoke again and said, "You'd better make it light on yourselves and let me have those seats." At this point, of course, the passenger who would have taken the seat hadn't said anything. In fact, he never did speak to my knowledge. When the three people, the man who was in the seat with me and the two women, stood up and moved into the aisle, I remained where I was. When the driver saw that I was still there, he asked if I was going to stand up. I told him, no, I wasn't. He said, "Well, if you don't stand up, I'm going to have you arrested." I told him to go on and have me arrested.

He got off the bus and came back shortly. A few minutes later, two policemen got on the bus, and they approached me and asked if the driver had asked me to stand up, and I said yes, and they wanted to know why I didn't. I told them I didn't think I should have to stand up. After I had paid my fare and occupied a seat, I didn't think I should have to give it up. They placed me under arrest then and had me get in the police car, and I was taken to jail and booked on suspicion, I believe. The questions were asked, the usual questions they ask a prisoner or somebody under arrest. They had to determine whether the driver wanted to press charges or swear out a warrant, which he did. Then they took me to jail and I was placed in a cell. In a little while I was taken from the cell, and my picture was made and fingerprints taken. I went back to the cell then, and a few minutes later I was called back again, and when this happened I found out that Mr. E. D. Nixon and Mrs. Clifford Durr had come to make bond for me. . . .

I was given permission to make a telephone call after my picture was taken and fingerprints taken. I called my home and spoke to my mother on the telephone and told her what had happened, that I was in jail. She was quite upset and asked me had the police beaten me. I told her, no. I hadn't been physically injured, but I was being held in jail, and I wanted my husband to come and get me out. . . . He didn't have a car at the time, so he had to get someone to bring him down. At the time he got down, Mr. Nixon and the Durrs had just made bond for me, so we all met at the jail and we went home. . . .

3.2 E. D. Nixon, who here recalls his initial contact with Parks following her arrest, played a pivotal though transitional role in the Montgomery bus boycott. For years Nixon had been a prominent black leader in the region. As local head of the NAACP and the Brotherhood of Sleeping Car Porters, he orchestrated voter registration campaigns, organized black workers, and spoke out against injustice. These actions prepared the ground for the seed that would sprout with Parks' arrest. Nixon and Clifford Durr bailed Parks out of jail and asked if she would be willing to turn her arrest into a challenge to segregation. Nixon also contacted Martin Luther King, Jr., a freshly arrived twenty-six-year-old preacher with no prior political involvement in the community. Recognizing that the various religious factions had yet to "lay their hands" on King, Nixon asked him to head the ad hoc boycott organization, the Montgomery Improvement Association (MIA). King agreed to do so. Ironically, Nixon ended up playing a marginal role in the boycott itself. Because of work commitments he missed the first days of the protest and soon found himself eclipsed by the very man he had tagged to take the helm.

3.2 E. D. Nixon, "How It All Started," *Liberation* (December 1956), p. 10.

On the night of December 1st, 1956, I sat for a long while on the edge of my bed. After a time I turned to my wife and said, "You know, I think every Negro in town should stay off the buses for one day in protest for Mrs. Parks' arrest." My wife looked at me as if I was crazy. Then I asked her, "What do you think?" "I think you ought to stop day dreaming, and turn out that light and get some sleep."

As I began to think about the three women who had been arrested in ten months for violating the Jim Crow law on the buses, my mind turned back thirty years. I began to think about the days when I first traveled out of Montgomery as a pullman porter. I remembered seeing Negroes in the North sitting anywhere they wanted on streetcars and trains. I remembered how I had seen black men holding public office—how they had freedoms which are still being denied us in Alabama. I began to wonder how long we were going to put up with being pushed around.

I remembered how, years ago, I had first asked myself. "What can I do to help bring freedom to the Negro in Alabama?" Naturally, one person alone could not bring about many changes in a deeply rooted tradition. But I believed that one person could kindle a spark that might cause others to see light and work.

I recalled that it had taken a long time before I had gained the courage to begin. Most of the people I talked to called me crazy. Others told me to take it easy if I wanted to live. They told me that Southern white people were different from those up North. Nevertheless I kept believing that Negroes could be free.

Then I thought of A. Philip Randolph, Congressman Oscar Depriest, Attorney Arthur A. Madison and Walter White—the four men who had encouraged me to go forward. I remembered how I first got started working for improvements in Montgomery. I had begun by working for better recreation for children; after that, for PWA and WPA jobs for Negroes, and then for the right to vote. Sometimes a few people would help but most of them were afraid. I recall how the NAACP and the Brotherhood of Sleeping Car Porters were always there to help. . . .

Then all of a sudden, as I sat there on the edge of my bed, some ideas came to me: Why not ask the people in Montgomery to stand up and be counted? Why not start a protest for Mrs. Parks? Why not stay out of the buses? Why not start a Montgomery Improvement Association? I decided that it was time for mass action in spite of my wife's reaction. I felt that the Negroes in Montgomery were at last anxious to move, prepared to sacrifice and ready to endure whatever came.

Although I felt the people in Montgomery had respect for me, I knew that a mass movement of 50,000 people required young, vigorous and well-educated leadership. I believed that if Rev. King and Rev. Abernathy could take over leadership of an improvement association, we could not fail. I rolled over and went to sleep. . . .

3.3 and 3.4 As head of the Women's Political Council (WPC), one of a handful of key civil rights groups in Montgomery, Jo Ann Gibson Robinson played a seminal behind-the-scenes role in the Montgomery struggle. Robinson had moved to Montgomery in 1949 after accepting a post to teach at Alabama State College. Shortly after her arrival she had been forced to give up her seat on a bus. The incident infuriated Robinson, and she committed herself to doing everything in her power to crack Jim Crow. She worked relentlessly to get the bus company and/or city commissioners to outlaw or at least modify the present bus regulations, though with no success. A tremendous amount of "drudge" work had to be done in order for the boycott to succeed and Robinson and the Women's Political Council did much of it. Robinson's description of the first day of the boycott is accompanied by a leaflet which the Women's Political Council distributed. Underlying the leaflet's appeal was the belief that almost all of Montgomery's blacks had both the motive and means to win.

3.3 David J. Garrow, ed., *The Montgomery Bus Boycott and the Women Who Started It: The Memoir of Jo Ann Gibson Robinson* (Knoxville: University of Tennessee Press, 1987), pp. 19-52.

It was Monday, December 5, 1955. For Negroes and whites alike among the 120,000 people who made up Montgomery, Alabama, the working day was beginning, busy with early morning activity. Meteorologically speaking, the day was not different from other winter days in the South—it was cold, threatening to rain. This day was no different to a casual, indifferent observer, or to most of the thousands of white people who were more or less indifferent or partly amused observers. Perhaps the personnel of the Montgomery City Lines, Incorporated, were a little concerned, because even one unfavorable day could cause a serious reduction in bus fare receipts.

But to Montgomery's fifty thousand black citizens, the cold, cloudy December day was different. None of them had slept very well the night before, for they had not been quite sure that their group would really cooperate in the "one-day bus boycott" of city buses. Then there was the cold and the threat of rain, neither of which was in their favor. And they—sleepy, tense with glorious expectancy, hopeful, even prayerful that all of them would endure for one day—were afraid. They were afraid

that their well-planned one-day protest against the Montgomery City
Lines would fail, that blacks in large numbers would ride the buses, and
that the proud black leaders of the boycott would be the laughingstock of
the town.

There would not have been such fear of embarrassment if the boycott
plans had not been discovered by whites and publicized in radio and television broadcast and in huge, black, glaring front-page headlines in local
newspapers. But the city did know of their plans, and black people were
on the spot.

At 5:30 A.M. Monday, December 5, dawn was breaking over Montgomery. Early morning workers were congregating at corners. There,
according to the plan, Negroes were to be picked up not by the Montgomery City Lines, but by Negro taxis driving at reduced rates of ten
cents per person, or by some two hundred private cars which had been
offered free to bus riders for Monday only.

The suspense was almost unbearable, for no one was positively sure
that taxi drivers would keep their promises, that private car owners would
give absolute strangers a ride, that Negro bus riders would stay off the
bus. And then there was the cold and the threat of rain!

The black Women's Political Council had been planning the boycott of
Montgomery City Lines for months, but the plans had only been known
publicly for the past three days. The idea itself had been entertained for
years. Almost daily some black man, woman, or child had an unpleasant
experience on the bus and told other members of his family about it at the
supper table or around the open fireplace or stove. These stories were
repeated to neighbors, who re-told them in club meetings or to ministers
of large church congregations.

At first the ministers would soothe the anger of their congregations with
recommendations of prayer, with promies that God would "make the
rough ways smooth" and with exhortations to "have patience and wait
upon the Lord."

The members had been patient and waited upon the Lord, but the rough
ways had gotten rougher rather than smoother. As months stretched into
years, the encounters with some of the bus drivers grew more numerous
and more intolerable. . . .

The news [of Rosa Parks' arrest] traveled like wildfire into every black
home. Telephones jangled; people congregated on street corners and in
homes and talked. But nothing was done. A numbing helplessness
seemed to paralyze everyone. Very few stayed off the buses the rest of
that day or the next. There was fear, discontent, and uncertainty. Everyone seemed to wait for someone to do something, but nobody made a

move. For that day and a half, black Americans rode the buses as before, as if nothing had happened. They were sullen and uncommunicative, but they rode the buses. There was a silent, tension-filled waiting. For blacks were not talking loudly in public places—they were quiet, sullen, waiting. Just waiting!

. . . Fred Gray [a black Montgomery attorney] was shocked by the news of Mrs. Parks' arrest. I informed him that I already was thinking that the WPC should distribute thousands of notices calling for all bus riders to stay off the buses on Monday, the day of Mrs. Parks' trial. "Are you ready?" he asked. Without hesitation, I assured him that we were. With that he hung up, and I went to work.

3.4 Women's Political Council, "Leaflet."

Another Negro woman has been arrested and thrown in jail because she refused to get up out of her seat on the bus for a white person to sit down. It is the second time since the Claudette Colvin case that a Negro has been arrested for the same thing. This has to be stopped. Negroes have rights, too, for if Negroes did not ride the buses, they could not operate. Three-fourths of the riders are Negroes, yet we are arrested, or have to stand over empty seats. If we do not do something to stop these arrests, they will continue. The next time it may be you, or your daughter, or mother. This woman's case will come up on Monday. We are, therefore, asking every Negro to stay off the buses Monday in protest of the arrest and trial. Don't ride the buses to work, to town, to school, or anywhere on Monday. You can afford to stay out of school for one day if you have no other way to go except by bus. You can also afford to stay out of town for one day. If you work, take a cab, or walk. But please, children and grown-ups, don't ride the bus at all on Monday. Please stay off all buses on Monday.

3.5 The initial one-day boycott proved more successful than anyone could have predicted, so much so that it encouraged Montgomery's black leaders to call for its continuation. The black community probably did not need that much prodding. Many had directly felt the sting of the segregated bus system and Rosa Parks' arrest provided them with the opportunity to demand that society treat them with dignity. This said, few can doubt that Martin Luther King, Jr. played a key role in the ensuing days, weeks, and months.

King was the son of a prominent Atlanta mininster. He had attended one of the most prestigious black institutions of higher learning in the nation, Morehouse College, and earned a Doctor in Theology from Boston University. He came to Montgomery with a young bride, Coretta, and had a newborn baby when the

boycott began. Until Parks' arrest, King had not displayed any particular incli-
nation to become politically involved and his comfortable background and family
circumstances provided reason alone for him not to do so. Yet, he hesitated only
for a moment.

The following excerpt, from his autobiographical account of the boycott, is
part of the rousing address that King delivered on the first night of the boycott at
the Holt Street Baptist Church. King also describes a key moment in his life, a
"communion" with God. As head of the MIA, King's life was placed in constant
danger. His house was bombed and he faced constant death threats. With a
young wife and child, he was compelled to wonder if he had the courage or the
right to continue to lead the boycott; perhaps he should withdraw to the comfort
of his father's church in Atlanta. He did not do so largely because of the
assurances he believed he received from God to persevere. This moment stayed
with him for the rest of his life.

3.5 Martin Luther King, Jr., *Stride Toward Freedom* (New York: Harper & Row, 1958), pp. 61-63 and 132-138.

When the meeting began [at the Holt Street Church] it was almost half an hour late. The opening hymn was the old familiar "Onward Christian Soldiers," and when that mammoth audience stood to sing, the voices outside swelling the chorus in the church, there was a mighty ring like the glad echo of heaven itself.

Rev. W. F. Alford, minister of the Beulah Church, led the congregation in prayer, followed by a reading of the Scriptures by Rev. U. J. Fields, minister of the Bell Street Baptist Church. Then the chairman introduced me. As the audience applauded, I rose and stood before the pulpit. Television cameras began to shoot from all sides. The crowd grew quiet.

Without manuscript or notes, I told the story of what happened to Mrs. Parks. Then I reviewed the long history of abuses and insults that Negro citizens had experienced on the city buses. "But there comes a time," I said, "that people get tired. We are here this evening to say to those who have mistreated us so long that we are tired—tired of being segregated and humiliated; tired of being kicked about by the brutal feet of oppression." The congregation met this statement with fervent applause. "We had no alternative but to protest," I continued. "For many years, we have shown amazing patience. We have sometimes given our white brothers the feeling that we liked the way we were being treated. But we come here tonight to be saved from that patience that makes us patient with anything less than freedom and justice." Again the audience interrupted with applause.

Briefly I justified our actions, both morally and legally. "One of the great glories of democracy is the right to protest for right." Comparing our methods with those of the White Citizens Councils and the Ku Klux Klan, I pointed out that while "these organizations are protesting for the perpetuation of injustice in the community, we are protesting for the birth of justice in the community. Their methods lead to violence and lawlessness. But in our protest there will be no cross burnings. No white person will be taken from his home by a hooded Negro mob and brutally murdered. There will be no threats and intimidation. We will be guided by the highest principles of law and order."

With this groundwork for militant action, I moved on to words of caution. . . . "Our method will be that of persuasion, not coercion. We will only say to the people, 'Let your conscience decide.' " Emphasizing the Christian doctrine of love, "our actions must be guided by the deepest principles of our Christian faith. Love must be our regulating ideal. Once again we must hear the words of Jesus echoing across the centuries: 'Love your enemies, bless them that curse you, and pray for them that despitefully use you.' If we fail to do this our protest will end up as a meaningless drama on the stage of history, and its memory will be shrouded with the ugly garments of shame. In spite of the mistreatment that we have confronted we must not become bitter, and end up by hating our white brothers. As Booker T. Washington said, 'Let no man pull you so low as to make you hate him.' " Then came my closing statement. "If you will protest courageously, and yet with dignity and Christian love, when the history books are written in future generations, the historians will have to pause and say, 'There lived a great people—a black people— who injected new meaning and dignity into the veins of civilization.' This is our challenge and our overwhelming responsibility." As I took my seat the people rose to their feet and applauded. I was thankful to God that the message had gotten over and that the task of combining the militant and the moderate had been at least partially accomplished. . . .

After the "get-tough" policy had failed to stop the movement the diehards became desperate, and we waited to see what their next move would be. Almost immediately after the protest started we had begun to receive threatening telephone calls and letters. Sporadic in the beginning, they increased as time went on. By the middle of January, they had risen to thirty and forty a day.

Postcards, often signed "KKK," said simply "get out of town or else." Many misspelled and crudely written letters presented religious half-truths to prove that "God do not intend the White People and the

Negro to gather if he did we would be the same.'' Others enclosed mimeographed and printed materials combining anti-Semitic and anti-Negro sentiments. One of these contained a handwritten postscript: ''You niggers are getting yourself in a bad place. The Bible is strong for segregation as of the jews concerning other races. It is even for segregation between the 12 tribes of Israel. We need and will have a Hitler to get our country straightened out.'' Many of the letters were unprintable catalogues of blasphemy and obscenity. . . .

When these incidents started, I took them in stride, feeling they were the work of a few hotheads who would soon be discouraged when they discovered that we would not fight back. But as the weeks passed, I began to see that many of the threats were in earnest. Soon I felt myself faltering and growing in fear. One day, a white friend told me that he had heard from reliable sources that plans were being made to take my life. . . .

One night toward the end of January I settled into bed late, after a strenuous day. Coretta had already fallen asleep and just as I was about to doze off the telephone rang. An angry voice said, ''Listen, nigger, we've taken all we want from you; before next week you'll be sorry you ever came to Montgomery.'' I hung up, but I couldn't sleep. It seemed that all of my fears had come down at once. I had reached the saturation point.

I got out of bed and began to walk the floor. Finally I went to the kitchen and heated a pot of coffee. I was ready to give up. With my cup of coffee sitting untouched before me I tried to think of a way to move out of the picture without appearing a coward. In this state of exhaustion, when my courage had all but gone, I decided to take my problem to God. With my head in my hands, I bowed over the kitchen table and prayed aloud. The words spoke to God that midnight are still vivid in my memory. ''I am here taking a stand for what I believe is right. But now I am afraid. The people are looking to me for leadership, and if I stand before them without strength and courage, they too will falter. I am at the end of my powers. I have nothing left. I've come to the point where I can't face it alone.''

At that moment I experienced the presence of the Divine as I had never experienced HIM before. It seemed as though I could hear the quiet assurance of an inner voice saying: ''Stand up for righteousness, stand up for truth; and God will be at your side forever.'' Almost at once my fears began to go. My uncertainty disappeared. I was ready to face anything. . . .

3.6 In general, southern whites adamantly resisted challenges to their way of life. However, there were some exceptions, including the Durrs. Clifford and Virginia Durr had a history of fighting for progressive causes, including the labor movement, and from the moment of Parks' arrest they became involved with the bus boycott. In her autobiography, Virginia Durr probes some of the games that whites and blacks played during the year-long struggle. White women could not admit that they sympathized with blacks. Yet, in numerous instances they abetted the boycott. Ironically, many black women played along with the game.

3.6 Hollinger F. Barnard, ed., *Outside the Magic Circle: The Autobiography of Virginia Foster Durr* (Tuscaloosa: University of Alabama Press, 1985), pp. 274-288.

The boycott lasted the entire year, December 1955 until December 1956. I would see the black women walking to work every morning and walking back at night. It was like the black tides would come up out of the black section of town and go to work and then sweep back again. We would offer the women rides when we saw them walking, particularly out in the country club area where the distances were rather great. I would say to a complete stranger, "Would you like a ride?" They'd say, "Yes, thank you very much." They'd get in the car, and I'd ask them where they lived. They always lived on the west part of town. I'd say, "I'm glad to see that you're supporting the boycott." "No ma'am. I hadn't nothing to do with that boycott. The lady I work for, she wasn't feelin' so good this afternoon so that's why I was walkin' home." "No ma'am, I don't have nothin' to do with that boycott. It's just that her little girl's sick." One reason after another, but they wouldn't admit they were supporting the boycott.

Then the policemen began giving tickets to the white women who were taking black women home. I had a washwoman who came once a week, an older lady who belonged to the Church of Christ. She admired Dr. King greatly. She said she had seen the angels come down and stand on his shoulders every Monday night. In everything he said he was speaking with the voice of God. Now, everything he did was also dictated by the voice of God. She got so she talked to God so much that she didn't do much ironing. She was really a sweet old lady, but she was a religious fanatic. I was taking her home one afternoon and we were stopped. I knew positively I had stopped at the stop sign, but a policeman came roaring up to me. He said that I had stopped too late. I'd gone two or three feet over the line. I knew there was no use in arguing, so I told him I was sorry and got my ticket and took this old lady home. I had to pay five dollars. This incident was typical of what happened over and over again all over town.

The mayor of the city, Tacky Gayle, issued a plea for the white women of Montgomery to stop taking their black maids home. He said they could break the boycott if the white women would stop taking their black maids home, or even stop hiring them. Well, you have never heard such a roar of indignation in your life as came from the white women of Montgomery. They were just furious at Tacky Gayle. They said, okay, if Tacky Gayle wants to come out here and do my washing and ironing and cleaning and cooking and look after my children, he can do it, but unless he does, I'm going to get Mary or Sally or Suzy. And they said, "Sally has never had a thing to do with that boycott in the first place. She told me she only stays off the buses because she's scared of those hoodlums that might hurt her."

A vast deceit went on. Everybody knew everybody else was lying, but to save face, they had to lie. The black women had to say they weren't taking any part in the boycott. The white women had to say that their maids didn't take part in the boycott. We had a good example of that in Mary, Mrs. Durr's old cook who came from Hardaway, in Macon County. She'd been with the Durrs for years and now was Mrs. Durr's nurse. Mrs. Durr by that time was quite old and feeble and had to stay in bed, but a lot of people would drop by in the afternoons. Mary would sit in the room.

Mrs. Durr was a beautiful old woman. . . . Her mind was failing her, but she was still able to carry on a conversation. One afternoon when I was in the room somebody said to Mary, "Mary, I hope you don't have anything to do with that boycott." Mary said, "No, ma'am, I hadn't had nothing to do with that boycott. There's my sister Olla. She don't live very far from her job so she just walks to work. And my brother, he's got a job at the cotton mill and he just goes to work with some other men who are driving a car. And my other sister she just walks to work cause it's so close. No, ma'am, none of us has a thing to do with that boycott. We just stays off the buses." The white people really believed that. They didn't see through it at all.

In truth, Mary was a passionate advocate of the boycott. She'd meet us as we came in the driveway to ask how the bus boycott was getting on, how Dr. King was. She couldn't read and write, but she listened to the radio. That afternoon after the guests had left and Mary was fixing supper, Cliff and I said to her, "Mary, you are the biggest storyteller in the world. You know very well you're supporting the boycott and all of your family are. Why in the world did you make up that tale about how none of you were, and you were all walking just because you wanted to?" She laughed and she said, "Well, I tell you, Mr. Cliff, I tell you, I learned one thing in my life and that is, when your hand's in the lion's mouth, it's just better to pat it on the head." That expressed the feeling of the black community. The black women needed those jobs. They weren't paid very much, but that's all the income many of them had. They couldn't afford to say, "I'm supporting the boycott." So the white women lied and the black women lied. And the maids kept coming and the white women kept driving them back and forth to work.

*1961 - realization
that Courts were ineffective*

c

stats

Chapter Four

THE SIT-INS
AND FREEDOM RIDES

If Rosa Parks' refusal to give up her seat on a bus in Montgomery, Alabama, symbolized a modern-day version of the "shot heard around the world" at Lexington and Concord, the decision of four North Carolina Agricultural & Technical College students to demand service at the lunch counter at Woolworth's in Greensboro, North Carolina, on February 1, 1960, represented an updated battle of Bunker Hill. On that eventful day, Joseph McNeil, Ezell Blair, Jr., David Richmond, and Franklin McCain sat down at the lunch counter, ordered coffee and doughnuts, and refused to leave until they were served. By the fall of 1961 every southern and border state—over one hundred communities—had experienced sit-ins. Over seventy thousand individuals participated. Still more donated money or wrote letters of support.

4.1 In the following interview, Franklin McCain, one of the four original sit-in participants describes their plans and feelings. The sit-ins took place against a backdrop of heightened but unfulfilled expectations. The Supreme Court's decision in the Brown *case had led young blacks to believe that Jim Crow was on its deathbed. Yet, segregation remained a fact of life. For example, as of 1961, only .026 percent of North Carolina's schools had desegregated, and North Carolina was considered a moderate state. The NAACP kept hammering away at Jim Crow in the courts, but all of its legal victories produced few tangible changes. Disgusted with local subterfuge, McCain and three other black students at North Carolina A&T decided that the time for waiting for the courts to bring about change had passed. It was time to act.*

4.1 Franklin McCain, "Interview," in Howell Raines, *My Soul Is Rested*, pp. 75-82.

The planning process was on a Sunday night, I remember it quite well. I think it was Joseph [McNeil] who said, "It's time that we take some action now. We've been getting together, and we've been, up to this point, still like most people we've talked about for the past few weeks or so—that is, people who talk a lot but, in fact, make very little action." After selecting the technique, then we said, "Let's go down and just ask for service." It certainly wasn't titled a "sit-in" or "sit-down" at that time. "Let's just go down to Woolworth's tomorrow and ask for service, and the tactic is going to be simply this: we'll just stay there." We never anticipated being served, certainly, the first day anyway. "We'll stay until we get served." And I think Ezell [Blair, Jr.] said, "Well, you know that might be weeks, that might be months, that might be never." And I think it was the consensus of the groups, we said, "Well, that's just the chance we'll have to take."

What's likely to happen? Now, I think that was a question that all of us asked ourselves. . . . What's going to happen once we sit down? Of course, nobody had the answers. Even your wildest imagination couldn't lead you to believe what would, in fact, happen. . . .

Once getting there . . . we did make purchases of school supplies and took the patience and time to get receipts for our purchases, and Joseph and myself went over to the counter and asked to be served coffee and doughnuts. As anticipated, the reply was, "I'm sorry, we don't serve you here." And of course we said, "We just beg to disagree with you. We've in fact already been served; you've served us already and that's just not quite true." The attendant or waitress was a little bit dumbfounded, just didn't know what to say under circumstances like that. And we said, "We wonder why you'd invite us in to serve us at one counter and deny service at another. If this is a private club or private concern, then we believe you ought to sell membership cards and sell only to persons who have a membership card. If we don't have a card, then we'd know pretty well that we shouldn't come in or even attempt to come in." That didn't go over too well, simply because I don't think she understood what we were talking about, and the second reason, she had no logical response to a statement like that. And the only thing that an individual in her case or position could do is, of course, call the manager. . . . Well, at this time, I think we were joined by Dave Richmond and Ezell Blair at the counter. . . .

Were you afraid at this point?

Oh, hell, yes, no question about that. At that point there was a policeman who had walked in off the street, who was pacing the aisle . . .

behind us, where we were seated, with his club in his hand, just sort of knocking it in his hand, and just looking mean and red and a little upset and a little bit disgusted. And you had the feeling that he didn't know what the hell to do. You had the feeling that this is the first time that this big bad man with the gun and the club has been pushed in a corner, and he's got absolutely no defense, and the thing that's killing him more than anything else—he doesn't know what he can or what he cannot do. . . .

There was virtually nothing that could move us, there was virtually nothing probably at that point that could really frighten us off. . . . If it's possible to know what it means to have your soul cleansed—I felt pretty clean at that time. I probably felt better on that day than I've ever felt in my life. Seems like a lot of feelings of guilt or what-have-you left me, and I felt as though I had gained my manhood, so to speak, and not only gained it, but had developed quite a lot of respect for it. Not Franklin McCain only as an individual, but I felt as though the manhood of a number of other black persons had been restored and had gotten some respect from just that one day. . . .

The only reason we did leave is the store was closing. We knew, of course, we had to leave when the store was closing. We said to him [Mr. Harris, the store manager], "Well, we'll have plenty of time tomorrow, because we'll be back to see you." I don't think that went over too well. But by the time we were leaving, the store was just crowded with people from off the streets. . . . As a matter of fact, there were so many people standin' in front of the store, we had to leave from the side entrance.

But back at the campus, there was just a beehive of activity. Word had spread. As a matter of fact, word was back on campus before we ever got back. There were all sorts of phone calls to the administration and to people on the faculty and staff. The mayor's office was aware of it and the governor was aware of it. I think it was all over North Carolina within a matter of just an hour or so. . . .

4.2 Prior to the Greensboro action a remarkable collection of black students had formed the Nashville movement. Under the direction of James Lawson, Jr., a student of Gandhi and the theory and practice of nonviolence, the Nashville (Tennessee) group, which included John Lewis, Marion Barry, and Diane Nash, prepared itself to challenge Jim Crow. Nash was from Chicago. She had come South for the first time in 1959 to study at Fisk University and was appalled by her firsthand contact with segregation. Rather than retreat to the North, however, she committed herself to toppling the "southern way of life."

4.2 Diane Nash, "Interview," in *The New Negro*, ed. by Mathew Ahman (Notre Dame: Fides, 1961).

My participation in the movement began in February 1960, with the lunch counter "sit-ins." I was then a student at Fisk University. . . . My occupation at present is coordinating secretary for the Nashville Non-violent Movement. . . .

In September, 1959, I came to Nashville as a student at Fisk University. This was the first time that I had been as far south as Tennessee; therefore, it was the first time that I had encountered the blatant segregation that exists in the South. I came then to see the community in sin. Seeing signs designating "white" or "colored," being told, "We don't serve niggers in here," and, as happened in one restaurant, being looked in the eye and told, "Go around to the back door where you belong," had tremendous psychological impact on me. To begin with, I didn't agree with the premise that I was inferior, and I had a difficult time complying with it. Also, I felt stifled and boxed in since so many areas of living were restricted. The Negro in the South is told constantly, "You can't sit here." "You can't work there." "You can't live here, or send your children to school there." "You can't use this park, or that swimming pool," and on and on and on. Restrictions extend into housing, schools, jobs (Negroes, who provide a built-in lower economic class, are employed in the most menial capacities and are paid the lowest wages). Segregation encompasses city parks, swimming pools and recreational facilities. . . . Oppression extends to every area of life.

Failure to comply with these oppressions results in beatings, in house-burnings and bombings, and economic reprisals, as we saw in Fayette County, Tennessee. . . .

As can easily be imagined, all this has a real effect upon the Negro. I won't attempt to analyze here the effect of the system upon the Negro, but I should like to make a few observations. An organism must make some type of adjustment to its environment. The Negro, however, continues to deny consciously to himself, and to his children, that he is inferior. Yet each time he uses a "colored" facility, he testifies to his own inferiority. . . .

Segregation has its destructive effect upon the segregator also. The most outstanding of these effects perhaps is fear. I can't forget how openly this fear was displayed in Nashville on the very first day that students there sat-in. Here were Negro students, quiet, in good discipline, who were consciously attempting to show no ill will, even to the point of making sure that they had pleasant and calm facial expressions. The demonstrators did nothing more than sit on the stools at the lunch counter. Yet, from the reaction of the white employees of the variety stores and from the onlookers, some dreadful monster might just as well have been about to devour them all. Waitresses dropped things. Store managers and personnel perspired. Several cashiers were led off in tears. One of the best remembered incidents of that day took place in a ladies restroom of a department store. Two Negro students, who had sat-in at the lunch counter, went into the ladies restroom which was marked "white" and were there as a heavy-set, older white lady, who might have been seeking refuge from the scene taking place at the lunch counter, entered. Upon opening the door and finding the two Negro girls inside, the women threw up her hands and, nearly in tears, exclaimed, "Oh Nigras everywhere!"

So segregation engenders fear in the segregator, especially needless fear of what will happen if integration comes; in short, fear of the unknown. Then Jim Crow fosters ignorance. The white person is denied the educational opportunities of exchange with people of a race other than his own. Bias makes for the hatred which we've seen stamped upon the faces of whites in newspaper pictures of the mob. . . .

Worst of all, however, is the stagnancy of thought and character—of both whites and Negroes—which is the result of the rationalization that is necessary in order that the oppressed and oppressor may live with a system of slavery and human abasement.

I can remember Nashville in this stage of sin when I first came there in September, 1959, a few months before the sit-in movement was to begin. As a new student at Fisk University that September, I was completely unaware that over the next few months I would really experience segregation; that I would see raw hatred; that I would see my friends beaten; that I would be a convict several times and, as is the case at the moment, that there would be a warrant out for my arrest. . . . Expecting my life to pursue a rather quiet course, I was also unaware that I would begin to feel part of a group of people suddenly proud to be called "black." To be called "Negro" had once been thought of as derogatory and had been softened by polite company to "colored person." At one time, to have been called "nigger" was a gross insult and hurt keenly. Within the movement, however, we came to a realization of our own worth. We began to see our role and our responsibility to our country and to our fellow men, so that to be called "nigger" on the picket line, or anywhere, was now an unimportant thing that no longer produced in us that flinch. As to the typical white southerner who compromises with "nigra" we only secretly wish for a moment when we could gracefully help him with his phonetics, explaining that it's "knee—grow. . . ."

Through the unity and purposefulness of the experience of the Nashville Negro, there was born a new awareness of himself as an individual.

There was also born, on the part of whites, a new understanding and awareness of the Negro as a person to be considered and respected.

4.3 On Easter weekend, 1960 (April 15-17), close to 175 students from 30 states, mostly southern, many of them sit-in participants, attended the Student Leadership Conference on Nonviolent Resistance at Shaw University in Raleigh, North Carolina. Sponsored by the Southern Christian Leadership Conference (SCLC), the meeting sought to enrich the students' understanding of nonviolent direct action and to coordinate their future efforts.

Ella Baker, whose firsthand report on the conference is reprinted here, was a graduate of Shaw University, a one-time assistant field secretary and president of the New York branch of the NAACP, and, as of 1960, executive director of SCLC. Baker played a seminal role in organizing the conference and in prodding the students to establish a new civil rights organization, the Student Nonviolent Coordinating Committee (SNCC). Both in public, as in the following article, and behind-the-scenes, Baker emphasized the necessity of developing a decentralized and democratic movement—one that did not rely upon a single charismatic personality (like SCLC).

4.3 Ella Baker, "Bigger than a Hamburger," *Southern Patriot*, Vol. 18 (1960).

The Student Leadership Conference made it crystal clear that current sit-ins and other demonstrations are concerned with some thing much bigger than a hamburger or even a giant-sized coke.

Whatever may be the difference in approach to their goal, the Negro and white students, North and South, are seeking to rid America of the scourge of racial segregation and discrimination—not only at lunch counters, but in every aspect of life.

In reports, casual conversations, discussion groups, and speeches, the sense and the spirit of the following statement that appeared in the initial newsletter of the students at Barber-Scotia College, Concord, N.C., were re-echoed time and again:

"We want the world to know that we no longer accept the inferior position of second-class citizenship. We are willing to go to jail, be ridiculed, spat upon and even suffer physical violence to obtain First Class Citizenship."

By and large, this feeling that they have a destined date with freedom, was not limited to a drive for personal freedom, or even freedom for the Negro in the South. Repeatedly it was emphasized that the movement was concerned with the moral implications of racial discrimination for the "whole world" and the "Human Race."

The universality of approach was linked with a perceptive recognition that "it is important to keep the movement democratic and to avoid struggles for personal leadership."

It was further evident that the desire for supportive cooperation from adult leaders and the adult community was also tempered by apprehension that adults might try to "capture" the student movement. The students showed willingness to be met on the basis of equality, but were intolerant of anything that smacked of manipulation or domination.

This inclination toward *group-centered leadership*, rather than toward a *leader-centered group pattern of organization* was refreshing indeed to those of the older group who bear the scars of the battle, the frustrations and the disillusionment that come when the prophetic leader turns out to have heavy feet of clay.

However hopeful might be the signs in the direction of group-centeredness, the fact that many schools and communities, especially in the South, have not provided adequate experience for young Negroes to assume the initiative and think and act independently accentuated the need for guarding the student movement against well-meaning, but nevertheless, over-protectiveness.

Here is an opportunity for adult and youth to work together and provide genuine leadership—the development of the individual to his highest potential for the benefit of the group.

Many adults and youth characterized the Raleigh meeting as the greatest or most significant conference of our period.

Whether it lives up to this high evaluation or not will, in a large measure, be determined by the extent to which there is more effective training in and understanding of non-violent principles and practices, in group dynamics, and in the re-direction into creative channels of the normal frustrations and hostilities that result from second-class citizenship.

4.4 Along with Baker, James Lawson played the lead role at SNCC's founding conference. Even more so than Martin Luther King, Jr., Lawson captured the student's imagination with his discussion of nonviolence. As he explained, non-violence and passivity were not identical. Nonviolence did not mean pursuing a moderate agenda through tame means. On the contrary, nonviolent direct action entailed a radical transformation of human relations.

4.4 James M. Lawson, Jr., "From a Lunch-Counter Stool," April 1960, Student Nonviolent Coordinating Committee Papers.

These are exciting moments in which to live. Reflect how over the last few weeks, the "sit-in" movement has leaped from campus to campus, until today hardly any campus remains unaffected. At the beginning of the decade, the student generation was "silent," "uncommitted," or "beat-nik." But after only four months, these analogies largely used by adults appear as hasty cliches which should not have been used in the first place. The rapidity and drive of the movement indicates that all the while American students were simply waiting in suspension; waiting for the cause, that ideal, that event, that "actualizing of their faith" which would cata-pult their right to speak powerfully to their nation and world. . . .

But as so frequently happens, these are also enigmatic moments. Enig-matic, for like man in every age who cannot read the signs of the times, many of us are not able to see what appears before us, or hear what is spoken from lunch counter stools, or understand what has been cried behind jail cell bars.

Already the paralysis of talk, the disobedience of piety, the frustration of false ambition, and the insensitivity of an affluent society yearns to diffuse the meaning and flatten the thrust of America's first non-violent campaign.

One great university equates the movement to simply another student fad similar to a panty raid, or long black stockings. . . . Amid this welter of irrelevant and superficial reactions, the primary motifs of the move-ment, the essential message, the crucial issues raised are often completely missed. So the Christian student who has not yet given his support or mind to the movement might well want to know what the issue is all about. Is it just a lot of nonsense over a hamburger? Or is it far more?

To begin, let us note what the issue is not. . . .

Police partiality is not the issue. Nashville has been considered one of those "good" cities where racial violence has not been tolerated. Yet, on a Saturday in February, the mystique of yet another popular myth vanished. For only police permissiveness invited young white men to take over store after store in an effort to further intimidate or crush the "sit-in." Law enforcement agents accustomed to viewing crime, were able to mark well-dressed students waiting to make purchases, as loitering on the lunch-counter stools, but they were unable even to suspect and cer-tainly not to see assault and battery. . . . Such partiality, however, is symptomatic of the diagnosis only—an inevitable by-product—another means of avoiding the encounter. But the "sit-in" does not intend to make such partiality the issue.

Already many well-meaning and notable voices are seeking to define the problem in purely legal terms. But if the students wanted a legal case, they had only to initiate a suit. But not a single sit-in began in this fashion. No one planned to be arrested or desired such. The legal battles which will be fought as a consequence of many arrests never once touch on the matter of eating where you normally shop, or on segregation *per se*. . . .

Let us admit readily that some of the major victories gained for social justice have come through the courts. . . . The Negro has been a law-abiding citizen as he has struggled for justice against many unlawful elements.

But the major defeats have occurred when we have been unable to convince the nation to support or implement the Constitution, when a court decision is ignored or nullified by local and state action. A democratic structure of law remains democratic, remains lawful only as the people are continuously persuaded to be democratic. Law is always nullified by practice and disdain unless the minds and hearts of a people sustain law. . . .

Eventually our society must abide by the Constitution and not permit any local law or custom to hinder freedom or justice. But such a society lives by more than law. In the same respect the sit-in movement is not trying to create a legal battle, but points to that which is more than law.

Finally, the issue is not integration. This is particularly true of the Christian oriented person. Certainly the students are asking in behalf of the entire Negro community and the nation that these eating counters become places of service for all persons. But it would be extremely short-sighted to assume that integration is the problem or the word of the "sit-in." To the extent to which the movement reflects deep Christian impulses, desegregation is a necessary next step. But it cannot be the end. If progress has not been at a genuine pace, it is often because the major groups seeking equal rights tactically made desegregation the end and not the means.

The Christian favors the breaking down of racial barriers because the redeemed community of which he is already a citizen recognizes no barriers dividing humanity. The Kingdom of God, as in heaven so on earth, is the distant goal of the Christian. That Kingdom is far more than the immediate need for integration. . . .

In the first instance, we who are demonstrators are trying to raise what we call the "moral issue." That is, we are pointing to the viciousness of racial segregation and prejudice and calling it evil or sin. The matter is not legal, sociological or racial, it is moral and spiritual. Until America (South and North) honestly accepts the sinful nature of racism, this cancerous disease will continue to rape all of us. . . .

In the second instance, the non-violent movement is asserting, "get moving." The pace of social change is too slow. At this rate it will be at least another generation before the major forms of segregation disappear. All of Africa will be free before the American Negro attains first-class citizenship. Most of us will be grandparents before we can live normal human lives.

The choice of the non-violent method, "the sit-in," symbolizes both judgment and promise. It is a judgment upon middle-class conventional, half-way efforts to deal with radical social evil. It is specifically a judgment upon contemporary civil rights attempts. As one high school student from Chattanooga exclaimed, "We started because we were tired of waiting for you to act. . . ."

But the sit-in is likewise a sign of promise: God's promise that if radical Christian methods are adopted the rate of change can be vastly increased. Under Christian non-violence, Negro students reject the hardship of disobedient passivity and fear, but embrace the hardship (violence and jail) of obedience. Such non-violence strips the segregationalist power structure of its major weapon: the manipulation of law or law-enforcement to keep the Negro in his place. . . .

4.5 At the Raleigh conference, SNCC drafted its "Statement of Purpose." Crafted largely by members of the Nashville movement, the manifesto displayed the organization's commitment to nonviolence. Heeding the advice of Ella Baker, SNCC decided to remain independent of SCLC and other adult organizations. It elected its first chairman, Marion Barry, a native of Itta Bena, Mississippi, a member of the Nashville movement, and the future mayor of Washington, D.C., and established an office in Atlanta, soon to be staffed by James Forman, Julian Bond, Jane Stembridge, and an assortment of other volunteers.

4.5 SNCC, "Statement of Purpose," April 1960.

We affirm the philosophical or religious ideal of nonviolence as the foundation of our purpose, the presupposition of our faith, and the manner of our action. Nonviolence as it grows from Judaic-Christian tradition seeks a social order of justice permeated by love. Integration of human endeavor represents the crucial first step toward such a society.

Through nonviolence, courage displaces fear; love transforms hate. Acceptance dissipates prejudice; hope ends despair. Peace dominates war; faith reconciles doubt. Mutual regard cancels enmity. Justice for all overthrows injustice. The redemptive community supersedes systems of gross social immorality.

Love is the central motif of nonviolence. Love is the force by which God binds man to Himself and man to man. Such love goes to the extreme; it remains loving and forgiving even in the midst of hostility. It matches the capacity of evil to inflict suffering with an even more enduring capacity to absorb evil, all the while persisting in love.

By appealing to conscience and standing on the moral nature of human existence, nonviolence nurtures the atmosphere in which reconciliation and justice become actual possibilities.

4.6 The Freedom Rides marked the spread of the nonviolent direct action (Fig. 4.1). The Supreme Court's decision in the Boynton *case (February 1, 1961), which expanded the ban against segregation in interstate travel, provided the immediate impetus for the rides. President Kennedy's reluctance to initiate civil rights reform added to the Congress of Racial Equality's decision to undertake the endeavor. By traveling on two separate buses and using various facilities, in the South, in an integrated manner, the riders sought to test the implementation of the Boynton decision. If southern authorities resisted, and CORE expected they would, the rides would generate publicity, which, in turn, could compel the federal government to intervene. In addition, CORE leaders sensed that the rides would revitalize its reputation. The Congress of Racial*

Figure 4.1
Route of Freedom Rides

Equality was an established civil rights organization. In the mid-1940s it had staged Freedom Rides, known as the Journey of Reconciliation, in the border states.

One of the thirteen freedom riders who departed from Washington, D.C., was James Peck, a veteran of CORE's 1947 Journey of Reconciliation. Peck's autobiographical account of the rides vividly describes the resistance that the riders met when they reached Anniston and Birmingham, Alabama. Though nearly killed by a white mob, Peck vowed to press on. As he noted, if whites could deter him through violence, then the southern way of life would remain in place.

4.6 James Peck, *Freedom Ride* (New York: Simon & Schuster, 1962), pp. 115-119 and 123-129.

The group which assembled May 1 at Fellowship House in Washington for training totaled thirteen. It was a very different type of group from the one which had gathered in Washington fourteen years previously for the same type of project. It included a number of what has become known as "the new Negro"—southern students who took part in the sit-in movement and for whom arrest or the threat thereof had become commonplace. Most of the group were young people in their twenties. Very few of them were pacifists. . . .

Danville, Virginia was the first place where testers were refused service. At the colored counter, Ed Blankenheim, a white, sat for ten minutes until his bus was ready for departure. Genevieve Hughes, a white, and I, aboard a later bus, were at first refused service but we—and Walter Bergman—finally got refreshments after a brief discussion with the manager.

Greensboro, though reputed for its liberalism, was the first city where the color signs started to become the rule. The first greeting to arriving bus passengers were oversized signs all around the building with arrows pointing to the colored waiting room. On the other hand, the colored lunch room which was no bigger than a good-sized closet and equally gloomy, had been closed permanently a week before our arrival. . . .

Charlotte was the scene of the trip's first arrest—and the birth of a new "in," the shoe in. Charles Person climbed onto a shoeshine chair and, after being refused service, remained seated until a cop with handcuffs arrived. . . .

Violence against the freedom riders erupted for the first time in Rock Hill, South Carolina, where the press had headlined our arrival and where hoodlums had recently attacked lunch-counter pickets. In fact, several of the hoodlums waiting at the Greyhound station were recognized as the same individuals who had assaulted the local student pickets.

As the Greyhound contingent of riders arrived, some twenty of these ruffians were waiting. When John Lewis, who is Negro, approached the entrance of the white waiting room, he was assaulted by two of them. Three started slugging Albert Bigelow, a white, who was next in line. . . .

In Atlanta, we were welcomed at the Greyhound terminal by a large group of students, many of whom had participated in the local lunch-counter picketing and sit-in's. The terminal restaurant was closed but we used the waiting room and rest rooms. The Trailway's terminal restaurant was open, and two of our teams tested it on departure without incident. . . .

The most nightmarish day of our freedom ride was Sunday, May 14, Mother's Day. I identify the date with Mother's Day because when Police Chief Connor was asked why there was not a single policeman at the Birmingham Trailway's terminal to avert mob violence, he explained that since it was Mother's Day, most of the police were off-duty visiting their mothers. That there was going to be a mob to meet us had been well known around Birmingham for several days. Reverend Fred Shuttles-worth told me so when I phoned to give him the scheduled arrival times of our two buses.

However, we did not know in advance that a similar mob was waiting in Anniston, a rest stop on the way. Our first contingent, aboard Grey-hound, learned of this when their bus stopped just outside of Anniston. . . .

When the Greyhound bus pulled into Anniston, it was immediately sur-rounded by an angry mob armed with iron bars. They set upon the vehicle, denting the sides, breaking the windows, and slashing tires. Finally police arrived, and the bus managed to depart. But the mob pursued it in cars. One car got ahead of the bus and prevented it from gathering speed. About six miles out, one of the tires went flat, and the bus was forced to pull over to a gas station.

Within minutes the pursuing mob was again hitting the bus with iron bars. Their rear window was broken and a bomb was hurled inside. Suddenly the vehicle became filled with thick smoke. The passengers, including the freedom riders, ducked toward the floor in order to breathe. A few climbed out of a window. Some tried to get out of the door, but it was being held shut from the outside.

As Henry Thomas tells it, he shortly succeeded in pushing the door open. As he stepped out, he walked toward a man who looked friendly. Suddenly the man wielded a club from behind his back and struck him over the head.

All the passengers managed to escape before the bus burst into flames and was totally destroyed. The extent of the destruction was shown in the grim newspaper photos. . . . Policemen, who had been standing by, be-latedly came on the scene. . . .

When the Trailways bus carrying our contingent arrived in Anniston an hour later, the other passengers learned of what had happened to the Greyhound bus and discontinued their trips. While waiting for the bus to proceed, we heard the sirens of ambulances taking the injured to the hospital, but we did not know what had happened.

We learned of it only when eight hoodlums climbed aboard and stood by the driver as he made a brief announcement. He concluded by stating that he would refuse to drive unless the Negroes in our group moved to the formerly segregated rear seats. They remained quietly in their front seat. The hoodlums cursed and started to move them bodily to the rear, kicking and hitting them. . . .

Walter Bergman, who is a retired professor, and I were seated toward the rear. We moved forward and tried to persuade the hoodlums to desist. We, too, were pushed, punched, and kicked. I found myself face downward on the floor of the bus. Someone was on top of me. I was bleeding. Bergman's jaw was cut and swollen. None of us realized that he also had received a crushing blow on the head which would bring him close to death. . . .

Finally, all of our group—whites and Negroes—and one Negro passenger who had not gotten off, had been forced to the back of the bus. The hoodlums . . . sat in the very front. . . . At that point the driver agreed to proceed to Birmingham. . . .

Upon arrival in Birmingham, I could see a mob line up on the sidewalk only a few feet from the loading platform. Most of them were young—in their twenties. Some were carrying ill-concealed iron bars. . . . All had hate showing on their faces. . . .

Now we stood on the Birmingham unloading platform with the segregationist mob only a few feet away. I did not want to put Person in a position of being forced to proceed if he thought the situation too dangerous. When I looked at him, he responded by saying simply, "Let's go."

As we entered the white waiting room . . . we were grabbed bodily and pushed toward the alleyway leading to the loading platform. As soon as we got into the alleyway and out of sight of onlookers in the waiting room, six of them started swinging at me with fists and pipes. Five others attacked Person a few feet ahead. Within seconds, I was unconscious on the ground. . . .

When I regained consciousness, the alleyway was empty. Blood was flowing down my face. I tried to stop the flow with a handkerchief but it soon became soaked. A white soldier came out of the waiting room to see whether I needed help. I declined, because I suddenly saw Bergman coming from the loading platform. He helped me to get a cab. . . .

The first thing Reverend Shuttlesworth said to me as I got out of the cab was, "You need to go to a hospital. . . ." I did not realize how seriously I had been hurt. My head required fifty-three stitches. . . .

Finally, after eight hours in the hospital, I was discharged, my face and head half hidden by bandages. . . . I said that for the most severely beaten rider to quit could be interpreted as meaning that violence had triumphed over nonviolence. . . . My point was accepted, and we started our meeting to plan the next lap. . . .

4.7 Though determined to continue, Peck and most of the other original riders were unable to do so because of their wounds. But, with Diane Nash leading the way, SNCC and other independent activists rushed to the deep South to complete the rides. They did so because, as Nash proclaimed: "We can't let violence overcome" (Taylor Branch, Parting the Waters, *p. 430). Among those to take part in the rides were numerous students from Howard University, especially members of the Nonviolent Action Group (NAG), a SNCC affiliate. In the following article, William Mahoney, a member of NAG, explained his decision to join the rides. Mahoney and hundreds of others landed in jail because of a deal struck between Attorney General Robert F. Kennedy and Mississippi Governor Ross Barnett. The governor agreed to protect the riders; in exchange, neither Robert nor John Kennedy intervened when Barnett proceeded to arrest the riders on trumped-up charges, such as trespass.*

4.7 William Mahoney, "In Pursuit of Freedom," *Liberation* (September 1961), pp. 7-11.

Monday, May 15th . . . , I saw pictures of a fellow Howard student with whom I had participated the past year and a half in the Non-Violent Action Group (N.A.G.) of Washington, leaving a flaming bus on the outskirts of Anniston, Alabama. The caption said that the student, whose name was Henry Thomas, had been struck on the head as he left the bus. I was infuriated. . . .

Late one evening, two members of N.A.G., Paul Detriecht and John Moody, called at my room to say goodbye before leaving for Montgomery. Paul and John joined the Freedom Riders. . . . [From Montgomery] Paul called N.A.G. and pleaded for as many as possible from the District to come down. . . . The project seemed to be at its most trying stage and my brothers in the South needed every person they could possibly muster, so I decided to go. I could quit the 60-cent-an-hour job and either take exams early or have them put off until I returned. . . .

I knew that my parents would oppose my decision, so I wrote them a letter of explanation (which I mailed while already on the way to

Alabama). I consoled myself with the thought that all revolutions have created such conflicts within families. . . . At 11 P.M. on Friday, May 26th, Frank Hunt, also a N.A.G. member, and I boarded a Greyhound bus in Washington with tickets for Montgomery.

. . . During our one-day journey Frank and I discussed race problems and eavesdropped on other passengers's conversations. An Air Force man just back from overseas sat in front of us talking to three other white passengers about the Freedom Riders. The consensus was that the integrationists should be hung from the nearest tree. . . . At one point a woman spoke loudly about the hardship she was suffering as a Negro, saying that she was the last hired at a job, the worst paid and the first fired. She complained about the rents one had to pay even to live in a slum. The whites in the front showed no reaction to the woman's loud despair. It was as though the bus riders were from two different worlds, the inhabitants of each being invisible to those of the other. . . .

At 7:00 Sunday Morning [May 28th], we entered the Montgomery bus station amidst a confusion of photographers, reporters, National Guardsmen and bus passengers. The white lunch counter was closed before we arrived and when we entered the colored waiting room, its lunch counter was quickly shut down.

With two rifle-carrying Guardsmen in the front seat and jeeps leading and following the bus we sped to the border. Waiting rooms at all stops along the way were closed. At the state line the commanding officer of the Guard boarded the bus and in a pleasant voice wished us luck, saying that we could expect a long stay in Mississippi. . . .

As we rolled toward Jackson, every blocked-off street, every back road taken, every change of speed caused our hearts to leap. Our arrival and speedy arrest in the white bus station in Jackson, when we refused to obey a policeman's order to move on, was a relief. A paddy wagon rushed us down the street to the police station.

While being interrogated I asked the detective if he knew that legally and by the moral standards America professes to the world we had a right to act as we did and that his actions were helping to tear down any respect that the world might have had for our country. He said that this might be so but that the South had certain traditions which must be respected.

On Tuesday, we were taken across the street to the county jail and locked up with the first group to have been arrested in Jackson. I had finally caught up with Henry Thomas, John Moody, and other friends. . . .

[The Riders were subsequently moved to Parchman Penitentiary.] The thirty or more of us occupied five cells and dining halls on the top floor. At night we slept on large bags of cotton and were locked in small, dirty, blood splattered, roach-infested cells. Days were passed in the hot, over-crowded, dining room playing cards, reading . . . and singing. . . .

On Saturday, June 24th the guards decided that the Freedom Riders' singing was too loud and took the mattresses away as punishment. At first this was taken as a joke and songs were made up about the incident, but after three days of sleeping on a cement floor or a steel shelf with an air-conditioning system on full blast the cell block became silent and gloomy. Another time when the Riders sang too loud for the guards, six of them were dragged down the hall with wrist-breakers (clamps tightened upon their wrists) and thrown into dark six-by-six boxes for a couple of days. As the spunky fellows were being taken to solitary they sang, "I'm Going to Tell God How You Treat Me."

When fellow prisoner Jim Farmer, national director of CORE, went before the superintendent to protest the treatment he was told that if we didn't cooperate conditions would deteriorate. A request was made for a written statement of rules to define what was meant by cooperation, but none was ever issued. Consequently, the imprisoned men drew up their own code of minimum standards for they felt that although they were obligated to respect the authorities, the authorities had an obligation to treat them as human beings. . . .

Most felt that the search for order and meaning in life could best be carried out in group devotion, where sermons could be delivered and group singing takes place. Phrases pertaining to the Freedom Rides were put to the tune of Negro spirituals, work songs, and union songs. When Henry Thomas finished with Harry Belafonte's "Day Oh," it became:

> Freedom, Freedom / Freedom come and I gonna go home.
> I took a trip down Mississippi way (Hey)
> Freedom come and I gonna go home.
> Met much violence on Mother's Day (Hey)
> Freedom come and I gonna go home. . . .

At 5 P.M. on July 7th those remaining of the first and second groups were released on appeal bonds after 40 days in jail. When we left, the number of Freedom Riders in jail was close to a hundred.

Before parting for our various destinations we stood in a circle, grasped hands and sang a song called "We Will Meet Again." As I looked round the circle into my companions' serious faces and saw the furrowed brows of the 19- and 20-year old men and women, I knew that we *would* meet again.

4.8 While in jail, the civil rights movement matured. Sustained by freedom songs, the freedom riders forged bonds that would help them withstand further travails. Inspired by the courage of the SNCC volunteers, young blacks flocked to the direct action campaigns against Jim Crow. SNCC and CORE flourished, with both organizations promoting themselves as the most militant and committed civil rights organizations. Jealousies and rivalries materialized, particularly between SNCC and the NAACP and SCLC. Initially, however, these differences did not hamper the fight for equality. The following promotional piece, issued by CORE in 1963, captures the bravery and commitment of many activists and presents a subtle criticism of the more moderate and established civil rights organizations. In time this critique would grow in importance.

4.8 CORE, "All About CORE," 1963, CORE Papers.

Twenty-seven CORE Freedom Riders, many of them fresh from beatings with fists, boots and iron bars, stood in their cells in the Hinds County, Mississippi, jail and sang. They sang new versions of old folk and gospel songs such as "We Shall Overcome Someday." "For the first time in history," wrote James Farmer, CORE's national director and one of the jailed Freedom Riders, "the Hinds County jail rocked with unrestrained singing of songs about freedom and brotherhood."

For the first time, too, the words of "We Shall Overcome" began to acquire reality for opponents of segregation in the Deep South. The Freedom Rides eventually desegregated 120 interstate bus terminals. But more important, they showed that non-violent action worked in the fight against racial discrimination even in the deepest part of the South. The Rides, like the sit-ins before them, demonstrated that anyone who opposed segregation—student, housewife or laborer—could drive a nail in the coffin of Jim Crow. They spurred the rapid spread of civil rights activity throughout the South and the entire country.

By the spring and summer of 1963, thousands of Americans, tired of waiting for their fellow-citizens to honor the Bill of Rights, had carried their protests into the streets. . . . Jail became a mark of honor. America was learning what Thoreau meant 120 years before when Emerson asked him why he was in jail for refusing to pay a poll tax and he replied, "Why are you *not* here?"

. . . In the North, demonstrators protested against de facto segregation in housing, education and employment, and filled government offices in patient but determined sit-ins to gain more than campaign promises from liberal politicians. Here, too, many went to jail. And here, too, the progress made was a hint of the progress to come. . . .

For too long, and for too many people, "segregation," "civil rights" and "racial equality" had been abstractions. They had inspired meetings, speeches and, sometimes, violent emotions, but very little constructive action. . . .

By the time sit-ins attracted national attention in 1960, direct action had been enabling CORE members to fight discrimination in their own communities for 18 years. CORE's action projects have been carried out by local people whenever appropriate, and they have always been non-violent. Why non-violent? CORE seeks understanding, not physical victory. It seeks to win the friendship, respect and even support of those whose racial policies it opposes. People cannot be bludgeoned into a feeling of equality. Integration, if it is not to be tense and artificial, must, in CORE's view, be more than an armed truce. Real racial equality can be attained only through co-operation; not the grudging co-operation one exacts from a beaten opponent, but the voluntary interaction of two parties working toward a solution of a mutual problem.

CORE sees discrimination as a problem for all Americans. Not just Negroes suffer from it and not just Negroes will profit when it is eliminated. Furthermore, Negroes alone cannot eliminate it. Equality cannot be seized any more than it can be given. It must be a shared experience.

CORE is an inter-racial group. Membership involves no religious affiliation. It is open to anybody who opposes racial discrimination, who wants to fight it and who will adhere to CORE's rules. The only people not welcome to CORE are "those Americans whose loyalty is primarily to a foreign power and those whose tactics and beliefs are contrary to democracy and human values." CORE has only one enemy: discrimination, and only one function: to fight that enemy. It has no desire to complicate its task by acquiring a subversive taint, and it avoids partisan politics of any kind. . . .

A great deal has been achieved for civil rights through the courts, and legal action has an important place in the civil rights movement. But legal action is necessarily limited to lawyers. CORE's techniques enable large numbers of ordinary people to participate in campaigns to end discrimination.

Direct action has a value that goes beyond its visible accomplishments. To those who are the target of discrimination, it provides an alternative to bitterness or resignation and, to others, an alternative to mere expressions of sentiment. . . .

Chapter Five

THE FIRES OF DISCORD

By the summer of 1963 hardly a day passed without new civil rights protests occurring. As President Kennedy observed in a nationally televised address: "The fires of frustration and discord are burning in every city, North and South." The protests were led by SNCC, CORE, SCLC, local chapters of the NAACP, and by independent community organizations. Young and old, men and women, college educated and the illiterate took part. America had not witnessed such social upheaval in years, if ever. While only a multivolume collection of documents could do justice to the breadth of the civil rights movement of the 1960s, this chapter seeks to provide a flavor of the many local insurgencies that dominated the landscape. This section also seeks to raise a set of interrelated questions: What was the significance of the local civil rights struggles? How were they connected, if at all? Did they share similar objectives and methods and face similar obstacles to success? What role did "outsiders" play? What role did blacks and whites indigenous to the region play?

5.1 One local movement which has received scant attention was centered in Fayette County, Tennessee. There, blacks committed themselves to registering to vote. As of 1959 less than one hundred blacks were registered in all of Fayette County; on election day in 1960 close to twelve thousand blacks voted. Contrary to the national trend, they overwhelmingly voted for the Republican Party, or against the local white supremacist Democratic Party. For daring to challenge white supremacy, former black sharecroppers were evicted—or threatened with eviction—refused service by local grocers and doctors, and shot at.

Many of Fayette County's blacks belonged to the Fayette County Civic and Welfare League. Led by John McFerren, the league promoted political activity and provided some protection to blacks who were harassed. Operating out of "McFerren's store and Tent City," a makeshift community of largely dispossessed black farmers, the Fayette League appealed to the outside world for help. One notable supporter was United Packinghouse Workers (UPWA), American Federation of Labor and Congress of Industrial Organization (AFL-CIO). Among the things that the UPWA did was to publish a pamphlet on the league, excerpts of which follow. (Throughout the 1960s the Packinghouse Workers remained a staunch ally of the civil rights movement, raising funds for SNCC, SCLC, and the NAACP, and taking part in numerous protests and sympathy demonstrations.) With labor's help, the Fayette League convinced the federal government to investigate the local situation. The investigation culminated with the filing of a suit by the Justice Department against local white officials under provisions outlined in the Civil Rights Act of 1957. It was one of the first such suits ever filed.

5.1 "Tent City: 'Home of the Brave' " (Washington, D.C.: AFL-CIO, IUD, 1961).

Less than two miles from the center of Somerville, on the old Macon road at a point where three roads intersect and hence known locally as Three-Way, is John McFerren's grocery store.

Here in this store, small and under-stocked, where the "quality" of Somerville would never deign to trade, is the GHQ of the greatest social revolution to occur in the rural Deep South since Reconstruction days.

It is from this store that the plans for mobilizing the under-advantaged Negroes of Fayette County went out, it is here that these people come today for assistance and a lift to their morale, and it is this simple crossroads grocery that has sent out the pleas that move the hearts and men and women of good will. . . .

The gentle people of Somerville pretend to ignore John McFerren's store—but there are some in their number who keep it under surveillance around the clock. With deep, brooding eyes they sit in their cars a short distance away and note the license numbers of every car that stops at McFerrens's. Then—if they can—they set in motion the machinery of reprisal; economic strangulation, threats, police harassment and sometimes even gunfire from their cowardly ambush. . . .

This is Fayette County, Tennessee, today, in March, 1961. . . .

A handful of families dominate Fayette County. Their attitude is that they govern almost by divine right and that nothing really has changed since Lincoln was "that man in the White House." Congress might come and go, the Supreme Court might rule what it would; but their dominance over a feudal system has gone along almost unchallenged and unchanged.

But a new wind is stirring through the County. . . . This is the wind of social change, bearing with it a new era not alone for Fayette County but for all of the South and some day for all of the nation. Against the wind, trying to stay its force, stand the big families of Fayette County and others whom prejudice, convention and blind fear have compelled to stand by their sides.

. . . The Negroes in Fayette County, from among the youngest to the oldest, can read; they know that the Constitution and its subsequent amendments give them *too* the right to register and vote. And they believe to this day that the Constitution of the United States is bigger, stronger and more respected than the big families . . . and the night riders of the White Citizens Council.

If they didn't, nearly 400 Negro families would not have been ordered from their homes of many years, pressured into near starvation, and forced to live on the alms of fellow Americans. . . .

Prior to 1959, only a handful, perhaps no more than ten of the County's more than 20,000 Negroes, had ever registered to vote. Even then, this tiny number did not always go to the polls on voting day. The insignificant number of Negro registered voters caused no concern to the white population, and perhaps even evoked a slight smug satisfaction that at least a token of equality existed in their area. . . .

On Election Day in 1959, when eligible Negroes attempted to vote, they were turned away from the polls. Each man or woman was handed a printed slip informing him that this was an "all-white primary" and that Negro voting was illegal.

That was when things really began to happen in Fayette County.
Twelve Negroes filed suit against the Democrat Committee in the County, charging that they had been barred illegally from exercising their franchise. They won their suit. The way was now clear, it would seem for Negro voting. . . .

Thus it was in Fayette County when a scant dozen Negroes combined to form the Fayette County Civic and Welfare League. . . .

Shortly after the mass registration drive got under way, leaders of the League began to suspect the existence of a secret blacklist of their membership. One day the list was discovered, a list of those who had been registered, with a special "X" by the names of those who were the ringleaders in the movement.

Now, when Negroes went to stores where they had traded for years, the white owner or manager scanned the list under the counter. If the Negro's name appeared on the list, the manager refused to sell. . . .

Filling stations refused to sell gasoline to Negroes who were suspect. Doctors and clinics in the County no longer would treat their Negro patients. . . .

Election Day, 1960 neared. Pressure on the Negro population, especially those who were now registered voters, grew heavier and more oppressive. . . . November 8, 1960, came and the Negroes trooped to the polls. For the first time in their lives they were voting as free Americans. . . . No attempts were made to turn them away from the polls but the looks of hate and menace made it clear that retribution would follow quickly.

Fayette County has had a long record of landing safely in the Democratic column. When the ballots were counted, the County gave its vote to the Republicans. . . .

It should have surprised no one. The Democratic machinery of Fayette County meant things to Negroes: the White Citizens Council, its predecessor the Klan. . . .

War was on. Retribution was not long in coming. On some of the huge plantations, on farms in the back districts of the country, summary notices to "get off my land" were given to Negroes even before all the states had completed the tabulation of their votes. In almost every instance, the commands were verbal—because in Fayette County there are no written leases or contracts between the landlord and the Negroes who farm as tenants or who sharecrop.

Most of the eviction notices were preemptory, "get the hell off by Saturday. . . ." The fortunate few were given until January 1 to find a new home. . . .

In all, 345 families were given eviction notices. . . . There were some who for one reason or another could not find accommodations.

It was for these that "Tent City" was established.

Tent City has become the outward symbol of the struggle by the Negroes of Fayette County to attain justice. . . . Some writers have called the place "Freedom Village" and for its symbolism it is as good a name as any. But to its residents and to the others in the County who share its fortunes, it remains Tent City.

Freedom though, is what the Negroes of Fayette County believe they have achieved through their vote—nearly one hundred years after the Emancipation Proclamation.

Surprisingly, there is little bitterness in Tent City. . . .

Not so well known is that there is a second Tent City. Its location is secret, "for security reasons."

. . . It was here, January 25, that Mrs. Jamie Lee Mason, 28, was delivered of her seventh child. Friendly neighbors attended at the birth, drawing on their own meager stores of supplies and fuel to have things in readiness for the new inheritor of the American dream. Outside the tent that night, unprotected against the icy wind, the family dog perished from the cold. . . .

5.2 In nearby Monroe, North Carolina, Robert F. Williams, a Marine Corps veteran, built a militant local movement, which at least temporarily grabbed the nation's attention. Williams had joined the local NAACP shortly after he left the military in the early 1950s. He quickly invigorated the nearly dead chapter and became its president. In 1957, he led a protest that forced the public library to integrate. Afterwards, Monroe's NAACP branch protested for better education, equal protection under the law, and equal access to public facilities, most importantly the public pool. As in Fayette, the local civil rights activists faced immediate and nearly unanimous opposition. Whites revitalized the KKK and red-baited Williams and the NAACP. The Klan held massive rallies, wantonly fired shots from cars into homes in the black community, and intimidated black and white women in broad daylight. In the following piece, Williams justified self-defense, as opposed to nonviolence. He wrote the piece from abroad, having been driven into exile—first to Cuba and then China—following a showdown with local authorities and his indictment on charges of kidnapping.

5.2 Robert Williams, *Negroes with Guns* (New York: Marzani & Munsell, 1962), pp. 35–41 and 102–124.

Why do I speak to you from exile? Because a Negro community in the South took up guns in self-defense against racist violence and used them. I am held responsible for this action, that for the first time in history American Negroes have armed themselves as a group, to defend their homes, their wives, their children in a situation where law and order had broken down, where the authorities could not, or rather would not, enforce their duty to protect Americans from a lawless mob. I accept this responsibility and am proud of it. I have asserted the right of Negroes to meet the violence of the Ku Klux Klan by armed self-defense—and have acted on it. It has always been an accepted right of Americans . . . that where the law is unable, or unwilling, to enforce order, the citizens can, and must, act in self-defense against lawless violence. I believe this right holds for black Americans as well as whites. . . .

Many people will remember that in the summer of 1957 the Ku Klux Klan made an armed raid on an Indian community in the South and were met with determined rifle fire from the Indians acting in self-defense. The nation approved of the action and there were widespread expressions of pleasure at the defeat of the Kluxers, who showed their courage by running away despite their armed superiority. What the nation doesn't know, because it has never been told, is that the Negro community in Monroe, North Carolina, had set the example two weeks before when we shot up an armed motorcade of the Ku Klux Klan, including two police cars, which had come to attack the home of Dr. Albert E. Perry, vice president of the Monroe chapter of the National Association for the Advancement of Colored People. The stand taken by our chapter resulted in the official re-affirmation by the NAACP of the right of self-defense. . . .

Because there has been much distortion of my position, I wish to make it clear that I do not advocate violence for its own sake, or for the sake of reprisals against whites. Nor am I against the passive resistance advocated by the Reverend Martin Luther King and others. My only difference with Dr. King is that I believe in flexibility in the freedom struggle. This means that I believe in non-violent tactics where feasible and the mere fact that I have a Sit-In case pending before the U.S. Supreme Court bears this out. . . . But where there is a breakdown of the law, the individual citizen has the right to protect his person. . . . When an oppressed people show a willingness to defend themselves, the enemy, who is a moral weakling and coward is more willing to grant concessions and work for a respectable compromise. Psychologically, moreover, racists consider themselves superior beings and they are not willing to exchange their superior lives for our inferior ones. They are most vicious and violent when they can practice violence with impunity. This we have shown in Monroe. Moreover, when because of our self-defense there is a danger that the blood of whites may be spilled, the local authorities in the South suddenly enforce law and order when previously they had been complacent toward lawless, racist violence. This too we have proven in Monroe. . . .

Furthermore, because of the international situation, the Federal Government does not want racial incidents which draw the attention of the world to the situation in the South. Negro self-defense draws such attention, and the federal government will be more willing to enforce the law and order if local authorities don't. When our people become fighters, our leaders will be able to sit at the conference table as equals, not dependent on whim and the generosity of the oppressor. . . .

The majority of white people in the United States have literally no idea of the violence with which Negroes in the South are treated daily—nay hourly. This violence is deliberate, conscious, condoned by the authorities. It has gone on for centuries and is going on today. . . . It is our way of life. Negro existence in the South has been one long travail, steeped in terror and blood—our blood. The incidents which took place in Monroe, which I witnessed and which I suffered, will give some idea of the conditions in the South, such conditions that can no longer be borne. That is why, one hundred years after the Civil War began, we Negroes in Monroe armed ourselves in self-defense and used our weapons. We showed that our policy worked. The lawful authorities of Monroe and North Carolina acted to enforce order *only after, and as a direct result of,* our being armed. . . . This is the meaning of Monroe and I believe it marks a historic change in the life of my people.

In 1961 and 1962 SNCC set down roots in some of the deepest backwaters of white supremacy with the goal of fomenting a decentralized grass-roots movement. Two of SNCC's better-known projects were in Southwest Georgia and the Mississippi Delta. The documents that follow provide a glimpse of these. They also describe the extensive resistance that SNCC and its local allies faced. Despite appeals for protection, the federal government provided little help. The FBI refused to make arrests, insisting that it was solely an investigatory agency. The documents also introduce the reader to some of the remarkable activists who joined or worked with SNCC. There were blacks native to the region, such as Charles Sherrod, Hollis Watkins, Cordell and Bernice Reagon. There were blacks from the North, who abandoned their studies or jobs in order to take part in the movement, such as Robert Moses and Don Harris. And there were whites from the North and South, including Bob Zellner, Casey Hayden, and Ralph Allen.

5.3 Tom Hayden, whose report on Mississippi is reprinted below, was one of the first Northerners to cover SNCC. While writing a story for the Michigan Daily, *his college newspaper, Hayden witnessed the meaning of white supremacy firsthand. This experience, watching SNCC activists and local blacks risk everything for rights which he took for granted, motivated him to abandon his dream of becoming an impartial journalist in favor of becoming an activist. Already a member of the Students for a Democratic Society (SDS), then a fledgling left-leaning student organization centered at the University of Michigan, Hayden went on to become its president and to help transform SDS into the best-known New Left organization in the country.*

5.3 Tom Hayden, "Revolution in Mississippi," SDS Papers, 1962.

. . . On August 7, 1961, the SNCC Voter Registration School opened in Burglundtown in a combination cinder block-and-paintless wood frame two-story structure which houses a grocery below and a Masonic meeting hall above. A typical voter registration (or citizenship) class involved a study of the Mississippi State Constitution, filling out of sample application forms, description of the typical habits of the Southern registrar—whose discretionary powers are enormous—and primarily attempted the morale building, encouragement and consequent group identification which might inspire the exploited to attempt registration.

On the first day of the school four persons went down to the registrar's office in nearby Magnolia, the county seat of Pike; three of them were registered. Nine went down on August 10th; one was registered. By this time, articles in the local press, the *Enterprise-Journal*, had increased awareness of the project, stirring a few Negroes from Walthall and Amite to come to the McComb classes. However, the thrust of the movement was somewhat blunted on the evening of August 10th when one of the Negroes who had attempted registration was shot by a white. (It is now clear that the shooting had nothing to do with the attempted registration that day. However, in the minds of the Negro community . . . the association was made between the two events. . . .)

Then on August 15th, the first of a still continuing series of "incidents" occurred. On that day, Moses drove to Liberty (yes, it is ironic), the county seat of Amite, with three Negroes (Ernest Issac, Bertha Lee Hughes and Matilda Schoby) who wished to register. Moses was asked to leave the registrar's office. . . . Upon completing the test, the applicants were told by the registrar that their attempts were inadequate . . . and [the registrar] asked the three not to return for at least six months. . . .

Leaving Liberty, driving toward McComb, the group was followed by a highway patrolman, Marshall Carwyle Bates of Liberty, who flagged them over to the side of the road. Bates asked the driver, Issac, to step out of his car and get inside of the police car in the rear. Issac complied. Then Moses left the car and walked back to the police car to inquire about the nature of the pull-over. Bates ordered Moses back to the car and shoved him in. . . . Moses, incidentally, was referred to as the "nigger who's come to tell the niggers how to register." Finally, the contingent of four Negroes was ordered to drive to the Justice of the Peace's office in McComb, where Moses was eventually charged with impeding an officer in the discharge of his duty, fined $50 and given a suspended sentence. . . .

On August 18th, Marion Barry from Nashville, a SNCC field representative particularly concerned with initiating direct action, arrived in McComb. The Pike County Non-Violent Movement was formed; workshops in the theory and practice of nonviolence were held. On August 26th two of the youths, Elmer Hayes and Hollis Watkins (both 18), sat-in at the lunch counter of the local Woolworth's, the first direct action incident in the history of the county. The two were arrested and remained in jail for 30 days. The charge: breach of peace. Their arrest set the stage for a mass meeting on August 29th. The Reverend James Bevel, of Jackson, spoke to a crowd of nearly 200. The paper the following day carried the story lead, in large type, and the local columnists warned the citizens that the Negroes were not engaged in a mere passing fad, but were serious in intention.

On August 30th, a sit-in occurred at the lunch counter of the local bus station. Issac Lewis, 20, Robert Talbert, 19, and Brenda Lewis, 16, were arrested on charges of breach of peace and failure to move on. They remained in jail for 28 days. By now, a current of protest had been generated throughout the counties. Subsequent events intensified the feeling. On August 29th, Bob Moses took two persons to the registrar's office in Liberty. They were met by Billy Jack Caston (cousin of the sheriff and son-in-law of State Representative Eugene Hurst) who was accompanied by another cousin and son of the sheriff. . . . Caston smashed Moses across the head and dropped him to the street. The other Negroes were not harmed. Moses' cuts required eight stitches. Moses filed assault and battery charges against Caston, perhaps the first time in the history of Amite that a Negro has legally contested the right of a white man to mutilate him at fancy. Approximately 150 whites attended the trial on August 31st. . . . Upon the suggestion of law officials, Moses left the trial, at which he was the plaintiff, before the "not guilty" verdict in order to escape mass assault. . . .

Several new SNCC people, returning from a successful national trip in quest of funds for bond . . . arrived in McComb on the morning of the 4th. Among those arriving was Robert Zellner, a white man from Alabama who, as a white, was even more susceptible to mob hostility than a Negro. . . .

The students . . . spent the mid-day preparing signs, and at about 2:30 P.M., they started to march downtown. . . . 119 in all, including 19 students over age 18, Bob Moses, Charles McDew and Robert Zellner. They walked through the Negro neighborhoods where families watched from the windows and steps and yards, through the downtown business district, down to the edge of McComb, and back up to City Hall. Then the march halted. Elmer Hayes, one of the original McComb sit-iners, began to pray on the steps. Three times the police asked him to move on. He refused and was arrested. . . . Too much time was being taken up, so the police blew their whistles and pronounced everyone under arrest.

The whole march started up the stairs on its way to be booked. As it did, a local white citizen reached out for Zellner and began to beat him.

Hurting Zellner with the first punch, the man then grabbed him around the neck and began choking him and gouging his eyes. Then Bob Moses and Charles McDew were there, one holding the white's wrists, one clasping Zellner in protection. Moses and McDew were struck and dragged into the station by police, who then pulled in Zellner. The first statement inside the Police Chief's office . . . was "Ought to leave you out there." Everyone was arrested and placed in jail. The nineteen over 18 years of age were arraigned on October 5th, after a night in Pike County jail. Before Robert W. Brumfield of McComb's Police Court, they pleaded innocent to charges of disturbing the peace; bond was $100 each. . . .

5.4 Bob Moses' "Letter," which follows, is one of the classic texts of the civil rights movement. Moses, a native of Harlem, who received an M.S. in philosophy from Harvard University, gave up his job teaching mathematics in New York to join the civil rights movement in 1960. Rather than sitting behind a desk at SCLC's or SNCC's headquarters in Atlanta, Moses ventured to the heart of Dixie, rural Mississippi, to initiate a freedom struggle. With the help of Amzie Moore, a World War II veteran and the head of the NAACP chapter in Cleveland, Mississippi, Moses established the voter registration campaign, discussed above by Hayden. His efforts dovetailed with a Justice Department plan to channel the energies of the freedom rides into voter registration but they did not mesh with the desires of the local white populace. Shortly after he arrived, just before a scheduled meeting with Justice Department attorney John Doar, one of his first recruits, Henry Lee, was murdered in cold blood. Afterwards, as Hayden noted, local authorities beat Moses and threw him in jail.

5.4 Robert Moses, "Letter from a Mississippi Jail Cell."

We are smuggling this note from the drunk tank of the county jail in Magnolia, Mississippi. Twelve of us are here, sprawled out along the concrete bunker; Curtis Hayes, Hollis Watkins, Ike Lewis and Robert Talbert, four veterans of the bunker, are sitting up talking—mostly about girls; Charles McDew ("Tell the story") is curled into the concrete and the wall; Harold Robinson, Stephen Ashley, James Wells, Lee Chester, Vick, Leotus Eubanks, and Ivory Diggs lay cramped on the cold bunker; I'm sitting with smuggled pen and paper, thinking a little, writing a little; Myrtis Bennett and Janie Campbell are across the way wedded to a different icy cubicle.

Later on Hollis will lead out with a clear tenor into a freedom song; Talbert and Lewis will supply jokes; and McDew will discourse on the history of the black man and the Jew. McDew—a black by birth, a Jew by choice and a revolutionary by necessity—has taken on the deep hates and deep loves which America, and the world, reserve for those who dare to stand in a strong sun and cast a sharp shadow.

In the words of Judge Brumfield, who sentenced us, we are "cold calculators" who design to disrupt the racial harmony (harmonious since 1619) of McComb into racial strife and rioting; we, he said, are the leaders who are causing young children to be led like sheep to the pen to be slaughtered (in a legal manner). "Robert," he was addressing me, "haven't some of the people from your school been able to go down and register without violence here in Pike county?" I thought to myself that Southerners are most exposed when they boast.

It's mealtime now: we have rice and gravy in a flat pan, dry bread and a "big town cake"; we lack eating and drinking utensils. Water comes from a faucet and goes into a hole.

This is Mississippi, the middle of the iceberg. Hollis is leading off with his tenor, "Michael, row the boat ashore, Alleluia; Christian brothers don't be slow, Alleluia; Mississippi's next to go, Alleluia." This is a tremor in the middle of the iceberg—from a stone that the builders rejected.

5.5 and 5.6 While Moses fought to register blacks in the Mississippi Delta, another contingent of SNCC activists established themselves in Albany, Georgia. In the summer of 1961, Charles Sherrod and Cordell Reagon arrived there with the goal of building a broad-based freedom movement. They struck a responsive audience among Albany State College students and a handful of prominent adult Albanians, most notably Slater King. By early winter they had built a vibrant organization, staging daily marches and vigils, sit-ins and mass meetings. The local sheriff, Chief Laurie Pritchett, however, sapped the movement's strength by arresting the protesters, en masse, and jailing them in every available facility in the region.

Subsequently, Albany's local leaders decided to call upon Martin Luther King for help. King came reluctantly and never intended to stay. But within one day of his arrival he too was in jail for taking part in a freedom march. Though he quickly made bond, he maintained a presence in Albany. Six months after his arrest he was sentenced to forty-five days in prison or a $170 fine. Feeling pressure from SNCC, which routinely chose jail over bail, King opted for imprisonment. Inexplicably, a day later, Chief Pritchett informed King that an anonymous person had paid his fine and that he was a free man. (Pritchett had arranged for the fine to be paid so that he could get King out of town.)

In the following months, sit-ins, protest marches, and mass meetings continued to dominate the Albany scene. But, in the process, tensions arose between SNCC and King, over, among other things, King's seeming timidity. In the long run, the Albany movement lost momentum; the national press tired of the story; the Kennedy administration refused to intervene, and King cut his ties with the community.

Many studies portray Albany as a setback for the civil rights movement, contending that King suffered a significant blow to his prestige. When compared to the Montgomery bus boycott and King's later success in Birmingham and Selma, Albany did represent a defeat. Few concrete changes took place and King's reputation and the allure of nonviolence diminished. Yet, as Slater King's and Bernice Reagon's pieces suggest, an alternative interpretation exists. Both King and Reagon describe the Albany movement from a perspective of the impact it had on the participants themselves. By daring to overthrow Jim Crow, Reagon contended, Albany residents toppled long-held psychological barriers and gained a sense of personal empowerment. In the long run, things would never be the same. Reagon also comments on the importance of music in the movement. Freedom songs, from the well-known "We Shall Overcome," to the less-known "Odinga, Odinga," united protestors, lifted their spirits in times of trouble, and became one of the primary mediums for expressing the goals and aspirations of the movement.

5.5 Slater King, "The Bloody Battleground of Albany," *Freedomways* (Winter 1964), pp. 93-101.

Around 1903 Dr. W.E.B. DuBois came to Albany, Dougherty County, Georgia, the heart of the black belt, to do a study on the views of the Blacks who inhabited the fertile black land. He viewed this study symbolically as applying to Blacks across the whole of America. He further stated, "In these chapters I have studied the struggles of the massed millions of the Black Peasantry."

Since this time, very little has been heard of Albany except that it was the home of a few Negro notables. . . .

Most people were amazed to read in December, 1961 of 700 Albany residents going to jail in protest demonstrations. What made people look at the Albany situation a little closer was that past civil rights demonstrations, such as the sit-ins and freedom rides, had involved mainly college youth, but here the total community was involved, both young and old. . . .

On November 17, 1961, The Albany Movement was founded. Dr. W. G. Anderson was elected president, M. S. Paige, secretary, and I, Slater King, vice president.

The aim of the organization is to totally desegregate all city facilities and secure equal educational and economic opportunities for every citizen. In an attempt to effect the aims of the organization, the Albany Movement has petitioned, attempted to negotiate and protested.

These protest demonstrations involved the whole of the Negro community and in the summer of 1962, they began anew, and approximately 2,000 people had been jailed.

After the dust had settled, many people began evaluating the situation. The whites said nothing had been gained and that the Negroes are now further behind than they had ever been. I think that the immediate reaction of most Negroes, right after the demonstrations, was the feeling of being let down. For most expected out of the great emotionalism and drama . . . that these few days of jailing would act as a penance and force the whites to accord to Negroes the privileges they had withheld so long. There are very few visible gains; the municipal buses agreed to desegregate . . . but the city stubbornly refused to give any written assurances to the Albany Movement that it would not harass and intimidate Negro passengers, so the bus line withdrew and Albany now has no municipal transit system.

The library has been integrated. The city has struck down all of its statutes involving segregation. . . . The public schools have been ordered to desegregate, by a court order, in September of 1964. Negroes gained the right to use the interstate bus station waiting rooms and restaurants. . . .

The tangible gains (if they can be called gains) are negligible and hardly worth mentioning. The main gain that I see are those that have internally shaken the Negro community.

There is more a sense of community and identity in the Negro community than ever before. Crime among Negroes has dropped. . . .

There has been a tremendous number of self-help organizations arising in the Negro community—such as, the teachers volunteering to teach night classes to the old and to those who were not able to receive education in the past; the Albany Movement has acted as the organization to see to those Negroes who are without, charity is extended in the form of clothes and food. It has also attempted to see that for those Negroes who have good minds and have been unable, because of economic reasons, to secure an education, some way may be found to help them scholastically to further their education. This has been done in attempting to propagate many of the policies of Dr. DuBois, who felt that the Negro could never advance as long as he allowed his best minds to wither and atrophy.

Another gain is the breaking down of the snobbishness with which professional Negroes formerly looked at the Negro masses. Out of the downtown boycott, the existing Negro businesses have been strengthened and new ones have been added.

For two years the Movement has been the place where the Negroes have come for inspiration, to learn Negro history, and to further the strong feeling of identity, to know that they are not alone, to learn how politics work, and how they have been taken advantage of. They have had speakers with opinions ranging from Dr. Lonnie X. Cross, representative of the Black Muslims to Dr. Martin Luther King, Jr., representing the integrationist. This has been a tremendous educative process for the masses. . . .

When DuBois wrote *The Soul of Black Folk*, in reference to this area . . . he stated that it had implications for millions of black people. We, too, in Albany, sixty years later, feel that what has taken place here in the past, and what takes place in the future will have heavy implications for twenty million blacks in America.

5.6 Bernice Reagon, "Interview," in *They Should Have Served That Cup of Coffee*, ed. by Richard Cluster (Boston: South End Press, 1979), pp. 11-31.

. . . Albany was not simply a student movement. There were just swarms of people who came out to demonstrate, from high school students to old people. And there was so much that you got from finding that some older people backed you and were wiling to put up bail and things of that sort. That made the Movement much stronger. It was a mass movement. . . .

The mass meetings had a level of music that we could recognize from other times in our lives. And that level of expression, that level of cultural power present in an everyday situation, gave a more practical or functional meaning to the music than when it was sung in church on Sunday. The music was a group statement. If you look at the music and the words that came out of the Movement, you will find the analysis that the masses had about what they were doing.

One song that started to be sung in Albany was, "Ain't gonna let nobody turn me 'round."

> Ain't gonna let Pritchett turn me round,
> I'm on my way to freedom land.
> If you don't go, don't hinder me.
> Come and go with me to that land where I'm bound.
> There ain't nothing but peace in that land,
> Nothing but peace.

. . . Singing voiced the basic position of the movement, of taking action on your life. . . .

In jail, the songs kept us together. I was in jail with about sixty women, and there were teachers in there, and educated people, a few people who had been drunk in Harlem and just ran. One lady said she was with her husband and the march was going by and she says, "Look there goes my people!" and he says, "You better stay here" and she ran and caught up with us and ended up in jail, and she says, "What did I do that for? I ain't never gonna drink no more."

So there was a real class difference between the Black women in jail, and music had a lot to do with breaking down those things because there were several women in there who could lead songs, of different ages, and everybody would back everybody up. It was the first time I led songs and felt totally backed up by a group of Blacks. . . .

There was a sense of power, in a place where you didn't feel you had any power. There was a sense of confronting things that terrified you, like jail, police, walking in the street—you know, a whole lot of Black folks couldn't even walk in the streets in those places in the South. So you were saying in some basic ways, "I will never again stay inside these boundaries." There were things asked for like Black police and fireper- sons and sitting where you wanted on the bus. . . . But in terms of what happened to me, and what happened to other people I know about, it was a change in my concept of myself and how I stood.

It was an experience that totally changed the lives of people who par- ticipated in it. . . .

The Civil Rights Movement gave me the power to challenge *any* line that limits me.

I got that power during the Albany Movement, and that is what it meant to me, just really to give me a real chance to fight and to struggle and not respect boundaries that put me down. Before then I struggled within a certain context but recognized lines. Across those lines were the powers that could do you in, so you just respected them and don't cross them. The Civil Rights Movement just destroyed that and said that if something puts you down, you have to fight against it. And that's what the Albany Move- ment did for Albany, Georgia.

5.7 SNCC's efforts in southwest Georgia included a project in "Terrible Terrell" county, so named because of its history of violence and repression. While Charles Sitton of the New York Times *and a handful of other national reporters sporadically covered the civil rights movement in such communities, most information on such struggles came from the alternative or New Left press, such as SNCC's* Student Voice, *CORE's* CORElator, *the* Activist, *an SDS-affiliated paper out of Oberlin College, and* Liberation. *Only by mining such sources and conducting intensive oral histories will we develop a full appreciation of these movements.*

5.7 SNCC, "Terrible Terrell," *The Student Voice*, October 1962.

One half of the southwest Georgia project was located in Terrell County—called "Terrible Terrell" by local residents. This county was the scene of the first prosecution of voting violations under the Civil Rights Act of 1957.

There Ralph Allen, a white student from Massachusetts, was arrested for vagrancy along with [Charles] Sherrod when the two brought a group of Negroes to the Terrell County Courthouse to register.

Allen and Joseph Pitts, a young man from Albany, were beaten by whites as they went to speak to Negroes in Dawson, Ga. about registering. Allen was unable to secure warrants from police authorities in order to prosecute his assailants.

On July 27, as Sherrod and other SNCC workers held a meeting at Mt. Olive Baptist Church in Sasser, Ga., Terrell County Sheriff Z. T. Mathews entered with several gun-toting, swearing deputies and threatened the crowd. In a front page story, New York *Times* reporter Claude Sitton quoted the Sheriff as saying, "We want our colored people to go on living like they have for years."

. . . In August, four Negro Churches in the area were burned to the ground, including the Mt. Olive Church in Sasser. SNCC pledged aid in rebuilding the churches, and donated a tent which was used for meetings in place of the destroyed buildings. At the end of the month and in early September, nightriders shot into the homes of those involved in the voter registration drive. James Mays, a Lee County teacher who had been fired from his job for his participation in the voter registration drive, reported 24 bullet holes in his house. Jack Chatfield, a white student from Connecticut was shot twice in the arm. Christopher Allen, a student from Oxford, England, and Pratha Hall were both grazed by the bullets.

But local Negroes and the SNCC workers who remained at the end of the summer vowed to continue the drive despite the terror and intimidation.

Sherrod commented, "We met in a tent on ground which has been cleared off for the rebuilding of the church. We had about fifty people from Albany. Six months ago, maybe less or more, you couldn't have paid these people of Albany enough to come to Dawson, Sasser, or anywhere in Terrell County. But something has happened here in Southwest Georgia which has a good chance of becoming the pattern of our grand strategy in the South. And so we go about our way feeling in the darkness for the best way, always too curtailed by lack of funds. And the world listens and looks on, wondering.''

5.8 The final selection in this chapter is an annotated tally of civil rights disturbances in the South during an eleven-week period in the spring of 1963, compiled by the Southern Regional Council, a longtime exponent of racial equality. Though less vivid than the previous readings, it provides an excellent sense of the breadth of the civil rights movement and substantiates President Kennedy's statement that the "fires of discord" were burning across the nation. By the spring of 1963, the civil rights movement was so widespread that neither the FBI nor the national media could keep track of it. The Southern Regional Council, which had contacts throughout the South, never contended that the following report was inclusive. For instance, the report did not mention the massive disturbances in Cambridge, Maryland, which compelled the governor of the state to call up the National Guard and to leave them in town for nearly one-and-a-half years—the longest occupation of a community during peacetime in U.S. history. Nor does the report list protests North of the Mason-Dixon line, from marches for fair employment in Cleveland and New York to protests against discrimination at San Francisco's elite Palace Hotel. Still, it is one of the best reports that we have.

5.8 Southern Regional Council, "The Civil Rights Crisis: A Synopsis of Recent Developments," April 1963 through June 24, 1963.

Alabama

Alabama-Georgia Border—May 3-10—Freedom marchers arrested as they entered Alabama to continue ill-fated march of William Moore. Found guilty of breach-of-peace charges in Fort Payne, June 3, fined $200 each and court costs. . . .

Anniston—May 12—Negro homes and a church fired into by a carload of whites. Former Ku Klux Klan member convicted for shooting into a church (May 30), sentenced to 180 days in jail. . . .

Attalla—April 24—William Moore, a Baltimore postman hiking to Jackson on a one-man civil rights crusade, found murdered near here. His bullet-pierced body, still carrying anti-segregationist signs, was discovered along U.S. Highway 11.

Birmingham—April 3-June 21—Weeks of mass Negro demonstrations in which thousands were arrested ended May 10, when a truce was reached between prominent white businessmen and Negro leaders. Truce

almost came apart May 11-12, when a riot broke out following two bombings of Negro property. Federal troops were alerted, remained near city
until May 31. . . .

Gadsden—June 18-21—More than 450 Negroes, many of them children, arrested June 18 for defying an injunction against sit-in demonstrations. Forty-two more arrested June 21. . . .

Arkansas

Hot Springs—April 4—Negroes attempted to integrate local bath house,
4 arrested.

Pine Bluff—April-June—1,300 Negroes participated in a march protesting all segregation (April 1). Thirty-nine arrested April 25 in demonstration to integrate local theater. Four Negroes served at Woolworth's
and Walgreen's lunch counters. . . .

Florida

Daytona Beach—June 1-9—At least 7 street demonstrations, also picketing and sit-ins, involving in one instance over 100 persons, at least 12
arrests. Targets are theaters, hotels, recreation facilities and restaurants
(beaches and some lunch counters are desegregated). . . .

Gainesville—June 2—Attempt of Negroes to buy movie tickets led to
gathering of 1000 persons, some violence . . . one shooting. . . .

Tallahassee—May 23-June 8—Large scale (75 pickets 1st day) demonstrations began, primarily aimed at theaters, but also chain stores (for
employment). By May 28, 29, 30 protest marchers numbering 300 and
400 and 5000 arrests in 3 days, tear gas used. During the first week of
June Court upheld right to picket, limited number of pickets. Picketing
subsequently continuous and with police guard. . . .

Winter Haven—June 1-7—Swim-ins, hostile white crowds, beaches
closed.

Georgia

Albany—May 7-June 24—Picketing and boycotting began May 7, with
Negro employment the goal and lasted for three consecutive days, then
sporadically through May 25, with over 100 arrests. . . .

Atlanta—April 12-June 24—After first sit-in attempt April 12, Atlanta
had demonstration—sit-ins, a prayer march (estimated 200 participants),
kneel-ins, picketing—on at least 32 days from April 27 to the present,
with at least 103 arrests. Demonstrations were usually in small groups, by
June 7 drawing some crowds of hostile whites and occasioning one
stabbing. . . .

Macon—April 2 and 3—Two rows initiated by whites resulted in one
stabbing, two arrests in integrated park. Mayor declined to close park, his

mailbox bombed April 6. April 22, 5 Negro girls sat-in at segregated (some are integrated) lunch counter and were arrested. . . .

Rome—April 2—Sixty-two high school students stood trial (51 of age received sentences) for lunch counter sit-ins of previous week, the first such activity in the northwest area of Georgia. . . .

Savannah—June 3-June 24—Current wave of demonstrations—marches, picketing, sit-ins, began June 3, continued daily through June 14, when the city announced some restaurants, theaters and hotels had agreed to desegregate. (On June 4, 3 movies had desegregated for a few hours, then re-segregated after a protest demonstration by whites.) June 13—Negro home shot into. When owners reneged demonstrations resumed June 18, 19, 20. Over 1000 arrests in 2½ weeks. Four restaurants have been granted injunctions against demonstrators on their property. . . .

Mississippi

Clarksdale—May 4-June 22—State NAACP President Aaron Henry's drugstore was damaged by an explosion which ripped a hole in the roof; no one was injured (May 4). A similar fire-bomb was tossed into Henry's home April 12 during a visit there by Negro Congressman Charles L. Diggs (D. Mich.). Negroes threatened to broaden their boycott of downtown merchants May 26, unless bi-racial talks were held. Henry announced the launching of a series of spot picketing and demonstrations in the city (June 22). . . .

Jackson—May 27-June 24—After talks between 13 Negro leaders and Mayor Allen C. Thompson broke off, a series of demonstrations began May 28, resulting in more than 600 arrests by June 6, when a state judge issued an injunction barring further demonstrations. Same day two Negro men integrated the municipal golf course, teeing off without incident. Local NAACP leader Medgar W. Evers murdered June 12. Following his funeral service June 15, Negroes clashed with police in downtown area; Justice Department Attorney John Doar helped bring demonstration under control. . . . Bryan de la Beckwith of Greenwood, was charged with the murder of Medgar Evers June 23. . . .

Winoa—June 9—Two Negro women and a 15-year old girl beaten by police at the local jail after trying to use the white facilities at town's bus station. The women, who were released a few days later, have been active in voter registration work. . . .

North Carolina

Charlotte—April 19-May 30—Proprietors of segregated hotels, restaurants, and theaters warned of mass picketing unless they agreed to desegregate. . . .

Durham—May 18-June 5—1,400 were arrested during demonstrations May 18-20. Temporary truce agreed upon. . . .

Fayetteville—May 14-June 19—Police dispersed mobs of Negroes and whites with tear gas May 14. Demonstrations lasting over a week began May 19, with some 1,500 persons participating in daily marches. . . .

Greensboro—May 10-June 23—Mass demonstrations began May 10, resulted in the arrest of some 440 persons by May 15. 420 arrested May 19 for sitting-in at Howard Johnson parking lot. Demonstrations continued through May 24, with approximately 1,500 arrested. . . .

Raleigh—April 4-June 5—Demonstrations began April 4, continued for over a month. By May 10 some 250 had been arrested. Following day 1,000 demonstrated; May 14, 750 marched, were mocked and cursed by about 200 whites. 347 were arrested, with 15 charged with assault and one for carrying a concealed weapon. . . .

Wilmington—June 7—Some 75 high school students staged a protest demonstration at cafeterias and theaters. . . .

South Carolina

Greenville—On May 27 city officials met with Negro leaders, and on May 28, in less than 15 minutes, City Council repealed segregation laws but passed a "trespass" city ordinance making it unlawful not to leave a business after being asked to do so by the owner. . . . On June 3, 11 lunch counters were voluntarily desegregated, two weeks after the Supreme Court made a Greenville case the key to a series of sit-in rulings by overturning the trespass convictions of ten Negroes arrested at a lunch-counter . . . .

Rock Hill—June 1-16—Negroes demonstrated in front of drive-in restaurant. . . .

Tennessee

Knoxville—May 9-28—Demonstrations began May 9, resulted in arrest of about 100 by May 11. . . . Two thousand citizens signed a petition May 22, to desegregate all public facilities; petition sponsored by Chamber of Commerce.

Maryville—June 24—A mountain training camp sponsored by CORE was found burned to the ground; no injuries reported. Camp had been raided by sheriff's deputies previous week; 28 whites and Negroes arrested. . . .

Nashville—May 8-June 5—Following demonstrations May 8 and 9, a clash between Negro students and white hecklers May 10, another demonstration May 13 in which two persons were hospitalized, a permanent bi-racial Metropolitan Human Relations Council was appointed. . . .

Virginia

Charlottesville—May 25-30—Sit-ins began at La Paree restaurant May 25, but the main target became Buddy's restaurant near the University of Virginia, with groups of about 50 Negroes and whites demonstrating through May 30, when a local Negro leader was beaten up by two white men and hospitalized. The "stand-ins" were temporarily called off as a result of this incident. . . .

Danville—May 31-June 22—Fifty-sixty Negro youths started demonstrations to force hiring of a Negro policeman. Demonstrations continued through June 10, when 50 Negroes were arrested and a rally broken up by police using fire hoses; about 45 persons were injured. City passed ordinance June 14 limiting number allowed to participate in demonstrations to 6; the following day 35 more Negroes were arrested. Ten leaders in the demonstrations, including 3 whites, were indicted by a special grand jury June 21 on a criminal charge of inciting to riot. Police seized three other leaders who had taken sanctuary in a local church June 22. Thus far about 150 persons have been arrested. June 19, 29 demonstrators broke three-day truce by marching downtown; all were arrested. Mayor Stinson announced 10 Negroes had been assigned to white schools. Motel operators met to discuss desegregation. . . .

Chapter Six

BIRMINGHAM AND
THE GREAT MARCH

While the "fires of discord" were widespread, two protests in the spring and late summer of 1963 catapulted the civil rights movement into the living rooms of most Americans, the Birmingham campaign and the March on Washington. One historian has termed Birmingham the Gettysburg of the second civil war. The March on Washington was the single largest protest to take place in the nation's capital since its creation and paved the way for a series of mass demonstrations. Both events deepened support for the civil rights movement and set the stage for the passage of the Civil Rights Act of 1964, the most significant piece of civil rights legislation since Reconstruction. The Birmingham campaign and the March on Washington also augmented Martin Luther King, Jr.'s reputation. This is not to suggest that these two protests were King's creation. On the contrary, they displayed the depth and breadth of a social movement that was much larger than any single individual.

6.1 Following their seeming defeat in Albany, Georgia, King and SCLC determined to plan their next action much more thoughtfully and thoroughly. Because of its long history of hostility to race reform, personified by Sheriff "Bull" Connor, an unreconstructed white supremacist who routinely used physical force against civil rights activists, SCLC chose Birmingham, Alabama, as its next target. (Recall that the Birmingham police force had mysteriously disappeared when the Freedom Riders arrived in town.) King and his top aides, Wyatt Walker, Andrew Young, and Ralph Abernathy, figured that if SCLC staged nonviolent demonstrations in Birmingham, Connor would respond with force, which would attract the attention of the mass media and the federal government.

In turn, the nation would awaken to the brutality of racism and prod their nation's leaders to enact civil rights legislation.

In the first week of April 1963, following some delay, SCLC put "Project C," for confrontation, as the Birmingham campaign was known, into action. One reason for the delay was that the city was in the midst of altering its city government. The business community and some moderates had begun to foster token reforms and several Birmingham blacks counseled in favor of giving them a chance to succeed. Simultaneously, the Kennedy administration prodded civil rights groups to accept a "cooling off" period. SCLC rejected all calls for caution. "The Birmingham Manifesto," written by local civil rights leader Reverend Fred Shuttlesworth—head of the Alabama Christian Movement for Human Rights (ACMHR), the local arm of the SCLC—explains why.

6.1 Fred L. Shuttlesworth and N. H. Smith, "The Birmingham Manifesto," *Freedomways* (Winter 1964), pp. 20-21.

The patience of an oppressed people cannot endure forever. The Negro citizens of Birmingham for the last several years have hoped in vain for some evidence of good faith resolution of our just grievances.

Birmingham is part of the United States and we are *bona fide* citizens. Yet the history of Birmingham reveals that very little of the democratic process touches the life of the Negro in Birmingham. We have been segregated racially, exploited economically, and dominated politically. Under the leadership of the Alabama Christian Movement for Human Rights, we sought relief by petition for repeal of city ordinances requiring segregation and the institution of a merit hiring policy in city employment. We were rebuffed. We then turned to the system of the courts. We weathered set-back after set-back, with all of its costliness, finally winning the terminal, bus parks and airport cases. The bus decision has been implemented begrudgingly and the parks decision prompted the closing of all municipally-owned recreational facilities with the exception of the Zoo and Legion Field. The airport case has been a slightly better experience. . . .

We have always been a peaceful people, bearing our oppression with super-human effort. Yet we have been the victims of repeated violence, not only that inflicted by the hoodlum element but also that inflicted by the blatant misuse of police power. Our memories are seared with painful mob experience of Mother's Day 1961 during the Freedom Rides. For years our homes and churches were being bombed, we heard nothing but the rantings and ravings of racist city officials.

The Negro protest for equality and justice has been a voice crying in the wilderness. Most of Birmingham has remained silent, probably out of fear. In the meanwhile, our city has acquired the dubious reputation of being the worst big city in race relations in the United States. Last fall, for a flickering moment, it appeared that sincere community leaders . . . discerned the inevitable confrontation in race relations approaching. . . . Solemn promises were made, pending a postponement of direct action. . . . Some merchants agreed to desegregate their rest-rooms as a good-faith start, some actually complying, only to retreat shortly thereafter. We hold in our hands now, broken faith and broken promises.

We believe in the American Dream of democracy, in the Jeffersonian doctrine that "all men are created equal and are endowed by their Creator with certain inalienable rights, among these being life, liberty and the pursuit of happiness."

Twice since September we have deferred our direct action thrust in order that a change in city government would not be made in the hysteria of community crisis. We act today in full concert with our Hebraic-Christian tradition, the law of morality and the Constitution of our nation. The absence of justice and progress in Birmingham demands that we make a moral witness to give our community a chance to survive. We demonstrate our faith that we believe that The Beloved Community can come to Birmingham. . . .

6.2 and 6.3 On Good Friday, April 12, 1963, Martin Luther King, Jr., along with his closest associate, Reverend Ralph Abernathy, openly defied a court injunction against marching, and they were promptly placed under arrest and thrown in jail. While incarcerated, King wrote the "Letter from Birmingham Jail," one of the most profound statements on the origins and goals of the civil rights movement. In part, King's letter was a direct response to a letter written by a group of white clergymen who urged him and Birmingham's blacks to stop demonstrating. In addition to calling for restraint, the clergymen condemned the entrance of outsiders into their community and the practice of civil disobedience. King found the letter, coming from his fellow clergymen, appalling. Ironically, King's letter, perhaps his greatest written work, initially received little attention. Over a month passed before either the black press or national media mentioned it. And not until mid-May 1963 did a New York magazine present excerpts from it.

6.2 "Letter to Dr. King," *New Leader* (June 24, 1963), p. 5.

We the undersigned clergymen are among those who, in January, issued "An Appeal for Law and Order and Common Sense," in dealing with racial problems in Alabama. We expressed understanding that honest convictions in racial matters could properly be pursued in the courts, but urged that decisions in those courts should in the meantime be obeyed.

Since that time there has been some evidence of increased forbearance and a willingness to face facts. Responsible citizens have undertaken to work on various problems. . . .

However, we are now confronted by a series of demonstrations by some of our Negro citizens, directed and led in part by outsiders. We recognize the natural inpatience of the people who feel that their hopes are slow in being realized. But we are convinced that these demonstrations are unwise and untimely.

We agree rather with certain local Negro leadership which has called for honest and open negotiation. . . . Just as we formerly pointed out that "hatred and violence have no sanction in our religious and political traditions," we also point out that such actions as incite hatred and violence, however technically peaceful those actions may be, have not contributed to the resolution of our local problems. We do not believe that these days of new hope are days when extreme measures are justified in Birmingham.

We commend the community as a whole . . . urge the public to continue to show restraint . . . [and] appeal to both our white and Negro citizenry to observe the principles of law and order and common sense.

6.3 Martin Luther King, Jr., "Letter from Birmingham Jail," reprinted in the *New Leader* (June 24, 1963), pp. 3-11.

My Dear Fellow Clergymen,

While confined here in the Birmingham City Jail, I came across your recent statements calling our present activities "unwise and untimely." . . . Since I feel that you are men of genuine good will . . . I would like to answer your statement in what I hope will be patient and reasonable terms.

I think I should give the reason for my being in Birmingham, since you have been influenced by the argument of "outsiders coming in." I have the honor of serving as president of the Southern Christian Leadership Conference. . . . We have some 85 affiliate organizations all across the South—one being the Alabama Christian Movement for Human Rights. . . . Several months ago our local affiliate here in Birmingham invited us to be on call to engage in a nonviolent direct-action program if such were deemed necessary. We readily consented and when the hour came we lived up to our promises. So I am here. . . . Beyond this, I am in Birmingham because injustice is here. Just as the 8th century prophets left their little villages and carried their "thus saith the Lord" far beyond the boundaries of their home town, and just as the Apostle Paul left his little village of Taurus and carried the gospel of Jesus Christ to practically every hamlet and city of the Greco-Roman world, I too am compelled to carry the gospel of freedom beyond my home town. . . .

Moreover . . . I cannot sit idly by in Atlanta and not be concerned about what happens in Birmingham. Injustice anywhere is a threat to justice everywhere. We are caught in an inescapable network of mutuality tied in a single garment of destiny. Whatever affects one directly affects all indirectly. Never again can we afford to live with the narrow, provincial "outside agitator" idea. Anyone who lives inside the United States can never be considered an outsider anywhere in this country.

You deplore the demonstrations that are presently taking place in Birmingham. But I am sorry that your statement did not express a similar concern for the conditions that brought the demonstrations into being. I am sure that each of you would want to go beyond the superficial social analyst who looks merely at effects, and does not grapple with underlying causes. I would not hesitate to say that it is unfortunate that so-called demonstrations are taking place in Birmingham at this time, but I would say in more emphatic terms that it is even more unfortunate that the white power structure of this city left the Negro community no other alternative. . . .

We know through painful experience that freedom is never voluntarily given by the oppressor; it must be demanded by the oppressed. Frankly, I have yet to engage in a direct-action campaign that was "well timed" in the view of those who have not suffered unduly from the disease of segregation. For years now I have heard the word "wait!" It rings in the ear of every Negro with piercing familiarity. This "Wait" has almost always meant "Never." We must come to see, with one of our distinguished jurists, that "justice too long delayed is justice denied."

We have waited for more than 340 years for our constitutional and God-given rights. The nations of Asia and Africa are moving with jet-like speed toward gaining political independence, but we still creep at horse-and-buggy pace toward gaining a cup of coffee at a lunch counter. Perhaps it is easy for those who have never felt the stinging darts of segregation to say, "Wait." But when you have seen vicious mobs lynch your mothers and fathers at will and drown your sisters and brothers at whim; when you have seen hate-filled policemen curse, kick and even kill your black brothers and sisters; when you see the vast majority of your twenty million Negro brothers smothering in an airtight cage of poverty in the midst of an affluent society; when you suddenly find your tongue twisted and your speech stammering as you seek to explain to your six-year old daughter why she can't go to the public amusement park that has just been advertised on television, and see tears welling up in her eyes when she is told that Funtown is closed to colored children, and see ominous clouds of inferiority beginning to distort her personality by developing an unconscious bitterness toward white people; when you have to concoct an answer for a five-year-old son who is asking: "Daddy, why do white people treat colored people so mean?"; when you take a cross-country drive and find it necessary to sleep night after night in the uncomfortable corners of your automobile because no motel will accept you; when you are humiliated day in and day out by nagging signs reading "white" and "colored"; when your first name becomes "boy" (however old you are) and your last name becomes "John," and your wife and mother are never given the respected title "Mrs."; when you are harried by day and haunted by night by the fact that you are a Negro, living constantly at tiptoe stance, never quite knowing what to expect next, and are plagued with inner fears and outer resentments; when you are forever fighting a degenerating sense of "nobodiness"—then you will understand why we find it difficult to wait. There comes a time when the cup of endurance runs over, and men are no longer willing to be plunged into the abyss of despair. I hope sirs, you can understand our legitimate and unavoidable impatience.

You express a great deal of anxiety over our willingness to break laws. This is certainly a legitimate concern. Since we so diligently urge people to obey the Supreme Court's decision of 1954 outlawing segregation in the public schools, it is rather strange and paradoxical to find us consciously breaking laws. One may well ask, "How can you advocate breaking some laws and obeying others?" The answer is found in the fact that there are *just* laws and there are *unjust* laws. I would be the first to advocate obeying just laws. One has not only a legal but a moral responsibility to obey just laws. Conversely, one has a moral responsibility to disobey unjust laws. I would agree with Saint Augustine that "An unjust law is no law at all."

. . . We can never forget that everything Hitler did in Germany was "legal" and everything the Hungarian freedom fighters did in Hungary was "illegal." It was "illegal" to aid and comfort a Jew in Hitler's Germany. But I am sure that, if I had lived in Germany during that time, I would have aided and comforted my Jewish brothers even though it was illegal. If I lived in a Communist country today where certain principles dear to the Christian faith are suppressed, I believe I would openly advocate disobeying these anti-religious laws.

I must make two honest confessions to you, my Christian and Jewish brothers. First I must confess that over the last few years I have been gravely disappointed with the white moderate. I have almost reached the regrettable conclusion that the Negroes' great stumbling block in the stride toward freedom is not the White Citizens' "Councilor" or the Ku Klux Klaner, but the white moderate who is more devoted to "order" than to justice; who prefers a negative peace which is the absence of tension to a positive peace which is the presence of justice; who constantly says "I agree with you in the goal you seek, but I can't agree with your methods of direct action"; who paternalistically feels that he can set the timetable for another man's freedom; who lives by myth of time and who constantly advises the Negro to wait until a "more convenient season." Shallow understanding from people of good will is more frustrating than absolute misunderstanding from people of ill will. . . .

I had hoped that the white moderate would understand that law and order exist for the purpose of establishing justice, and that when they fail to do this they become the dangerously structured dams that block the flow of social progress. . . .

In your statement you asserted that our actions, even though peaceful, must be condemned because they precipitate violence. But can this assertion be logically made? Isn't this like condemning the robbed man because his possession of money precipitated the evil act of robbery? . . . Isn't this like condemning Jesus because His unique God consciousness and never-ceasing devotion to His will precipitated the evil act of crucifixion? . . .

You spoke of our activity in Birmingham as extreme. At first I was rather disappointed that fellow clergymen would see my nonviolent efforts as those of the extremist. I started thinking about the fact that I stand in the middle of two opposing forces in the Negro community. One is a force of complacency made up of Negroes who, as a result of long years of oppression, have been so completely drained of self-respect and a sense of "somebodiness" that they have adjusted to segregation, and of a few Negroes in the middle class who, because of a degree of academic and economic security, and because at points they profit by segregation, have unconsciously become insensitive to the problems of the masses. The other force is one of bitterness and hatred and comes perilously close to advocating violence. It is expressed in the various black nationalist groups that are springing up over the nation. . . . This movement is nourished by the contemporary frustration over the continued existence of racial discrimination. It is made up of people who have lost faith in America, who have absolutely repudiated Christianity, and who have concluded that the white man is an incurable "devil." . . .

I must admit that I was initially disappointed in being so categorized. . . . But as I continued to think about the matter I gradually gained a bit of satisfaction from being considered an extremist. Was not Jesus an extremist in love? . . . Was not Martin Luther an extremist? . . .Was not Abraham Lincoln . . . Thomas Jefferson. . . .

So the question is not whether we will be extremist but what kind of extremist will we be. Will we be extremists for hate or will we be extremists for love? Will we be extremists for the preservation of injustice—or will we be extremists for the cause of justice? . . .

Before closing I am impelled to mention one other point in your statement that troubled me profoundly. You warmly commended the Birmingham police force for keeping "order" and "preventing violence." I don't believe you would have so warmly commended the police force if you had seen its angry violent dogs literally biting six unarmed, non-violent Negroes. . . . It is true that they have been rather disciplined in their public handling of the demonstrations. In this sense they have been rather publicly "nonviolent." But for what purpose? To preserve the evil system of segregation. . . .

I wish you had commended the Negro sit-inner and demonstrators for their sublime courage, their willingness to suffer, and their amazing discipline in the midst of the most inhuman provocation. One day the South will recognize its real heroes. They will be the James Merediths, courageously and with a majestic sense of purpose, facing jeering and hostile mobs. . . .They will be old, oppressed, battered Negro women, symbolized in a 72-year-old woman of Montgomery, Alabama, who rose up with a sense of dignity and with her people decided not to ride the segregated buses, and responded to one who inquired about her tiredness with ungrammatical profundity: "My feets is tired, but my soul is rested. . . ." One day the South will know that . . .they were in reality standing up for the best in the American dream and the most sacred values in our Judeo-Christian heritage. . . .

6.4 Rather than deterring the protesters, King's imprisonment emboldened them. Shortly afterward, Birmingham experienced unparalleled protest, highlighted by the daring freedom marches of school children. Thousands of them were arrested; others were set upon by Sheriff Bull Connor's police dogs and knocked down by torrents of water shot at them from fire hoses. The mass media captured this vicious side of segregation, broadcasting pictures of it across the airwaves. Americans from all regions of the nation proclaimed their horror and demanded that President Kennedy intervene. As a result, city authorities and the business community negotiated an accord, which King and others proclaimed a tremendous victory. However, a day after it was announced, the KKK held a massive rally and later, that same day, bomb blasts ripped through the homes of Reverend A. D. King and the Gaston Motel, owned by Birmingham's wealthiest

black citizen. A miniriot broke out and SCLC averted a major one only by plead-
ing with the citizens to remain nonviolent. The campaign was successful.
According to Shuttlesworth, if one placed it in its historical context, then the
black community had made considerable strides forward.

6.4 Fred L. Shuttlesworth, "Birmingham Shall Be Free Some Day," *Freedomways* (Winter 1964), pp. 16-19.

. . . Much has been written about Birmingham since the demonstrations, and what the Birmingham Direct Action has meant to the nation and
the world. "But you ought to have seen and known how bad and terrible
Birmingham was before the demonstrations," says a typical Negro citizen, "and it ain't much better now. If it hadn't been for the Movement,
we would now be back in complete slavery." This reflects the sentiment
of most of the Birmingham Negro community. Birmingham, for many
years, has been so afflicted with bleakness, and like Tombstone Territory
of old, it has been "not good enough to live and too sinful to die."

Years ago, only a few Negro citizens dared to speak out, and there
could be no consistent challenge to segregation; the Ku Klux Klan saw to
that, and back of them were the police. The unwritten rule was "if the
mobs don't stop Negroes, the police will." Not only was there no vocif-
erous clamor for civil rights; the Negro's existence depended upon his
keeping quiet and upon the white man's paternalism.

Dialogue between the white and Negro community was non-existent,
except that between servant and master. . . . Indeed, men were arrested
for holding interracial meetings. . . . When a reporter interviewed
"Bull" Connor about his attitude and obedience to law, the commissioner
was quoted in the *Afro-American* newspaper as saying "Damn the law;
down here I am the Law."

With such an official attitude prevailing in Birmingham, one can understand why there have been over 50 bombings in 30 years. The city has
sanctioned "keeping Negroes in their place," and so the police were considered to be acting intelligently when they slapped, beat, or abused hundreds of colored people; or when they made it untenable for Negroes to
be in the streets late at night—even when coming from jobs. . . .

Despite this and other things, "Bull" was again elected commissioner
(1956-58) and he felt this a mandate to continue leading the city back-
wards. The other commissioners were not better, just more dignified. . . .

At the inception of the "Movement," it was common practice for
police to issue a hundred or more parking tickets on meeting nights. We
have been used to police attending mass meetings since 1958; but they
came many times with sirens screaming, lights flashing, fire axes, rush-

ing into buildings hunting "fires" which were not there—but failing to stampede Negroes, or to extinguish the fire that wouldn't go out.

We have challenged segregation so thoroughly that a few days ago in federal court the city claimed to have no barriers at all. The challenges have indeed been costly. The KKK castrated Mr. Jud Aaron, a common ordinary citizen, just like a man would a hog. They beat Rev. Charles Billups with chains. In the early days of our Movement countless Negroes went to jail and lost their jobs. Some even lost their homes, and many left for other cities. Time would fail to tell of the personal involvement of my family and myself. The thousands of crank and very real telephone threats, the mobs at Terminal Station, and at Phillips High School, before which I was dragged and beaten in the streets and my wife stabbed in the hip; the two dynamite explosions, through which we lived by the grace of God; the agonies of having to crusade almost alone, at first; the brutal tactics unleashed upon us by the city—all of these things did not move us, nor deter us from our goal.

They rather proved the mettle of the Birmingham Negro and lay the basis for the massive assault which took place last summer. Birmingham ought to be a better city. . . .

I like to feel, despite the fearlessness and vacillations of the new city council, that the massive demonstrations, led by the illustrious Dr. Martin Luther King, Reverend Ralph Abernathy, Reverend Wyatt Walker, and others who assisted me, have brought Birmingham to her senses; and that further persistence by our Movement will finally make it a City of Brotherhood.

I look back to the 3,300 who went to jail, and take pride in my people. And I think way back to the dark, dismal days of 1956 to 1963, and see Negroes trekking through snow and cold, rain and heat, persecution and peril, sacrifice and hardship, and then I say "thank God for knowing them, and the power of Faith." . . .

6.5 Project C had an even more profound affect on race relations outside of Birmingham. According to the Justice Department, there were at least 758 demonstrations in 186 cities across the South in the ten weeks following the Birmingham campaign. Nearly fifteen thousand persons were arrested in eleven southern states and protests. In mid-June, a month after the Birmingham demonstrations ended, Alabama Governor George Wallace vowed to personally block the desegregation of the state university. Faced with Wallace's open defiance of the law in combination with the swelling tide of indignation against segregation, President Kennedy decided that it was time to speak out. In a tele-

vised address, JFK delivered his strongest endorsement of civil rights and one of the most important presidential speeches on race relations in the history of the United States. Afterward, Kennedy presented an omnibus civil rights bill to Congress (eventually passed as the Civil Rights Act of 1964).

6.5 John F. Kennedy, "Address," June 11, 1963.

Good evening my fellow citizens. This afternoon, following a series of threats and defiant statements, the presence of Alabama National Guardsmen was required on the campus of the University of Alabama to carry out the final and unequivocal order of the United States District Court of the Northern District of Alabama.

The order called for the admission of two clearly qualified young Alabama residents who happened to have been born Negro.

That they were admitted peacefully on the campus is due in good measure to the conduct of the students of the University of Alabama who met their responsibilities in a constructive way.

I hope that every American, regardless of where he lives, will stop and examine his conscience about this and other related incidents.

This nation was founded by men of many nations and backgrounds. It was founded on the principle that all men are created equal, and that the rights of every man are diminished when the rights of one man are threatened.

Today we are committed to a worldwide struggle to promote and protect the rights of all who wish to be free. And when Americans are sent to Vietnam or West Berlin we do not ask for whites only.

It ought to be possible, therefore, for American students of any color to attend any public institution they select without having to be backed up by troops. It ought to be possible for American consumers of any color to receive equal service in places of public accommodation, such as hotels and restaurants, and theaters and retail stores without being forced to resort to demonstrations in the street.

And it ought to be possible for American citizens of any color to register and to vote in a free election without interference or fear of reprisal.

It ought to be possible, in short, for every American to enjoy the privileges of being American without regard to his race or his color.

In short, every American ought to have the right to be treated as he would wish to be treated, as one would wish his children to be treated. But this is not the case.

The Negro baby born in America today, regardless of the section or the state in which he is born, has about one-half as much chance of completing high school as a white baby, born in the same place, on the same day . . . twice as much chance of becoming unemployed . . . a life expectancy which is seven years shorter. . . .

This is not a sectional issue. Difficulties over segregation and discrimination exist in almost every city . . . producing . . . a rising tide of discontent that threatens the public safety.

Nor is this a partisan issue. In a time of domestic crisis, men of goodwill and generosity should be able to unite regardless of party or politics.

This is not even a legal or legislative issue alone. It is better to settle these matters in the courts than on the streets, and new laws are needed at every level. But law alone cannot make men see right.

We are confronted primarily with a moral issue. It is as old as the Scriptures and is as clear as the American Constitution. The heart of the question is whether all Americans are to be afforded equal rights and equal opportunities; whether we are going to treat our fellow Americans as we want to be treated.

If an American, because his skin is dark, cannot eat lunch in a restaurant open to the public; if he cannot send his children to the best public school available; if he cannot vote for the public officials who represent him; if, in short, he cannot enjoy the full and free life which all of us want, then who among us would be content to have the color of his skin changed and stand in his place?

Who among us would then be content with the counsels of patience and delay. One hundred years of delay have passed since President Lincoln freed the slaves, yet their heirs, their grandsons, are not fully free. . . .

And this nation, for all its hopes and all its boasts, will not be fully free until all its citizens are free.

We preach freedom around the world, and we mean it. And we cherish our freedom here at home. But are we to say to the world—and more importantly to each other—that this is the land of the free, except for the Negroes. . . .

Now the time has come for this nation to fulfill its promise. The events in Birmingham and elsewhere have so increased the cries for equality that no city or state or legislative body can prudently choose to ignore them.

The fires of frustration and discord are burning in every city, North and South. Where legal remedies are not at hand, redress is sought in the streets in demonstrations, parades and protests, which create tensions and threaten violence—and threaten lives.

We face, therefore, a moral crisis as a country and a people. It cannot be met by repressive police action. It cannot be left to increased demonstrations in the streets. It cannot be quieted by token moves or talk. It is time to act in the Congress, in your state and local legislative body, in all of our daily lives.

It is not enough to pin the blame on others, to say this is a problem of one section of the country or another, or deplore the facts that we face. A great change is at hand, and our task, our obligation is to make that revolution, that change peaceful and constructive for all.

Those who do nothing are inviting shame as well as violence. Those who act boldly are recognizing right as well as reality.

Next week I shall ask the Congress of the United States to act, to make a commitment it has not fully made in this century to the proposition that race has no place in American life or law. . . .

But legislation, I repeat, cannot solve this problem alone. It must be solved in the homes of every American in every community across our country.

In this respect, I want to pay tribute to those citizens, North and South, who've been working in their communities to make life better for all. They are acting not out of a sense of legal duty but out of a sense of human decency. Like our soldiers and sailors in all parts of the world, they are meeting freedom's challenge on the firing line and I salute them for their honor—their courage. . . .

We have a right to expect that the Negro community will be responsible, will uphold the law. But they have a right to expect that the law will be fair, that the Constitution will be color blind, as Justice Harlan said at the turn of the century.

This is what we're talking about. This is a matter which concerns this country and what it stands for, and in meeting it I ask the support of all our citizens. . . .

6.6 Even before Kennedy delivered his address, A. Philip Randolph and most of the major civil rights organizations had prepared plans for staging a mass demonstration in Washington, D.C. Randolph, whose proposed March on Washington Movement in 1941 had prompted Franklin Roosevelt to desegregate the defense industry, saw the new March as a vehicle for advancing the civil rights movement. However, in a meeting with Randolph and other civil rights leaders, President Kennedy urged that the protest be called off, arguing that it threatened to strip away support for the civil rights bill. Randolph unequivocally rebuffed the president's plea, declaring that the main issue was who would lead the protest and whether it would be nonviolent or violent, not whether it would take place.

Once the movement had committed itself to sponsoring the March, the time-consuming details of orchestrating it were left to Bayard Rustin. On August 28,

1963, Rustin's painstaking work paid off beyond his highest expectations, as over 200,000 Americans, from all across America, black and white, old and young, poured into the nation's capital. The final stage of the event took place in front of the Lincoln memorial. With thousands massed around the reflecting pools, A. Philip Randolph introduced the speakers, including Roy Wilkins of the NAACP, Whitney Young of the National Urban League, clerics representing American Protestants, Catholics, and Jews, Walter Reuther of the United Automobile Workers (UAW), and a panoply of performers and dignitaries, from Peter, Paul, and Mary to Mahalia Jackson. The breadth and depth of those assembled, with their banners, buttons, hats, and signs, all pledged to freedom and jobs, served as a fitting tribute to Randolph, who had dreamed of such an event for years.

Though Randolph's introduction and the scene in front of the Lincoln memorial spoke of unity, not all was calm and triumphant. The prepared speech of John Lewis (SNCC), reprinted below, engendered cries of outrage from some of the moderate sponsors. Archbishop O'Boyle declared that he would not present the opening invocation unless Lewis altered his remarks. In the name of unity, Rustin pleaded with Lewis to redraft the speech, to edit out his direct attacks on the Kennedy administration and the civil rights bill and to tone down some of the harsher rhetoric. Lewis did so. Even in its final form, Lewis' speech was the most militant of many delivered that day. It signified that serious differences existed within the civil rights movement, over the pace of change, the value of coalition with liberals, and the Kennedy administration. This said, Lewis, and his SNCC colleagues, such as SNCC executive secretary James Forman, who helped him modify the speech, reported favorably on the march in its immediate aftermath.

6.6 John Lewis, "Address at the March on Washington" [pre-edited draft], SNCC Papers.

We march today for jobs and freedom, but we have nothing to be proud of, for hundreds and thousands of our brothers are not here—they have no money for their transportation, for they are receiving starvation wages . . . or no wages, at all.

In good conscience, we cannot support the Administration's civil rights bill, for it is too little, and too late. There's not one thing in the bill that will protect our people from police brutality.

The voting section of the bill will not help the thousands of citizens who want to vote; will not help the citizens of Mississippi, of Alabama, and Georgia who are qualified to vote, who are without a 6th grade education. "One Man, One Vote," is the African cry—it is ours, too.

People have been forced to move for they have exercised their right to register to vote. What is in the bill that will protect the homeless and starving people of this nation? What is there in this bill to insure the equality of a maid who earns $5.00 a week in the home of a family whose income is $100,000 a year?

The bill will not protect young children and old women from police dogs and fire hoses for engaging in peaceful demonstrations. This bill will not protect the citizens in Danville, Virginia, who must live in constant fear in a police state. This bill will not protect the hundreds of people who have been arrested on trumped-up charges, like those in Americus, Georgia, where four young men are in jail, facing a death penalty, for engaging in peaceful protests.

For the first time in 100 years this nation is being awakened to the fact that segregation is evil and it must be destroyed in all forms. Our presence today proves that we have been aroused to the point of action.

We are now involved in a serious revolution. This nation is still a place of cheap political leaders allying themselves with open forms of political, economic and social exploitation.

In some parts of the South we have worked in the fields from sun-up to sun-down for $12 a week. In Albany, Georgia, we have seen our people indicted by the Federal government for peaceful protest, while the Deputy Sheriff beat Attorney C. B. King and left him half-dead; while local police officials kicked and assaulted the pregnant wife of Slater King, and she lost her baby.

It seems to me that the Albany indictment is part of a conspiracy on the part of the federal government and local politicians for political expediencey.

I want to know—which side is the federal government on?

The revolution is at hand, and we must free ourselves of the chains of political and economic slavery. The non-violent revolution is saying, "We will not wait for the courts to act, for we have been waiting hundreds of years. We will not wait for the President, nor the Justice Department, nor Congress, but we will take matters into our own hands, and create a great source of power, outside of any national structure that could and would assure us victory." For those who have said, "Be patient and wait!" we must say, "Patience is a dirty and nasty word." We cannot be patient, we do not want to be free gradually, we want our freedom, and we want it now. We can not depend on any political party, for both the Democrats and the Republicans have betrayed the basic principles of the Declaration of Independence.

We all recognize the fact that if any radical social, political and economic changes are to take place in our society, the people, the masses must bring them about. In the struggle we must seek more than mere civil rights; we must work for the community of love, peace, and true brotherhood. Our minds, souls, and hearts cannot rest until freedom and justice exist for all the people.

The revolution is a serious one. Mr. Kennedy is trying to take the revolution out of the streets and put in in the courts. Listen, Mr. Kennedy, listen. Mr. Congressman, listen, fellow citizens—the black masses are on the march for jobs and freedom, and we must say to the politicians that there won't be a "cooling-off period."

We won't stop now. All of the forces of Eastland, Barnett and Wallace won't stop this revolution. The next time we march, we won't march on Washington, but will march through the South, through the Heart of Dixie, the way Sherman did. We will make the action of the past few months look petty. And I say to you, WAKE UP AMERICA!!

All of us must get in the revolution—get in and stay in the streets of every city, village and hamlet of this nation, until true freedom comes, until the revolution is complete. The black masses in the Delta of Mississippi, in Southwest Georgia, Alabama, Harlem, Chicago, Detroit, Philadelphia and all over this nation are on the march.

6.7 Martin Luther King, Jr.'s address provided a fitting climax to the March. In contrast to his "Letter from Birmingham Jail," King aimed this speech to a very broad audience—not just those assembled but also millions who were watching the event on television. He sought to unite a diverse country in the cause of civil rights. At least for the moment he succeeded, especially with his closing extemporaneous remarks.

6.7 Martin Luther King, Jr., "I Have a Dream," August 28, 1963.

Five score years ago, a great American, in whose symbolic shadow we stand, signed the Emancipation Proclamation. This momentous decree came as a great beacon of light of hope to millions of Negro slaves who had been seared in the flames of withering injustice. It came as a joyous daybreak to end the long night of captivity.

But one hundred years later, we must face the tragic fact that the Negro is still not free. One hundred years later, the life of the Negro is still sadly crippled by the manacles of segregation and the chains of discrimination. One hundred years later, the Negro lives on a lonely island of poverty in the midst of a vast ocean of material prosperity. . . . So we have come here today to dramatize an appalling condition.

In a sense we have come to our nation's Capital to cash a check. When the architects of our republic wrote the magnificent words of the Constitution and the Declaration of Independence, they were signing a promissory note to which every American was to fall heir. This note was a promise that all men would be guaranteed the unalienable rights of life, liberty, and the pursuit of happiness.

It is obvious today that America has defaulted on this promissory note insofar as her citizens of color are concerned. Instead of honoring this sacred obligation, America has given the Negro people a bad check; a check which has come back marked "insufficient funds." But we refuse to believe that the bank of justice is bankrupt. We refuse to believe that there are insufficient funds in the great vaults of opportunity of this nation. So we have come to cash this check. . . .

We have also come to this hallowed spot to remind America of the fierce urgency of now. This is no time to engage in the luxury of cooling off or to take a tranquilizing dose of gradualism. Now is the time to make real the promises of Democracy. Now is the time to rise from the dark and desolate valley of segregation to the sunlit path of racial justice. Now is the time to open the doors of opportunity to all of God's children. Now is the time to lift our nation from the quicksands of racial injustice to the solid rock of brotherhood.

It would be fatal for the nation to overlook the urgency of the moment and to underestimate the determination of the Negro. The sweltering summer of the Negro's legitimate discontent will not pass until there is an invigorating autumn of freedom and equality. 1963 is not an end, but a beginning. Those who hope that the Negro needed to blow off steam and will now be content will have a rude awakening if the Nation returns to business as usual. There will be neither rest nor tranquility in America until the Negro is granted his citizenship rights. The whirlwinds of revolt will continue to shake the foundations of our Nation until the bright day of justice emerges.

But there is something that I must say to my people who stand on the warm threshold which leads into the palace of justice. In the process of gaining our rightful place we must not be guilty of wrongful deeds. Let us not need to satisfy our thirst for freedom by drinking from the cup of bitterness and hatred. We must forever conduct our struggle on the high plane of dignity and discipline. . . . The marvelous new militancy which has engulfed the Negro community must not lead us to distrust white people, for many of our white brothers, as evidenced by their presence here today, have come to realize that their destiny is tied up with our destiny and their freedom is inextricably bound to our freedom. We cannot walk alone. . . .

There are those who are asking the devotees of civil rights, "When will you be satisfied?" We can never be satisfied as long as the Negro is the victim of the unspeakable horrors of police brutality. . . . We cannot be satisfied as long as the Negro's basic mobilty is from a smaller ghetto to a larger one. We can never be satisfied as long as a Negro in Mississippi cannot vote and a Negro in New York believes he has nothing for which to vote. No, no we are not satisfied, and we will not be satisfied until justice rolls down like waters and righteousness like a mighty stream.

I am not unmindful that some of you have come here out of great trials and tribulations. Some of you have come fresh from narrow jail cells. Some of you have come from areas where your quest for freedom left you battered by the storms of persecution. You have been the veterans of creative suffering. Continue to work with the faith that unearned suffering is redemptive.

Go back to Mississippi, go back to Alabama, go back to South Carolina, . . . go back to the slums and ghettos of our modern cities, knowing that somehow this situation can and will be changed. Let us not wallow in the valley of despair.

I say to you today, my friends, that in spite of the difficulties and frustrations of the moment I still have a dream. It is a dream deeply rooted in the American dream.

I have a dream that one day this nation will rise up and live out the true meaning of its creed: "We hold these truths to be self-evident; that all men are created equal."

I have a dream that one day on the red hills of Georgia the sons of former slaves and the sons of former slaveowners will be able to sit down together at the table of brotherhood.

I have a dream that one day even the state of Mississippi, a desert state sweltering with the heat of injustice and oppression, will be transformed into an oasis of freedom and justice.

I have a dream that my four children will one day live in a nation where they will not be judged by the color of their skin but by the content of their character.

I have a dream today.

I have a dream that one day the state of Alabama, whose governor's lips are presently dripping with the words of interposition and nullification, will be transformed into a situation where little black boys and black girls will be able to join hands with little white boys and white girls and walk together as sisters and brothers.

I have a dream today.

I have a dream that one day every valley shall be exalted, every hill and mountain shall be made low, the rough places will be made plains, and the crooked places will be made straight, and the glory of the Lord shall be revealed, and all flesh shall see it together.

This is our hope. This is the faith with which I return to the South. With this faith we will be able to hew out of the mountain of despair a stone of hope. With this faith we will be able to transform the jangling discords of our nation into a beautiful symphony of brotherhood. With this faith we will be able to work together, to pray together, to struggle together, to go to jail together, to stand up for freedom together, knowing that we will be free one day.

This will be the day when all God's children will be able to sing with new meaning "My country 'tis of thee, sweet land of liberty, of thee I sing. Land where my fathers died, land of the pilgrim's pride, from every mountainside, let freedom ring."

And if America is to be a great nation this must come to be true. So let freedom ring from the prodigious hilltops of New Hampshire. Let freedom ring from the mighty mountains of New York. Let freedom ring from the heightening Alleghenies of Pennsylvania!

. . . But not only that; let freedom ring from Stone Mountain of Georgia! Let freedom ring from Lookout Mountain, Tennessee! Let freedom ring from every hill and mole hill of Mississippi. From every mountainside, let freedom ring.

When we let freedom ring, when we let it ring from every village and every hamlet, from every state and every city, we will be able to speed up that day when all of God's children, black men and white men, Jews and Gentiles, Protestants and Catholics, will be able to join hands and sing in the words of the old Negro spiritual, "Free at last! Free at last! thank God almighty, we are free at last!"

6.8 On September 15, 1963, less than three weeks after the Great March, a bomb exploded in the Sixteenth Street Baptist Church in Birmingham, Alabama. Four young black girls, all dressed in their Sunday white—Denise McNair, Addie Mae Collins, Cynthia Wesley, and Carole Robertson—were killed. Nearly twenty others were seriously wounded. Earlier that same week, Sonnie Hereford IV, age four, had become the first black student to attend a white school in Alabama. The bombing tested the metal of the civil rights movement and the nation. Coming so soon after the March on Washington, it cast a somber mood on King and his allies and just as importantly laid doubt as to the feasibility of his dream. Birmingham, which had barely averted a major riot in the spring, seemed ready to explode. Meanwhile, President Kennedy's civil rights bill was stalled in the Senate by a filibuster, and many felt that at best Congress would pass another watered-down law.

The following editorial which appeared in the Atlanta Constitution *reflected the extent to which the church bombing shook many Americans to their core. Even many Southerners who heretofore opposed the civil rights movement or remained silent now spoke out. The killing was so senseless that it compelled Eugene Patterson to demand that Southerners reconsider their way of life. Perhaps because individuals like Patterson reacted the way he did, King was able to retain his faith in nonviolence. He wrote to President Kennedy following the fatal blast: "I still have faith in the vast possibilities of Birmingham. There are many white people of good will" (quoted in Taylor Branch,* Parting the Waters, *p. 894). Less than two months later, President Kennedy, too, lay dead in a pool of blood, shot by an assassin while touring Dallas, Texas, in part to gain support for his civil rights bill.*

6.8 Eugene Patterson, "A Flower for the Graves," *Atlanta Constitution*, September 16, 1963.

A Negro mother wept in the street Sunday morning in front of a Baptist Church in Birmingham. In her hand she held a shoe, one shoe, from the foot of her dead child. We hold that shoe with her. Every one of us in the white South holds that small shoe in his hand.

It is too late to blame the sick criminals who handled the dynamite. The FBI and the police can deal with that kind. The charge against them is simple. They killed four children. Only we can trace the truth. Southerner—you and I. We broke those childrens bodies. We watched the stage set without saying it. We listened to the prologue unbestirred. We saw the curtain opening with disinterest. We have heard the play.

We—who go on electing politicians who beat the kettles of hate. We—who raise no hand to silence the mean and little men who have their nigger jokes. We—who stand aside in imagined rectitude and let the mad dogs that run in every society slide their leashes from our hand, and spring. We—the heirs of a proud South, who protest its worth and demand its recognition—we are the ones who have ducked the difficult, skirted the uncomfortable . . . rationalized the unacceptable, and created the day surely when these children would die.

This is not time to load our anguish onto the murderous scapegoat who set the cap in dynamite of our own manufacture. He didn't know any better. Somewhere in the dim and fevered recess of an evil mind he feels right now that he has been a hero. He is only guilty of murder. He thinks he has pleased us.

We of the white South who know better are the ones who must take a harsher judgment. We, who know better, created a climate for child-killing by those who don't. We hold that shoe in our hand, Southerner. Let us see it straight, and look at the blood on it. Let us compare it with the unworthy speeches of Southern public men who have traduced the Negro; match it with the spectacle of shrilling children whose parents and teachers turned them free to spit epithets at small huddles of Negro school children for a week before this Sunday in Birmingham; hold up the shoe and look beyond it to the state house in Montgomery where the official attitudes of Alabama have been spoken in heat and anger.

Let us not lay the blame on some brutal fool who didn't know any better. We know better. We created the day. We bear the judgment. May God have mercy on the poor South that has been so led.

The Sunday school play at Birmingham is ended. With a weeping Negro mother, we stand in the bitter smoke and hold a shoe. If our South is ever to be what we wish it to be, we will plant a flower of nobler resolve for the South now upon these four small graves that we dug.

Chapter Seven

MISSISSIPPI:
OPENING THE CLOSED SOCIETY

You know, it may sound funny, but I love the South. I don't choose
to live anywhere else. There's land here, where a man can raise coffee, and I'm going to do that some day. There are lakes where a man
can sink a hook and fight for bass. . . . There is room here for my
children to play and grow, and become good citizens—if the white
man will let them. . . . I'll be damned . . . if I'm going to let the
white man beat me. There's something out here that I've got to do
for my kids, and I'm not going to stop until I've done it.

—Medgar Evers, "Why I Live in Mississippi"

In August 1955, the summer after the Brown *decision, Emmett Till, of Chicago,
age fourteen, traveled to Money, Mississippi, to visit with his mother's family.
Shortly after he arrived, Till and his cousins went to the town drugstore and
bought some candy. On his way out of the store, Emmett allegedly yelled out to
the female storekeeper: "Bye baby." Later that night, the storekeeper's husband, Roy Bryant and his buddy, J. W. Milam, knocked on the door of Mose
Wright, Till's great uncle and asked for the boy. They proceeded to drag Emmett
out of the house, interrogated, beat, and then shot him in the skull from point-
blank range. Then they dumped his corpse into the Tallahatchie River.*

Till's murder outraged black America. Jet *magazine published a graphic
photograph of his mutilated body. His mother had insisted on an open casket
funeral service so that "the whole world could see what they've done." Protests
took place and the NAACP kept the case in the limelight to generate support for*

the fight against segregation. Bryant and Milam were arrested and brought to trial for murder. At the end of the trial, Bryant's and Milam's defense attorney declared to the jury: "I am sure that every last Anglo-Saxon one of you will have the courage to free these men." Within an hour they did, ignoring virtually all the evidence, as had whites in countless other murders or lynchings of blacks. In a paid interview with William Bradford Huie, Bryant and Milam admitted that they had killed Till in cold blood. As Milam recalled: "I just decided it was time a few people got put on notice. As long as I live and can do anything about it, niggers are gonna stay in their place."

7.1 In the following excerpt from her autobiography, Coming of Age in Mississippi, *Anne Moody, who grew up near Money, describes the impact that Till's murder had on her. The piece hints at the origins of the movement in Mississippi. While Milam hoped to keep blacks "in their place," the murder had the exact opposite impact on Moody. She became convinced that she had to fight to crack the social and legal barriers that had been imposed on blacks by whites in Mississippi for centuries. With the help of a basketball scholarship Moody went away to college, ending up at Tougaloo State, the black university in Jackson, Mississippi. There she befriended several civil rights activists and worked with Medgar Evers, CORE, and SNCC in the local freedom fight. Her autobiography remains one of the best firsthand accounts of the movement.*

7.1 Anne Moody, *Coming of Age in Mississippi* (Garden City, N.Y.: Doubleday, 1968), pp. 121-138.

Not only did I enter high school with a new name, but also with a completely new insight into the life of Negroes in Mississippi. I was now working for one of the meanest white women in town, and a week before school started Emmett Till was killed.

Up until his death, I had heard of Negroes found floating in a river or dead somewhere with their bodies riddled with bullets. But I didn't know the mystery behind these killings then. I remember once when I was only seven I heard Mama and one of my aunts talking about some Negro who had been beaten to death. "Just like them lowdown skunks killed him they will do the same to us," Mama had said. When I asked her who killed the man and why, she said, "An Evil Spirit killed him. You gotta be a good girl or it will kill you too." So since I was seven, I had lived in fear of that "Evil Spirit." It took me eight years to learn what that spirit was. . . .

That evening when I stopped off at the house on the way to Mrs. Burke's, Mama was singing. . . . I wondered if she knew about Emmett Till. The way she was singing she had something on her mind and it wasn't pleasant either. . . . "Mama, did you hear about that fourteen-year-old Negro boy who was killed a little over a week ago by some white men?" I asked her.

"Where did you hear that?" she said angrily. "Boy, everybody really thinks I am dumb or deaf or something. I heard Eddie them talking about it this evening coming from school." "Eddie them better watch how they go around here talking. These white folks git hold of it they gonna be in trouble," she said. "What are they gonna be in trouble about, Mama? People got a right to talk, ain't they?" "You go on to work before you is late. And don't you let on like you know nothing about that boy being killed before Miss Burke them. . . . That boy's a lot better off in heaven than he is here," she continued. . . .

On my way to Mrs. Burke's that evening, Mama's words kept running through my mind. "Just do your work like you don't know nothing." "Why is Mama acting so scared?" I thought. "And what if Mrs. Burke knew we knew? Why must I pretend I don't know? Why are these people killing Negroes? What did Emmett Till do besides whistle at that white woman?"

By the time I got to work, I had worked my nerves up some. I was shaking as I walked on the porch. "Do your work like you don't know nothing." But once I got inside, I couldn't have acted normal if Mrs. Burke were paying me to be myself.

I was so nervous, I spent most of the evening avoiding them going about the house dusting and sweeping. . . . I went to the bathroom to clean the tub. . . . I spent a whole hour scrubbing it. I had removed the stains in no time but I kept scrubbing until they had finished dinner.

When they had finished and gone into the living room. . . . Mrs. Burke called me to eat. I took a clean plate out of the cabinet and sat down. Just as I was putting the first forkful of food in my mouth, Mrs. Burke entered the kitchen. "Essie, did you hear about the fourteen-year-old boy who was killed in Greenwood?" . . . "No, I didn't hear that," I answered, almost choking on the food. "Do you know why he was killed?" she asked and I didn't answer. "He was killed because he got out of his place with a white woman. A boy from Mississippi would have known better than that. This boy was from Chicago. Negroes up North have no respect for people. They think they can get away with anything. He just came to Mississippi and put a whole lot of notions in the boys' heads here and stirred up a lot of trouble," she said passionately.

"How old are you, Essie?" she asked. . . . "Fourteen. I will soon be fifteen though," I said. "See, that boy was just fourteen too. It's a shame he had to die so soon." She was so red in the face, she looked as if she was on fire.

When she left the kitchen I sat there with my mouth open and my food untouched. I couldn't have eaten now if I were starving. . . . I went home shaking like a leaf on a tree. For the first time out of all her trying, Mrs. Burke had made me feel like rotten garbage. Many times she had tried to instill fear within me and subdue me and had given up. But when she talked about Emmett Till there was something in her voice that sent chills and fear all over me.

Before Emmett Till's murder, I had known the fear of hunger, hell, and the Devil. But now there was a new fear known to me—the fear of being killed just because I was black. This was the worst of my fears. I knew once I got food, the fear of starving to death would leave. I also was told that if I was a good girl, I wouldn't have to fear the Devil or hell. But I didn't know what one had to do or not do as a Negro not to be killed. Probably just being a Negro period was enough, I thought. . . .

7.2, 7.3, and 7.4 As Robert Moses and other activists in McComb discovered, most white Mississippians displayed a fierce commitment to white supremacy. The White Citizens Council came to dominate state politics. In 1960, Ross Barnett, a damage-suit lawyer, who had twice failed miserably to become governor, was elected to the top post in the state by promising to resist integration. Two years after he was elected, Barnett made good on his promise, defying court orders to allow James Meredith to enroll at the University of Mississippi. In the same time period, the number of registered black voters actually declined. As of 1962, in five counties with black majorities, not a single black was registered to vote. Without a doubt, physical intimidation was one of the main reasons for this. The following affidavits—taken from E. W. Steptoe, a brave ally of SNCC; Aaron Henry, Medgar Evers' successor as head of the state chapter of the NAACP; and June Johnson, one of many homespun Mississippi freedom fighters—demonstrate that activism had its costs. These affidavits, along with countless others, were collected by the Council of Federated Organizations (COFO) and published as the Mississippi Black Paper *(Random House, 1965).*

7.2 E. W. Steptoe, "Affidavit."

In 1954 I organized the Amite County Chapter of the NAACP. We held several meetings in a school building. . . . One night . . . the sheriff, Ira Jenkins, his deputy, and a member of the school board, and 15 or 20 other white men came out and surrounded the building. Then the sheriff, deputy, and school board member came into the meeting. This was about 8 P.M. These three did not take off their hats or anything; they just sat down. Then the school board member turned to different people and asked them what they were doing at the meeting. They didn't answer him. Then he said: "My advice to you is to take this money and put it into the school building.'' He apparently thought the group was collecting some money, though this was not the case. When they were ready to leave, the sheriff without asking reached on the table and took the secretary's book. Then they left the building and drove off. Because of their presence, the people were frightened and the meeting ended.

Ever since that time, whenever we have held meetings, the sheriff or his deputy drives around. . . . It is hard to get people to come to the meetings because they are so afraid. . . .

I live far off the highway, and the white people never come out to threaten me at my house. But in September, 1963, a cross was burned where the road to my house leads off from the highway. . . . It is extremely dangerous for anyone to work for civil rights there [Amite Co.] without protection from outside the county. . . . I feel that my life is in danger. . . . I have felt this since I began working for the NAACP in 1954. . . .

7.3 Aaron Henry, "Affidavit."

I am a Negro and reside in Clarksdale, Mississippi. . . . I have had my life threatened by telephone, by carrier of word, and other means. . . .

On Good Friday of 1962, while sleeping in the dead of night, our home was bombed and set afire. In the house at that time besides my wife and daughter was Congressman Charles Diggs of the State of Michigan. . . . The fact that he was staying with me had been circulated in the local paper, the Clarksdale *Press Register*, the day before. Immediately following that the house was fired upon with several slugs sticking in the walls. Three months after that, the Fourth Street Drug Store, my place of business, was bombed. The plate glass windows in the front of the store have been repeatedly broken out in the past few years. As a result of these attacks, all of the insurance we have carried on the store and on our home has been canceled. . . .

7.4 June Johnson, "Affidavit."

I am 16 years old and live in Greenwood, Mississippi. A group of civil rights workers was travelling from Charleston, South Carolina, to Greenwood, Miss., by bus on June 9, 1963. The group consisted of Mrs. Fannie Lou Hamer, Miss Annell Ponder, Mr. James West, Miss Euvester Simpson, Miss Rosemary Freeman, and myself. On the trip from Columbus, Miss., to Winona, Miss., our group sat in the front of the bus and occasionally sang freedom songs.

When we got to Winona, the bus stopped at the terminal there. Everybody went into the terminal except Mrs. Hamer. When we got inside the terminal, our group sat down on the "white" side. [A] Winona [police officer] came in and told us to "get over where you belong." We got up and went outside the terminal. Soon the [police officer] and a state trooper came outside and arrested us. When she saw us getting into the trooper's car, Mrs. Hamer got out of the bus and asked us, "Should I go on to Greenwood?" We told her to go ahead, but the trooper called out, "Get that woman," and an unidentified white man grabbed her and put her in his car. The trooper took us to the Montgomery County Jail. Mrs. Hamer arrived in the other car about the same time.

We were taken inside. The trooper said, "What you niggers come down here for—a damn demonstration?" We all shook our heads and answered "No." Then he said, "You damn niggers don't say 'No' to me—you say 'Yes, sir.' " While he was saying this, Officer A____ and the Winona [police officer] came in, accompanied by the same white man that brought Mrs. Hamer in.

Officer A____ walked over and stamped James West's toe and hit Euvester in the side with a ring of heavy keys. Then the trooper questioned us. While questioning Annell Ponder, he found out that she lived in Atlanta, Ga. He told her, "I knew you wasn't from Mississippi 'cause you don't know how to say 'Yes, sir' to a white man." Then he turned to the rest of us and said, "I been hearing about you black sons-of-bitches over in Greenwood raising all that hell. You come over here to Winona, you'll get the hell whipped out of you."

He opened the door to the cell block and told everybody to get inside. I started to go in with the rest of them and he said, "Not you, you black-assed nigger." He asked me, "Are you a member of the NAACP?" I said yes. Then he hit me on the cheek and chin. I raised my arm to protect my face and he hit me in the stomach. He asked, "Who runs that thing?" I answered, "The people." He asked, "Who pays you?" I said, "Nobody." He said, "Nigger, you're lying. You done enough already to get your neck broken." Then the four of them . . . brought Mrs. Hamer in—threw me on the floor and beat me. After they finished stomping me, they said, "Get up, nigger." I raised my head and the white man hit me on the back of the head with a club wrapped in black leather. Then they made me get up. My dress was torn off and my slip was coming off. Blood was streaming down the back of my head and my dress was all bloody. They put me in a cell with Rosemary Freeman, and called Annell Ponder. I couldn't see what they did to Annell, but I could hear them trying to make her say "Yes, sir." When they brought her back, she was bloody and her clothes were torn. . . . A little while later we heard Mrs.

Hamer hollering, "Don't beat me no more. . . ." Later they brought her back to her cell crying. She cried at intervals during the night, saying that the leg afflicted with polio was hurting her terribly.

We stayed in that jail cell day and night from Sunday till Tuesday, when they booked us and informed us that we were charged with disorderly conduct and resisting arrest. We then went back to jail until Wednesday afternoon, when a group of SNCC people came from Greenwood to get us out of jail. We got back to Greenwood about 7 P.M. on June 12, 1963.

7.5 In early 1964, SNCC decided to undertake a major campaign which became known as Mississippi or Freedom Summer. Working with CORE, the NAACP, and SCLC, under the umbrella of COFO, SNCC brought hundreds of volunteers to Mississippi to test the implementation of the Civil Rights Act, to register blacks to vote, and to extend its activities in the state. SNCC decided to go forward with Freedom Summer only after careful deliberation. Some SNCC veterans warned that bringing masses of volunteers to the state, including a large number of whites, would undermine the objective of building up a grass-roots movement. But Robert Moses, James Forman, and several others countered that the advantages of such an endeavor outweighed the disadvantages. One potential advantage was that if a white person was killed, the nation could be expected to react. Whereas when blacks had been killed, it had not. That might sound cold, remarked CORE's David Dennis, "but that was also speaking the language of the country" (quoted in Howell Raines, My Soul Is Rested, p. 274).

Before embarking on their mission, the volunteers gathered in Oxford, Ohio, for intensive training in nonviolence. Robert Moses, James Forman, and other SNCC leaders were the teachers. While in Oxford, the volunteers learned about the disappearance of Michael Schwerner, a CORE veteran, James Chaney, a native of Mississippi, and Andrew Goodman, one of the new recruits. From the moment that the three did not report their whereabouts, SNCC worried that they had been killed. Mississippi authorities scoffed at this. President Johnson decided to undertake a massive manhunt for them, mobilizing 150 FBI investigators and 200 Navy men. On August 4, the bodies of the three activists were uncovered in an earthfill dam near Philadelphia, Mississippi. An autopsy revealed that they had all been dead when buried and that they had been killed on or around the date of their initial disappearance.

7.5 Sally Belfrage, *Freedom Summer* (New York: Viking, 1965), pp. 15-21.

Then Bob Moses, the Director of the Summer Project, came to the front of the floor. He didn't introduce himself, but somehow one knew who he was. Everyone had heard a little—that he was twenty-nine, began in Harlem, had a Master's degree in philosophy from Harvard, and that he had given up teaching in New York to go South after the sit-ins. He had been in Mississippi for three years, and he wore its uniform: a T-shirt and denim overalls, in the bib of which he propped his hands. He began as though in the middle of a thought. "When Mrs. Hamer sang, 'If you miss me from the freedom fight, you can't find me nowhere; Come on over to the graveyard, I'll be buried over there . . .' that's true."

Moving up to the stage, he drew a map of Mississippi on a blackboard and patiently, from the beginning, outlined the state's areas and attitudes. The top left segment became the Delta; industry was cotton; power in the Citizens' Councils. . . . The segment beneath the Delta was the hill country, mostly poor white farmers who had been organizing since the March on Washington. Amite County, McComb: Klan territory, where violence was indiscriminately aimed at "keeping the nigger in his place" and no one was safe. Five Negroes had been murdered there since December. No indictments.

Mississippi gained texture and dimension. . . . "When you come South, you bring with you the concern of the country—because the people of the country don't identify with Negroes. The guerrilla war in Mississippi is not much different from that in Vietnam. But when we tried to see President Johnson, his secretary said that Vietnam was popping up all over his calendar and he hadn't time to talk to us. Now," he said, "because of the Summer Project, because whites were involved, a crack team of FBI men was going down to Mississippi to investigate. We have been asking them for three years. Now the federal government is concerned; there will be more protection for us, and hopefully for the Negroes who live there." . . .

"Our goals are limited. If we can go and come back alive, then that is something. If you can go into Negro homes and just sit and talk, that will be a huge job. We're not thinking of integrating the lunch counters. The Negroes in Mississippi haven't the money to eat in those places anyway. . . ."

"Mississippi has been called 'The Closed Society.' It is closed, locked. We think the key is in the vote. Any change, and possibility for dissidence and opposition, depends first on a political breakthrough." . . .

There was an interruption then at the side entrance: three or four staff members had come in and were whispering agitatedly. . . . Time passed. When [Moses] stood and spoke, he was somewhere else; it was simply that he was obliged to say something, but his voice was automatic. "Yesterday morning, three of our people left Meridian, Mississippi, to investigate a church-burning in Neshoba County. They haven't come back, and we haven't had any word from them. We spoke to John Doar in the Justice Department. He promised to order the FBI to act, but the local FBI still says they have been given no authority.'' . . .

Then a thin girl in shorts was talking to us from the stage: Rita Schwerner, the wife of one of the three.

She paced as she spoke, her eyes distraught and her face quite white, but in a voice that was even and disciplined. It was suddenly clear that she, Moses, and others on the staff had been up all the night before. The three men had been arrested for speeding. Deputy Sheriff Price of Neshoba claimed to have released them at 10 P.M. the same day. All the jails in the area had been checked, with no results. The Jackson FBI office kept saying they were not sure a federal statute had been violated.

Rita asked us to form groups by home area and wire our congressmen that the federal government, though begged to investigate, had refused to act, and that if the government did not act, none of us was safe. Someone in the audience asked her to spell the names. . . .

No one was willing to believe that the event involved more than a disappearance. It was hard to believe even that. Somehow it seemed only a climatic object lesson, part of the morning's lesson, an anecdote to give life to the words of Bob Moses. To think of it in other terms was to be forced to identify with the three, to be prepared, irrevocably, to give one's life.

The volunteers broke up into their specialized units. . . . Each day began with an announcement like Vincent Harding's on Tuesday: ''There has been no word of the three people in Neshoba. The staff met all night. When we sing 'We are not afraid,' we mean we are afraid. We sing 'Ain't gonna let my fear turn me round,' because many of you might want to turn around now.'' . . .

The lectures and classes continued. . . . Tuesday night. Bob Moses came in quietly, turned on the microphone and said, ''The car has been found outside Philadelphia [Miss.]. It was badly burned. There is no news of the three boys.'' . . .

The President sent two hundred sailors to search for the missing boys. Rita Schwerner and all the staff members who could be spared were in Meridian and Philadelphia. Nothing visible was being done by the authorities to prevent the same thing from happening to anyone else. We clung to the television set. . . .

Then Moses, said, ''The kids are dead.''

He paused—quite without regard for dramatic effect. But long enough for it to hit us: this was the first time it had been spoken: they are dead. Up to now they had simply "disappeared." . . .

"There may be more deaths." He waited, seeking the words he needed. "I justify myself because I'm taking risks myself, and I'm not asking people to do things I'm not willing to do. And the other thing is, people were being killed already, the Negroes of Mississippi, and I feel, anyway, responsible for their deaths. Herbert Lee killed, Louis Allen killed, five others killed this year. In some way you have to come to grips with that. . . . If you are going to do anything about it, other people are going to be killed. No privileged group in history has ever given up anything, without some kind of blood sacrifice." . . .

"The way some people characterize this project is that it is an attempt to get some people killed so the federal government will move into Mississippi. And the way some of us feel about it is that in our country we have some real evil, and the attempt to do something about it involves enormous effort . . . and therefore tremendous risks. If for any reason you're hesitant about what you're getting into, it's better for you to leave. Because what has got to be done has to be done in a certain way, or otherwise it won't get done. You have to break off a little chunk of a problem and work on it, and try to see where it leads, and concentrate on it." . . .

He finished, stood there, then walked out the door. The silence which followed him was absolute. It lasted a minute, two; no one moved. They know, now, what could not be applauded. Suddenly, a beautiful voice from the back of the room pierced the quiet.

> They say that freedom is a constant struggle.
> They say that freedom is a constant struggle.
> They say that freedom is a constant struggle,
> Oh, Lord, we've struggled so long,
> We must be free, we must be free.

It was a new song to me and the others. But I knew it, and all the voices in the room joined as though the song came from the deepest part of themselves, and they had always known it.

7.6 Freedom Summer had two main foci, (1) the Mississippi Freedom Democratic Party or MFDP and (2) the Freedom Schools. The MFDP was built on the Freedom Vote of 1963, an effort organized by SNCC and independent activist Allard Lowenstein, whereby blacks voted for a slate of candidates in a mock election. Like the Freedom Vote, COFO figured that the MFDP could be used as a means to register blacks, increase their political acumen, and build for the future. The fact that tens of thousands of blacks risked economic and physical threats to vote for MFDP suggests that the strategy worked very well.

In addition, COFO determined to challenge the Regular Democratic Party of the state at the National Democratic Convention in Atlantic City. A slate of delegates headed by Aaron Henry went before the credentials committee of the party to argue that they were the only legitimate Democratic Party in the state. Joe Rauh, a liberal lawyer, counsel of the UAW, and head of the Americans for Democratic Action (ADA), wrote a brief in MFDP's favor, introduced its members to leading Democrats and presented its case before the credentials committee. MFDP's challenge climaxed with the testimony of Fannie Lou Hamer, a Mississippi sharecropper and one of the most respected civil rights activists in the movement. Her testimony is reproduced below.

7.6 "Testimony of Fannie Lou Hamer Before the Credentials Committee of the Democratic National Convention," August 22, 1964, Atlantic City, New Jersey.

Mr. Chairman, and the Credentials Committee, my name is Mrs. Fannie Lou Hamer, and I live at 626 East Lafayette Street, Ruleville, Mississippi, Sunflower County, the home of Senator James O. Eastland, and Senator Stennis.

It was the 31st of August in 1962 that 18 of us traveled 26 miles to the county courthouse in Indianola to try to register to try to became first-class citizens. We was met in Indianola by Mississippi men, Highway Patrolmen and they allowed two of us in to take the literacy test at the time. After we had taken the test and started back to Ruleville, we was held up by the City Police and the State Highway Patrolmen and carried back to Indianola where the bus driver was charged that day with driving a bus the wrong color.

After we paid the fine among us, we continued on to Ruleville, and Reverend Jeff Sunny carried me the four miles in the rural area where I had worked as a time-keeper and sharecropper for 18 years. I was met there by my children, who told me the plantation owner was angry because I had gone down to try to register.

After they told me, my husband came, and said the plantation owner was raising cain because I had tried to register and before he quit talking the plantation owner came, and said, "Fannie Lou, do you know—did Pap tell you what I said?" And I said, "Yes sir." He said, "I mean that . . . If you don't go down and withdraw . . . well—you might have to go because we are not ready for that." . . .

And I addressed him and told him and said, "I didn't try to register for you. I tried to register for myself."

I had to leave that same night.

On the 10th of September, 1962, 16 bullets was fired into the home of Mr. and Mrs. Robert Tucker for me. That same night two girls were shot in Ruleville, Mississippi. Also Mr. Joe McDonald's house was shot in.

And in June, the 9th, 1963, I had attended a voter registration workshop, was returning back to Mississippi. Ten of us was traveling by the Continental Trailways bus. When we got to Winona, Mississippi, which is Montgomery County, four of the people got off to use the washroom. . . . I stepped off the bus to see what was happening and somebody screamed from the car that four workers was in and said, "Get that one there," and when I went to get in the car, when the man told me I was under arrest, he kicked me.

I was carried to the county jail and put in the holding room. They left some of the people in the booking room and began to place us in cells. I was placed in a cell with a young woman called Miss Euvester Simpson. After I was placed in the cell I began to hear sounds of licks and screams. I could hear the sounds of licks and horrible screams, and I could hear somebody say, "Can you say, yes, sir, nigger?" "Can you say yes, sir?"

And they would say horrible names. She would say. "Yes, I can say yes, sir." . . . They beat her, I don't know how long, and after a while she began to pray and asked God to have Mercy on those people. And it wasn't too long before three white men came to my cell. One of these men was a State Highway Patrolmen and he asked me where I was from, and I told him Ruleville; he said, "We are going to check this."

And they left my cell and it wasn't too long before they came back. He said, "You are from Ruleville all right," and he used a curse word, he said, "We are going to beat you until you wish you was dead."

I was carried out of that cell into another cell where they had two Negro prisoners. The State Highway patrolmen ordered the first Negro to take the blackjack. The first Negro prisoner ordered me, by orders from the State Highway Patrolmen, for me to lay down on a bunk bed on my face, and I laid on my face.

The first Negro began to beat, and I was beat by the first Negro until he was exhausted, and I was holding my hands behind at this time on my left side because I suffered polio when I was six years old. After the first Negro had beat until he was exhausted the state Highway Patrolman ordered the second Negro to take the blackjack. The second Negro began to beat and I began to work my feet, and the State Highway Patrolmen ordered the first Negro who had beat to set on my feet to keep me from working my feet. I began to scream and one white man got up and began to beat me in my head and tell me to hush.

One white man—my dress had worked up high, he walked over and pulled my dress down and he pulled my dress back, back up. . . .

All of this on account we want to register, to become first-class citizens, and if the freedom Democratic Party is not seated now, I question America, is this America, the land of the free and the home of the brave where we have to sleep with our telephones off the hooks because our lives be threatened daily because we want to live as decent human beings, in America?

7.7 Worried about the damage that the MFDP challenge would do to his re-election bid, President Johnson moved quickly to squelch it. He stripped Hamer of her televised audience by scheduling an emergency press statement. Afterward, working through Hubert Humphrey, the presumed vice-presidential nominee, and the longtime darling of liberals, Johnson demanded that MFDP accept a compromise of two at-large delegates and promises of reform for future conventions. Though it had come a long way, MFDP refused to accept LBJ's offer. As James Forman observed, MFDP refused to sell out those who had worked so hard and risked so much for so little in return.

7.7 James Forman, *The Making of Black Revolutionaries* (Seattle: Open Hand, 1985), pp. 386-396.

At the 1964 Democratic National Convention in Atlantic City Hubert Humphrey, Walter Reuther, Senator Wayne Morse, Roy Wilkins, Bayard Rustin, Martin Luther King, Jr., Ralph Abernathy, Allard Lowenstein and many other forces in the liberal-labor syndrome said that the Student Nonviolent Coordinating Committee did not understand politics.

We did not understand the political process, they said. We did not know how to "compromise." . . . We did not understand the Democratic Party." . . .

We in SNCC understood politics and political process. We could compromise—but not sell out the people. And we knew a great deal about the Democratic Party. But the way the liberal-labor syndrome looked at life was not the way we looked at. We did not see the Democratic Party as the great savior of black people in this country. Therefore we did not have the habit of following blindly the ass, no matter how stupid he became . . . or how many times he kicked you . . . or did not move forward . . . or lost his way. . . . We understood, we understood all too well.

When I arrived at Atlantic City, two days after the others from Mississippi, Mrs. Fannie Lou Hamer had already testified before the Credentials

Committee—the first step in the battle of the Mississippi Freedom Democratic Party delegation to be recognized as the rightful representatives at this convention. Mrs. Hamer has a way of describing her own life and the lives of other poor people in the Delta with such force that they become very real. Her testimony, carried over national television, stirred the hearts of many viewers. She brought to life the legal brief prepared by Joseph Rauh, general counsel for the UAW, whose true character we did not yet know, and by Eleanor Norton, a skilled black attorney. The brief argued that the regular delegates could not represent the Democrats of Mississippi because almost half of the state's population was excluded from the entire political process, including the election of delegates; that the regular delegation, aside from its racist basis, could not even be considered "loyal" to the national party because the state Democrats had several times bolted—most recently by coming out for Goldwater. These were solid arguments, but would they be heeded? We knew better, and went on pushing. . . .

We had worked an entire summer, done a tremendous amount of organizing, but we had not done enough to prepare people in Mississippi and in SNCC for the kind of political machinations, double crosses, and treachery that always went on at these conventions. . . .

The delegates from Mississippi . . . refused the crumbs offered them. They had come from Mississippi to challenge the seating of the regular Democratic Party and they felt they were entitled to the regular seats. "We didn't come all this way for no two seats!" Fannie Lou Hamer exclaimed. . . .

7.8 and 7.9 The other major focus of the summer, the Freedom Schools, are reviewed below by one of their organizers, Liz Fusco. The schools, under the direction of Staughton Lynd, a young white history professor at Spelman College, and staffed by experienced and novice teachers, taught the three R's and material relevant to the students' experiences, particularly African-American history. Fusco's piece is followed by several poems written by the Freedom School's students, compiled by COFO and published in book form, with a moving introduction by Langston Hughes.

7.8 Liz Fusco, "Deeper than Politics: The Mississippi Freedom Schools," *Liberation* (November 1964), pp. 17-19.

The original plan for Freedom Schools developed from Charles Cobb's dream that what could be done in Mississippi could be deeper, more fundamental, more far-reaching, more revolutionary than voter registration alone: more personal, and in a sense more transforming, than a political program. The validity of the dream is evidenced by the fact that people trying desperately to keep alive while working on voter registration could take seriously the idea that Mississippi needs more than for Negroes to have the right to vote.

The decision to have Freedom Schools in Mississippi seems to have been a decision, then, to enter into every phase of the lives of the people of Mississippi. It seems to have been a decision to set the people free for politics in the only way that people can become live and that is totally. It was an important decision for the staff to be making, and so it is not surprising that the curriculum for the proposed schools became everyone's concern. They worked and argued about what should be taught, about what the realities of Mississippi are, and how these realities affect the kids, and how to get the kids to discover themselves. And then, Staughton Lynd, the director, came in to impose a kind of beautiful order on the torment that the curriculum was becoming—torment because it was not just curriculum: it was each person on the staff painfully analyzing what the realities of the world were, and asking . . . what right he had to keep it from them until now. And because of these sessions, the whole concept of what could be done in Mississippi changed. It was because the people trying to change Mississippi were asking themselves the real questions about what is wrong with Mississippi that the summer project in effect touched every aspect of the lives of Negroes in Mississippi, and started to touch the lives of the whites as well. . . .

The so-called "Citizenship Curriculum" set up two sets of questions. The "primary" set was: (1) Why are we (teachers and students) in Freedom Schools? (2) What is the Freedom Movement? (3) What alternative does the Freedom Movement offer us? The "secondary" set of questions (which seemed to me more important because more personal) was: (1) What does the majority culture have that we want? (2) What does the majority culture have that we don't want? (3) What do we have that we want to keep?

The continual raising of these questions in many contexts may be said to be what the Freedom Schools were about. This was so because in order to answer them it was necessary for the students to confront other questions of who he is, what his world is like, and how he fits into or is alienated from it. . . .

The kids began to see two things at once: that the North was no real escape, and that the South was not some vague white monster doomed irrationally to crush them. Simultaneously, they began to discover that they themselves could take action against injustices which have kept them unhappy and impotent.

Through the study of Negro history they began to have a true sense of themselves as a people who could produce heroes. . . . Beginning to sense the real potency of organized Negroes in Mississippi, the kids in the Freedom Schools found an immediate area of concern in the Negro schools they attended or had dropped out of: the so-called "public" schools. They had grievances, but until drawn into the question-asking, had only been able to whine, accept passively, or lash out by dropping out of school or getting expelled. By comparing the Freedom Schools with the regular schools, they began to become articulate about what was wrong in the regular schools and the way things should be instead. "Why don't they do this at our school?" was the first question asked; and then there began to be answers which led to further questions, such as "Why don't our teachers register to vote, if they presume to teach us about citizenship?" "Why can't our principal make his own decisions instead of having to follow the order of the white superintendent?" "Why do we have no student government?" or "Why doesn't the administration take the existing student government seriously?"

Always in the end, the main question was why are we not taken seriously—which came also out of why there are no art classes, no language classes, why there is no equipmennt in the science labs, why the library is inadequate, the classes overcrowded. This is of course the question that the adults were asking about the city, county, and state, and the question that the Freedom Democratic Party asked—at the Democratic National Convention. . . .

7.9 SNCC, *Freedom School Poetry*, 1965.

"I am Mississippi Fed," Ida Ruth Griffin, age 12, Harmony, Carthage.

I am Mississippi fed, I am Mississippi bred, Nothing but a poor,
   black boy.
I am a Mississippi slave, I shall be buried in a Mississippi grave,
Nothing but a poor, dead boy.

"Fight on Little Children," Edith Moore, age 15, McComb.

Fight on little children, fight on
You know what you're doing is right.
Don't stop, keep straight ahead
You're just bound to win the fight.

Many hardships there will be;
Many trials you'll have to face.
But go on children, keep fighting
Soon freedom will take hardship's place.
Sometimes it's going to be hard;
Sometimes the light will look dim.
But keep it up, don't get discouraged
Keep fighting, though chances seem slim.
In the end you and I know
That one day the fact they'll face.
And realize we're human too
That freedom's taken slavery's place.

"Freedom in Mississippi," David March, age 16, Indianola.

In the middle of the night,
a stressive bell of Hope is ringing
Everyone is on the eve of fear and success
is not yet come
Until Everyone Wakes up and Speaks out
in an overcoming voice, the slums will Remain.
Let Not the pulling out of a few
go down the whole crowd.
If this remains we will forever be
under bowed.

"Mr. Turnbow," Lorenzo Wesley, Milestone.

I know a man who has no foe
His name is Mr. Turnbow
He is about five feet six
Every time you see him he has a gun or a brick.
If you want to keep your head
Then you'd better not come tripping around his bed.
When he talks to you
His fingers talk too.
Some people will never understand
But Mr. Turnbow is a good old man.

"Mine," Alice Jackson, age 17, Jackson.

I want to walk the streets of town
Turn into any restaurant and sit down
And be served the food of my choice,
And not be met by a hostile voice.
I want to live in the best hotel for a week,

Or go for a swim at a public beach.
I want to go to the best University
and not be met with violence or uncertainty.
I want the things my ancestors
thought we'd never have.
They are mine as a Negro, an American;
I shall have them or be dead.

7.10   On one level, Freedom Summer represented the apex of the civil rights movement. The campaign mobilized thousands of volunteers (if one includes support outside of Mississippi), tackled injustice in its most entrenched and repressive form, touched the lives of hundreds of thousands of black Mississippians, and gripped the attention of the entire nation. Yet, on another level, Freedom Summer stood as the crossroads of an era. Tensions that had simmered below the surface before the summer came out into the open afterward. Militant activists in and around SNCC and CORE grew disillusioned with liberal allies, tired of the nonviolent method, and even came to question the value of integration. Bringing white volunteers to the state brought valuable national attention and manpower, yet it also reinforced a sense of dependency on whites.

Regardless of the impact that Freedom Summer had on the national scene, Mississippi would never again be the same. In the following piece, Mike Thelwell and Lawrence Guyot, two MFDP leaders, mapped out a strategy for black Mississippians to follow. They called for organizing an independent political party, one which would operate within the democratic system but which would be built by and for Mississippi blacks. MFDP followed this advice, building an independent political movement, which, on occasion, allied with another reform caucus in the state. In 1968 the two groups successfully challenged the regular Democrats at the Democratic convention in 1968. And in 1972, as part of the Loyal Democrats, former Mississippi activists—such as, Aaron Henry and Charles Evers (Medgar's brother)—represented the state at the Democratic convention, pledged to George McGovern.

7.10   Lawrence Guyot and Mike Thelwell, "Toward Independent Political Power," *Freedomways* (Summer 1966), pp. 246-254.

It is not possible here to go into the machinations of the leadership of the National Democratic Party which managed to avoid any vote of the convention on the issue. The important fact that emerged was that the leadership of the Democratic party—which is to say the political leadership of the nation, at this time—was not prepared to end or even amend its relationship of fraternal coexistence with Mississippi racism. The public relations gesture of offering the MFDP delegation two seats "at large" was at best a slap on the wrists of the "regulars" a pat on the head of Mississippi's Negroes. It made no pretense of meeting the claims of the MFDP delegation for representation for Mississippi's black population.

One side effect of the MFDP delegation's rejection of the token offer should be mentioned. This is the response of truly surprising vindictiveness—and scarcely disguised contempt for the members of the MFDP delegation—with which "liberals" in the National Democratic Party greeted our rejection of the compromise. Inherent in the charge that the delegation was "manipulated" to reject this gesture is the notion that the members of the delegation who were present at the risk of jail, loss of livelihood, and even life, were somehow unable to recognize that they had been deprived of a vote by the full convention, and were being asked to accept a meaningless gesture that meant no change in the condition that had brought them to Atlantic City in protest.

Back in Mississippi people across the State were watching on every available television set and saw that the "system" was vulnerable. That week of TV coverage did more than a month of mass meetings in showing people that there was nothing necessary and eternal about white political supremacy, and that they—who had been told by the system that they were nothing—could from the strength of organization affect the system.

Of equal importance was the fact that we emerged from the campaign with *a state-wide network of precinct and county organizations* and an Executive Committee representative of all five Congressional districts. It is possible that with all the national furor caused by the Convention challenge, this legacy of grass-root, structured organization on a statewide basis will prove to be the most lasting, effective product of that challenge. . . .

It is the MFDP's position that the route to effective political expression in Mississippi lies, at least in the immediate future, in *independent* political organization in the black community. For one thing, there are just no other possibilities. Behind its facade of moderation, the racist state Democratic party appears unable to moderate its actions or policies, or even to give a convincing appearance of having done so, in order to appeal to the Negro voter. . . .

While waiting for the vote to become a reality, we can use the time to strengthen and deepen the level of organization across the state, and develop the political consciousness in the community. Mississippi is the only state in which there is a state-wide, active and viable framework of organization in the Negro community. Our job now is to establish and entrench in every Negro community the tradition of active participation in politics, in which the people will understand that their involvement and control of *their own* political organization is their strongest weapon. . . .

Our job must be, then, to continue organizing these black voters into an independent political organ capable of unified action on the state level. If this appears to "introduce racial politics and further polarize the state," as the national Democrats like to claim, that's all right. Once we have this organization functioning, white allies of all stripes, moderates, liberals and even radicals, can blossom in the ranks of the white party, for ultimately no politician is going to ignore that kind of political strength. . . .

Chapter Eight

SELMA:
THE BRIDGE TO FREEDOM

In the decade that followed the Brown *decision, blacks made tremendous strides. Not only did their problems and concerns become the focal point of the nation, with the passage of the Civil Rights Act of 1964, they won the most significant reform in race relations since Reconstruction. The law outlawed discrimination in employment, secured equal access to public accommodations, and provided the federal government with the authority to enforce these and other laws. Moreover, Lyndon Baines Johnson's landslide victory in the 1964 election seemed to display broad support for the liberal agenda, including further civil rights legislation and the War on Poverty.*

Yet, the strains of the civil rights struggle were beginning to show. Freedom Summer left SNCC, CORE, and many of their friends disillusioned with the Democratic Party and liberalism in general. Founded as multiracial organizations dedicated to the principle of nonviolence, SNCC and CORE engaged in heated debates over the value of both. In the North, urban riots took place in Harlem and Rochester, New York, revealing the deep frustrations of millions of blacks for whom the civil rights movement had had little affect. In addition, even in defeat, Barry Goldwater's campaign (the Republican presidential nominee), along with George Wallace's limited though surprisingly successful primary efforts, provided hints of a nascent backlash against the civil rights movement.

Before internal strains tore the civil rights movement apart or backlash congealed, however, a broad coalition emerged in Selma, Alabama. Spearheaded by the Southern Christian Leadership Conference (SCLC) and Martin Luther King, Jr., the Selma campaign captured the nation's attention and produced the greatest outpouring of support for the civil rights movement in history. Ultimately, President Johnson called for and won passage of voting rights legislation.

8.1 King and SCLC built their campaign on the efforts of local activists, most notably those of Amelia Platts Boynton. Along with a core of dedicated men and women she worked tirelessly to forge a community movement aimed at registering blacks to vote. In the early 1960s, SNCC activists came to town to help in the struggle. While the going was tough—Selma was infamous for its police brutality—Boynton and SNCC managed to make small but significant inroads. For instance, in October 1963, on "Freedom Day," over three hundred of Selma's blacks patiently waited at the courthouse door to register to vote. They did so despite the threatening presence of helmeted and gun-wielding police officers, who refused to allow SNCC workers to bring food or drink to the prospective registrants. The authorities, led by Sheriff Jim Clark, even used electric cattle prods to intimidate the activists. Meanwhile, federal authorities did nothing except take notes. The protesters' willingness to "not be moved" revealed that Selma's blacks were overcoming their historic fear and reservations about challenging white supremacy. In the following piece drawn from her autobiography, Boynton describes the emergence of an indigenous voting rights campaign, from the late 1950s, when she worked in near unanimity, to January 1965, when King and the national news media arrived in town. As in Montgomery, Little Rock, Nashville, and the Delta, Boynton's activism confirmed the prominent role that women played in the civil rights movement.

8.1 Amelia Platts Boynton, *Bridge Across Jordan* (New York: Carlton, 1979), pp. 138-140.

In 1958 Bill and I had gone to Montgomery and testified before the Civil Rights Commission, telling of the many atrocities that blacks had endured and how they were afraid. We told about the blacks who had to get off the plantations because they tried to register. We told how some were beaten because they went to voter registration clinics my husband had held in the counties. We told them of the Negroes in the city who had lost their jobs and the officers who would constantly walk by meeting places and intimidate the people.

Many of the men of the Commission complimented us on our courage but were afraid for us. This was five years before Dallas County's civil rights struggle was known to the nation. They advised us not to go home on highway 80 but to take the back road, which we did, leaving Montgomery early enough to get to Selma before dark.

Keeping the registration fires burning was no easy task. Six years later we staged mass meetings in the county or in the city nightly and often because of the crowds we had them in two or three places the same night. Black people came from surrounding counties to hear how they could win their freedom. They felt they couldn't afford to stay at home although their day's work was hard and the hours long. This was particularly true of the farming people in spring and fall.

Teaching the black people to hold up their heads, stand tall, and be counted kept an ever increasing flow of young people attending the meetings. They were easily convinced that something needed to be done about their parents' civil rights and they placed themselves in the line of duty. Convincing the black ministers that the time to help their people was now and the place was right here was harder. Almost all ministers had to be begged to let us have meetings in their churches (we could not go to the armory, schools, courthouse, and other public places as did the White Citizens' Council and other political groups) and when we first persuaded them the church would be opened by the sexton but the ministers would conveniently disappear at meeting time.

During these trying times of getting Selma and Dallas County Negroes together, I was often greeted with sneers and jeers as I came home late at night. For weeks I received anonymous phone calls all night long. The callers would let out a volume of the worst curses and threats I have ever heard in my life. But such threats were not new; during the Fikes trial the phone rang one morning about 3 o'clock and when I answered a heavy voice said "Nigger, we ain't gonna have you all trying to change things around here. Git out of town and damn quick." . . .

All of these threats made me more determined to fight for what I knew was right. Not once did I become frightened nor did I fear going into my own home. There were many friends who stood guard at all times and they gave me the strength to continue. But more than anything else, I depended on the guidance of God, whom I felt had groomed me for this struggle. The struggle of the Negroes was also that of the white man, and far beyond my expectations, from across the country there came black and white people to help us. . . .

In spite of the atrocities the Negro had to endure there were many, for a wonder, who had no hate or malice in their hearts. Fear and ignorance, but not hate. They wanted only to know where to turn for help, so when Dr. King came into the city, along with SNCC and others, to help unshackle those in bondage, he was welcomed by all blacks of Dallas County. Most of the prisoners and the people who had been to jail for some slight provocation made up their minds that this time they would go for something important—their rights which had been taken away. This explains why the marchers and demonstrations were so successful. . . .

8.2 One of the keys to the Selma campaign's success was Sheriff Jim Clark who had a reputation as an arch-segregationist. As in Birmingham, SCLC felt that mass protests would prompt law enforcement authorities to explode, which in turn would garner the attention of the media and the nation. After careful preparation, King made an initial appearance in Selma on January 2, 1965.

Despite the efforts of Joseph Smitherman and Wilson Baker, the newly elected "reform" mayor and public safety director, respectively, to maintain calm, violence erupted. On January 22 over one hundred black teachers, generally considered the most conservative segment of the black community, staged a silent protest at the courthouse. Sheriff Clark and his deputies indiscriminately used clubs and cattle prods to clear the streets. Clark personally pinned Annie Lee Cooper to the ground and pummeled her with his fists before onlooking cameramen. On February 1, King, Abernathy, and over seven hundred demonstrators, many of them schoolchildren, staged a mass protest. All of them were placed under arrest. More demonstrators were arrested the following day.

Among the things that appalled the nation were the deplorable conditions endured by the arrestees. In the following article, SNCC activist Ralph Featherstone describes Selma's prisons. Like other members of SNCC, Featherstone's commitment to nonviolence was already fragile before his arrest. Jail, along with the beatings and killings he witnessed in the Selma campaign, led him to wonder even more if the gains were worth the costs.

8.2 Ralph Featherstone, "The Stench of Freedom," *The Negro History Bulletin* (March 1965), p. 130.

On Monday, February 8, 1965, about 55 local people, 3 visiting Northern ministers, James Bevel, and I, were arrested. After a speedy trial (held without benefit of legal counsel) we were convicted of contempt of court and whisked off to the county jail. The following is a partial account of the eight days that ensued in the Dallas County jail and in a state prison camp.

We were ushered into the Dallas County jail at about 4:00 P.M. On the way in, Rev. Ira Blaylock from Boston was attacked from behind by one of Sheriff Jim Clark's possemen; he managed to escape without apparent injury. After being subjected to finger-printing and photographing (accompanied by verbal insults and abuses), we were all jammed into a cell with about 25 men who had been arrested and convicted of the same "crime" a week earlier. This meant that over 50 men were being housed in an area I paced off to be 25 feet long and 12 feet wide. This cell contained a commode, which was not enclosed, and a shower. We exchanged pleasantries with our fellow warriors and attempted to bring them up to date on the latest news from the outside, over dinner, which consisted of black-eyed peas and corn bread. As the evening wore on into the night, the group settled down into some serious singing and preaching. When the jailer informed us at twenty minutes to nine that the lights would be turned off at nine, the search for sleeping space commenced. The men who had been jailed earlier had first call on the eleven mattresses, and the rest of us stretched out on the concrete floor, and on the metal benches. None of us had any cover.

The next morning, after eating our black-eyed peas and corn bread, we were marched into a school bus and transported seven miles to Camp Selma, a state prison. The bus on which we travelled to Camp Selma had a normal capacity for thirty-two people, but when the possemen had finished herding us into the bus with their electric cattle prods, fifty-five of us had been crammed into the now bulging vehicle.

Before we were allowed to enter the compound, all beds, blankets, and mattresses were removed. The bed frames were stored outside, visible from inside our prison. The mattresses were stored in the hall that led to the dining room. The compound itself was forty-seven feet long and nineteen feet wide. In one corner was a commode (not enclosed) that became stopped up at least three times a day, and almost always at night. As a result, people using the commode could not avoid walking in the overflow and tracking it all over the floor, on which we had to sleep. People were not allowed to take but one shower, so it isn't hard to imagine the sanitary condition of people sleeping in human discharge and not being allowed to wash.

Sleeping on the concrete floor was considerably worsened by two things: (1) We had an all-night rain; (2) We had no heat. At night temperatures were in the thirties. Each night one attempted to develop a "sleeping plan": Do I sleep with my jacket on? . . . Do I put it under my head? . . . But still each morning I woke up barely able to speak, and my entire body aching so that I could barely walk. My difficulty in walking was contributed in no small part by the inadequate diet provided.

We were fed beans and corn bread twice a day. The only variation in this diet was the type of bean—black-eyed peas, navy beans, lima beans, and great northern beans. We were helped (if not truly sustained) by some local churches who sent food to us each night.

One of the advantages of being "in jail" is that people can do a lot of talking, thinking, and listening. So after a few days I attempted some freedom school classes, with very good response. People talked about their lives, and how much say they have in governing their lives. We talked about how Negroes got into the situation in which we find ourselves. We talked about the home of the first Negro slaves in America. We also defined words—words like ownership, stealing, and murdering, and people in this country who are guilty of theft and murder. People talked about money and who controls it, and who gives value to it.

After five days we were transported to the county jail to await release, which took three days. When we were released Monday evening at 4:30, most of us had only time to get a meal and go to 7:30 mass meeting, to continue dealing with some of the problems the country faces. Who really steals? Who are the real murderers? Who owns natural resources? How is it that we have so much ''surplus'' food and people are dying of starvation? Why do we keep talking about training people for jobs, when in fact jobs are on a fast decline? When is this country going to seriously deal with a guaranteed annual income? When?

8.3 As time passed the protests spread to neighboring communities, such as Marion, Alabama. During one midnight vigil, Jimmy Lee Jackson, a black protester, was shot to death by an Alabama state trooper. Jackson had been attempting to protect his mother from being wantonly beaten by authorities. His death enraged Selma's blacks. Partly with the aim of channeling Selma's blacks' anger into something constructive, SCLC proposed leading a march from Selma to Montgomery. Alabama Governor George Wallace announced that he utterly opposed the idea and that he would take whatever measures necessary to halt it. SCLC proceeded with its plans nonetheless.

On Sunday, March 7, 1965, approximately six hundred blacks, led by Hosea Williams (SCLC), and John Lewis (SNCC), marched toward the Edmund Pettus Bridge, the main artery out of town. There they encountered local and state authorities, including Sheriff Clark's infamous posse and Colonel Al Lingo's state troopers. One of the marchers, Sheyann Webb, age six at the time, described the scene in her memoir.

8.3 Sheyann Webb, *Selma, Lord, Selma* (Tuscaloosa: University of Alabama Press, 1980), pp. 92-99.

Now the Edmund Pettus Bridge sits above the downtown; you have to walk up it like it's a hill. We couldn't see the other side, we couldn't see the troopers. So we started up and the first part of the line was over. I couldn't see all that much because I was so little; the people in front blocked my view.

But when we got up there on that high part and looked down we saw them. I remember the woman [next to her] saying something like, ''Oh, My Lord'' or something. And I stepped out to the side for a second and I saw them. They were in a line—they looked like a blue picket fence—stretched across the highway. There were others gathered behind that first line and to the sides, along the little service road in front of the stores and drive-ins, there was a group of white people. And further back were some of Sheriff Jim Clark's possemen on their horses. Traffic had been blocked.

At that point I began to get a little uneasy about things. I think everyone did. People quit talking; it was so quiet then that all you could hear was the wind blowing and our footsteps on the concrete sidewalk.

Well, we kept moving down the bridge. I remember glancing at the water in the Alabama River, and it was yellow and looked cold. I was told later that Hosea Williams said to John Lewis, "See that water down there? I hope you can swim, 'cause we're fixin' to end up in it."

The troopers could be seen more clearly now. I guess I was fifty to seventy-five yards from them. They were wearing blue helmets, blue jackets, and they carried clubs in their hands; they had those gas-mask pouches slung across their shoulders. The first part of the march line reached them and we all came to a stop. For a few seconds we just kept standing, and then I heard this voice speaking over the bullhorn saying that this was an unlawful assembly and for us to disperse and go back to the church.

I remember I held the woman's hand who was next to me and had it gripped hard. I wasn't really scared at that point. Then I stepped out a way and looked again and saw the troopers putting on their masks. That scared me. I had never faced the troopers before, and nobody had ever put on gas masks during the downtown marches. But this one was different; we were out of the city limits and on a highway. Williams said something to the troopers asking if we could pray—I didn't hear it but was told later that we could—and then I heard the voice again come over the bullhorn and tell us we had two minutes to disperse.

Some of the people around me began to talk then, saying something about, "Get ready, we're going to jail," words to that effect.

But I didn't know about that; the masks scared me. So the next thing I know—it didn't seem like two minutes had gone by—the voice was saying, "Troopers advance and see that they are dispersed." Just all of a sudden it was beginning to happen. I couldn't see for sure how it began, but just before it did I took another look and saw this line of troopers moving toward us; the wind was whipping at their pant legs. . . .

All I knew is I heard all this screaming and the people were turning and I saw this first part of the line running and stumbling back toward us. At that point, I was just off the bridge and on the side of the highway. And they came running and some of them were crying out and somebody yelled, "Oh, God, they're killing us!" I think I just froze then. There were people everywhere, jamming against me, pushing against me. Then, all of a sudden, it stopped and everyone got down on their knees, and I did too, and somebody was saying for us to pray. But there was so much excitement it never got started, because everybody was talking and they were scared and we didn't know what was happening or was going to happen. I remember looking toward the troopers and they were backing up, but some of them were standing over some of our people who had been knocked down or had fallen. It seemed like just a few seconds went by and I heard a shout. "Gas! Gas!" And everybody started screaming again. And I looked and I saw the troopers charging us again and some of them were swinging their arms and throwing canisters of tear gas. And beyond them I saw the horsemen starting their charge toward us. I was terrified. What happened then is something I'll never forget as long as I live. Never. In fact, I still dream about it sometimes.

I saw those horsemen coming toward me and they had those awful masks on; they rode right through the cloud of gas. Some of them had clubs, others had ropes or whips, which they swung about them like they were driving cattle. I'll tell you, I forgot about praying, and I just turned and ran. And just as I was turning the tear gas got me; it burned my nose first and then got my eyes. I was blinded by tears. So I began running and not seeing where I was going. I remember being scared that I might fall over the railing and into the water. I don't know if I was screaming or not, but everyone else was. . . . It was like a nightmare seeing it through the tears. I just knew then that I was going to die, that those horses were going to trample me. So I kind of knelt down and held my hands and arms up over my head. . . .

All of a sudden somebody was grabbing me under the arms and lifting me up and running. The horses went by and I kept waiting to get trampled on or hit, but they went on by and I guess they were hitting at somebody else. And I looked up and saw it was Hosea Williams who had me and he was running but we didn't seem to be moving, and I kept kicking my legs in the air, trying to speed up, and I shouted at him, "Put me down! You can't run fast enough with me!"

But he held on until we were off the bridge and down on Broad Street and he let me go. I didn't stop running until I got home. All along the way there were people running in small groups; I saw people jumping over cars and being chased by the horsemen who kept hitting them. . . .

When I got into the house my momma and daddy were there and they had this shocked look on their faces and I ran in and tried to tell them what had happened. I was maybe a little hysterical because I kept repeating over and over, "I can't stop shaking, Momma, I can't stop shaking," and finally she grabbed me and sat down with me on her lap. But my daddy was like I'd never seen him before. He had a shotgun and yelled. "By God, if they want it this way, I'll give it to them!" And he started out the door. Momma jumped up and got in front of him shouting at him. And he said, "I'm ready to die; I mean it! I'm ready to die!" I was crying on the couch, I was so scared. But finally he put the gun aside and sat down. I remember just laying there on the couch, crying and feeling so disgusted. They had beaten us like we were slaves.

8.4 "Bloody Sunday," as the massacre on Pettus Bridge came to be known, outraged the nation. The national media highlighted the brutality of the police, including a blow to John Lewis' skull. ABC-TV broke into Judgment at Nuremberg, *the award-winning movie on the Nazi war-crime trials, to show film footage of the attacks. SNCC, which as an organization had not endorsed the first march, determined to stage a second one. King agreed that blacks and their allies could not allow themselves to be defeated by violence. Hence, on Tuesday, March 9, King led a second group to Pettus Bridge. Once again they came face to face with armed state troopers. Much to the surprise of most of the marchers, King turned the protest around. Singing freedom songs, he led the group back to Selma, explaining that he did not wish to risk another massacre nor break a federal court injunction. SNCC was outraged at King's maneuver; others were befuddled. King promised that another march would take place, as soon as the federal injunction was rescinded.*

Later that same evening, four Unitarian ministers were brutally assaulted in Selma by white ruffians; one of them, James Reeb died from the attack. The nation was horrified. American men and women cabled President Johnson and their congressmen demanding action and rushed to Alabama to take part in the promised third march. Among those to arrive was Daniel Berrigan, then a relatively unknown priest, later a prominent antiwar activist, who described the scene.

8.4 Daniel Berrigan, "Selma and Sharpeville," *Commonweal* (April 1965), pp. 71-75.

Monday, March 15. We came in, thirty-five strong, from New York, in time for the memorial service for Reverend Reeb. We were from Harlem and Manhattan and Brooklyn, Negroes, and whites, laymen and priests. Selma was quiet as a mill pond; but the quiet was ominous; the pin had been pulled, the depth charge dropped. Children wandered in the sun, the stores were open, the fresh tourist-signs were out: Welcome to Selma. . . . Then we approached Browns Chapel, the reality of Selma hit like a tight fist.

The church was ringed with Clark's troopers. They lounged in the open cars, feet hung out of doors and windows, eyes half closed in the sunlight; helmets, billy clubs, a stereotype of sleepy brutal power; the day of the iguana. Our car circled the church for blocks—no way in. Finally, we parked and walked through.

The church was packed. The TV cameras, the newsmen were there in force, tired out but still there. The nation needed to see this; better, since Sunday, it even wanted to see. A shabby backwater church, that had sheltered and comforted generations of Negroes, and had rung with the passion and anguish of a trodden people, was for this week, the heart and focus of America. In it, the most astounding ironies were being taken for granted. Black store-hands and field workers sat beside distinguished theologians. Hawaiians met New Yorkers, believers shook hands with the unchurched, beatniks sang along with nuns. Men who differed in every conceivable respect—faith and race and culture—found themselves bewildered by a sudden unity whose implications went far beyond the unpredictable days they were enduring together. But they knew beyond any doubt that they would never again be the same men who had lived Before Selma. . . .

One thing was clear. This was the Negro's day. We were, at long last, at his side. But even the newsmen were not sure why we were there. They were not even convinced that we knew why: one of them asked us, in words that were not especially flattering: why have the Catholics gotten into the act? We were not sure either in a way that could easily be formulated. But it was something like an ethic of the guts; some things cannot be disposed of, in peace, by moral tics over headlines, even in 1965. . . .

In any case, it was the black man's day, his week; one might say, his week of creation. He had been conceived and born at Bloody Bridge, at all the bloody crossroads of the nation, weeks and years before Selma. Could he, this week, bring us over that Bridge, to birth? He might; love is a marvelous midwife. . . .

Monday, March 15, Selma. The long memorial service is almost over. Hardly any discomfort is evident. . . . The benediction has been pronounced over the memory of Reeb. Flowers bank the speakers' stand. Someone has pinned to the front of the pulpit a drawing from a Northern newspaper; it shows a wreath of thorns fastened to the gravestone, the tomb of James Reeb. Martin King has spoken. And then, the announcement comes; the march is permitted by court order. Three by three, in silence, we are allowed by the courts of Alabama to march on the courthouse of Selma. It is to be a memorial march for James Jackson and James Reeb. Prayers at the courthouse are permitted; we can even sing.

Whites and Negroes, after all the bitter years, after black heroism and white anger, after Birmingham and Marion . . . after all this, both sides are fused together by one fact, a bitter event which neither side wanted, but which each side knew in its heart must come to pass. Each side now had a martyr.

For the Negroes, the irony is nearly complete. They have had to wait and wait for the whites—when will they stand with us, or march with us? And the whites have waited for death, before they could be moved. For the Negroes, martyrdom was nothing new at all; it was old as their American history. It had begun with lynchings and disappearances and bodies pulled from rivers. Most of the Negro martyrs were nameless. But one of them, otherwise obscure and humble, had died in Selma; and Selma, by a convergence of happenings beyond all prediction, had exploded.

The explosion was triggered by a white man's death. The blow had been launched by whites; they had struck down a minister of the Gospel. It was a wound with a difference; it lay on the body of the white community.

Time indeed might heal it. Give us time . . . you can't push this thing too fast. . . . But no time was allowed. The Negroes granted time no place. They had been clocked too long by whites; Clark and Lingo had had too much time; time for troopers, time for gas, time for Bloody Bridge. The end was in sight. . . .

8.5 The night of Reeb's memorial service, President Johnson delivered a nationally televised address before a joint session of Congress. It was probably the strongest speech on civil rights by a president in U.S. history. One of the highlights of the speech came when Johnson invoked the words of the civil rights movement, declaring "we shall overcome." In addition, Johnson called upon Congress to pass voting rights legislation, which it did in relatively short order.

8.5 Lyndon B. Johnson, "Address Before a Joint Session of Congress," March 15, 1965.

I speak tonight for the dignity of man and the destiny of democracy. I urge every member of both parties, Americans of all religions and of all colors, from every section of this country, to join me in that cause.

At times history and fate meet at a single time in a single place to shape a turning point in man's unending search for freedom. So it was at Lexington and Concord. . . . So it was last week in Selma, Alabama. There, long-suffering men and women peacefully protested the denial of their rights as Americans. Many were brutally assaulted. One good man, a man of God, was killed. There is no cause for pride in what happened in Selma. There is no cause for self-satisfaction in the long denial of equal rights of millions of Americans. But there is cause for hope and for faith in our democracy in what is happening here tonight. For the cries of pain and the hymns and protests of oppressed people, have summoned into convocation all the majesty of this great government of the greatest nation on earth.

Our mission is at once the oldest and the most basic of this country: to right wrong, to do justice, to serve man. . . . Rarely in any time does an issue lay bare the secret heart of America itself. Rarely are we met with a challenge, not to our growth or abundance, or our welfare or our security, but rather to the values and the purposes and the meaning of our beloved nation.

The issue of equal rights for American Negroes is such an issue. And should we defeat every enemy and should we double our wealth and conquer the stars and still be unequal to this issue, then we will have failed as a people and as a nation. For with a country as with a person, "What is a man profited, if he shall gain the whole world, and lose his own soul?"

There is no Negro problem. There is no Southern problem. There is no Northern problem. There is only an American problem. And we are met here tonight as Americans, not as Democrats or Republicans, we are met here as Americans to solve the problem.

This was the first nation in the history of the world to be founded with a purpose. The great phrases of that purpose still sound in every American heart, North and South: "All men are created equal"—"government by consent of the governed"—"give me liberty or give me death." Those are not just clever words. These are not just empty theories. In their name Americans have fought and died for two centuries, and tonight around the world they stand there as guardians of our liberty, risking their lives.

These words are a promise to every citizen that he shall share in the dignity of man. . . . It says that he shall share in freedom, he shall choose his leaders, educate his children, provide for his family according to his ability and his merits as a human being. To apply any other test—to deny a man his hopes because of his color or race, or his religion, or the place of his birth—is not only to do injustice, it is to deny America and to dishonor the dead who gave their lives for American freedom.

Our fathers believed that if this noble view of the rights of man was to flourish, it must be rooted in democracy. The most basic right of all was the right to choose your own leaders. The history of this country in large measure is the history of expansion of that right to all of our people.

Many of the issues of civil rights are very complex and most difficult. But about this there can and should be no argument. Every American citizen must have an equal right to vote. There is no reason which can excuse the denial of that right. There is no duty which weighs more heavily on us than the duty we have to ensure that right.

Yet the harsh fact is that in many places in this country men and women are kept from voting simply because they are Negroes. Every device of which human ingenuity is capable has been used to deny this right. . . .

The Constitution says that no person shall be kept from voting because of his race or his color. We have all sworn an oath before God to support and to defend that Constitution. We must now act in obedience to that oath.

Wednesday, I will send to Congress a law designed to eliminate illegal barriers to the right to vote. . . . To those who seek to avoid action by their national government in their own communities, who want to and who seek to maintain purely local control over elections, the answer is simple. Open your polling places to all your people. Allow men and women to register and vote whatever the color of their skin. Extend the rights of citizenship to every citizen of this land. There is no constitutional issue here. The command of the Constitution is plain. There is no moral issue here. It is wrong to deny any of your fellow Americans the right to vote in this country. There is no issue of states rights or national rights. There is only the struggle for human rights. . . .

We cannot, we must not refuse to protect the right of every American to vote in every election that he may desire to participate in. And we ought not, we must not wait another eight months before we get a bill. We have already waited a hundred years and more and the time for waiting is gone. . . .

Even if we pass this bill, the battle will not be over. What happened in Selma is part of a far larger movement which reaches into every section and state of America. It is the effort of American Negroes to secure for themselves the full blessings of American life. Their cause is our cause too. Because it is not just Negroes, but really it is all of us, who must overcome the crippling legacy of bigotry and injustice. And, we shall overcome.

As a man whose roots go deeply into Southern soil I know how agonizing racial feelings are. I know how difficult it is to reshape attitudes and the structure of our society. But a century has passed, more than a hundred years, since the Negro was freed. And he is not fully free tonight. . . .

The time of justice has now come. I tell you that I believe sincerely that no force can hold it back. It is right in the eyes of man and God that it should come. And when it does, I think that the day will brighten the lives of every American. For Negroes are not the only victims. How many white children have gone uneducated, how many white families have lived in stark poverty, how many white lives have been scarred by fear because we wasted our energy and substance to maintain the barriers of hatred and terror.

So I say to all of you here and to all in the nation tonight, that those who appeal to you to hold on to the past do so at the cost of denying you your future. This great, rich, restless country can offer opportunity and education and hope to all—all black and white, all North and South, share-cropper, and city dweller. These are the enemies—poverty, ignorance, disease. They are enemies, not our fellow man, not our neighbor, and these enemies too . . . we shall overcome. . . .

This is one nation. What happens in Selma or in Cincinnati is a matter of legitimate concern to every American. But let each of us look within our hearts and our own communities, and let each of us put our shoulder to the wheel to root out injustice wherever it exists.

The real hero of this struggle is the American Negro. His actions and protests, his courage to risk safety and even to risk his life, have awakened the conscience of this nation. His demonstrations have been designed to call our attention to injustice, designed to provoke change, designed to stir reform. He has called upon us to make good the promise of America. And who among us can say that we would have made the same progress if not for his persistent bravery, and his faith in democracy.

8.6 Two days after President Johnson's address, Federal Judge Frank Johnson, no relation to the president, rescinded the injunction against the march. Hence, on March 21 thousands of marchers set out from Selma to Montgomery, protected by state troopers who had been federalized by President Johnson. Without incident, they arrived five days later in the city where King had first emerged as a leader in 1955. As Coretta Scott King observed, it was somewhat of a homecoming. From the steps of the state capitol, the place that George Wallace had called the "cradle of the confederacy," King delivered a ringing address in which he noted the distance that blacks had traveled in a decade.

8.6 Martin Luther King, Jr., "Our God Is Marching On!"

Last Sunday, more than eight thousand of us started on a mighty walk from Selma, Alabama. We have walked on meandering highways and rested our bodies on rocky byways. Some of our faces are burned from the outpourings of the sweltering sun. Some have literally slept in the mud. We have been drenched by the rains. . . .

They told us we wouldn't get here. And there were those who said that we would get here only over their dead bodies, but all the world today knows that we are here and that we are standing before the forces of power in the state of Alabama saying, "We ain't goin' let nobody turn us around."

The Civil Rights Act of 1964 gave Negroes some part of their rightful dignity, but without the vote it was dignity without strength. Once more the method of nonviolent resistance was unsheathed from its scabbard and once again an entire community was mobilized to confront the adversary.

And again the brutality of a dying order shrieks across the land. Yet Selma, Alabama, became a shining moment in the conscience of man.

There never was a moment in American history more honorable and more inspiring than the pilgrimage of clergymen and laymen of every race and faith pouring into Selma to face danger at the side of its embattled Negroes.

Confrontation of good and evil compressed in the tiny community of Selma generated the massive power to turn the whole nation to a new course. A president born in the South had the sensitivity to feel the will of the country, and in an address that will live in history as one of the most passionate pleas for human rights ever made . . . he pledged the might of the federal government to cast off the centuries-old blight. President Johnson rightly praised the courage of the Negro for awakening the conscience of the nation.

On our part we must pay our profound respects to the white Americans who cherish their democratic traditions over the ugly customs and privileges of generations and come forth boldly to join hands with us. . . .

So I stand before you this afternoon with the conviction that segregation is on its deathbed in Alabama and the only thing uncertain about it is how costly the segregationists and Wallace will make the funeral. . . .

We have come a long way since that travesty of justice was perpetuated upon the American mind. Today I want to tell the city of Selma, today I want to say to the state of Alabama, today, I want to say to the people of America and the world: We are not about to turn around. We are on the move now. Yes, we are on the move and no wave of racism can stop us.

We are on the move now. The burning of our churches will not deter us. . . . Like an idea whose time has come, not even the marching of mighty armies can halt us. We are moving to the land of freedom.

Let us therefore continue our triumph and march to the realization of the American dream. Let us march on segregated housing, until every ghetto of social and economic depression dissolves and Negroes and whites live side by side in decent, safe and sanitary housing. Let us march on segregated schools. . . . Let us march on poverty. . . . Let us march on the ballot boxes . . . until the Wallaces of our nation tremble in silence. . . . For all of us today the battle is in our hands. The road ahead is not altogether a smooth one. There are no broad highways to lead us easily and inevitably to quick solutions. We must keep going. . . .

I know you are asking today, "How long will it take?" I come to say to you this afternoon however difficult the moment, however, frustrating the hour, it will not be long, because the truth pressed to earth will rise again. How long? Not long, because no lie can live forever. How long? Not long, because you still reap what you sow. How long? Not long, because the arm of the moral universe is long but it bends toward justice. How long? Not long, 'cause mine eyes have seen the glory of the coming of the Lord, trampling out the vintage where the grapes of wrath are stored. He has loosed the fateful lightening of his terrible swift sword. His truth is marching on.

He has sounded forth the trumpets that shall never call retreat. He is lifting up the hearts of man before His judgment seat. Oh, be swift, my soul, to answer Him. Be jubilant, my feet. Our God is marching on.

8.7, 8.8, and 8.9 The period following the Selma campaign was one of reflection, introspection and debate. Whereas ten years earlier southern blacks faced a rigid set of Jim Crow laws and could not vote, in the fall of 1965 they enjoyed at least de jure *equal citizenship rights. Yet blacks, nationwide, were still not equal. Economically blacks faced double the unemployment and poverty rates as whites; many lived in festering ghettos and even when they had the resources to move to middle-class neighborhoods they often were barred from doing so. School integration still had not been implemented in the South and was becoming less feasible in the North. Moreover, blacks faced persistent discrimination and open prejudice in their everyday encounters with whites.*

Most civil rights leaders were well aware of this. These same activists also faced a dangerous dilemma: white complacency and self-admiration, on the one hand and growing black frustration, especially in the North, on the other. Most Americans expected that with the vote secured civil rights protests would subside. Yet, the reality of life for millions of black Americans insured that protest, in one form or another, would continue. Indeed, five days after President Johnson signed the Voting Rights Act, Watts, the black ghetto of Los Angeles, burst into flames, in one of the worst riots in U.S. history.

The following selections, by Bayard Rustin, longtime civil rights activist and organizer of the March on Washington, James Farmer, co-founder and director of CORE, and Staughton Lynd, a white history professor at Spelman College and former head of the Mississippi Freedom Schools, represent part of the dialogue amongst blacks and their white allies on the course that the civil rights movement should take. Should blacks continue to protest in the streets? Was nonviolence still viable? Could blacks and whites continue to ally?

Rustin was convinced that blacks and whites had to continue to work together, that the coalition which had staged the March on Washington and the Selma to Montgomery march had to be maintained, although, he added, it needed to shift its focus from protest to politics. Staughton Lynd directly criticized Rustin's argument, recalling the stabs in the back that blacks had received from their liberal "allies." Lynd also asserted that with the escalation of the war in

Vietnam, coalition meant cooperating with American imperialism, which was directly against the interest of black Americans, and their allies. Farmer's essay, directed to a larger audience than either Rustin's or Lynd's, tended to support Lynd's argument. Farmer warned that whites could not expect the protests to stop since black Americans still faced countless barriers to full equality. Yet, the tone of Farmer's essay was different than Lynd's, and he tended to remain more open to coalition and committed to nonviolence and integration than many of his counterparts in CORE and SNCC.

8.7 Bayard Rustin, "From Protest to Politics," *Commentary* (February 1965), pp. 21-23.

The decade spanned by the 1954 Supreme Court decision on school desegregation and the Civil Rights Act of 1964 will undoubtedly be recorded as the period in which the legal foundations of racism in America were destroyed. To be sure, pockets of resistance remain; but it would be hard to quarrel with the assertion that the elaborate legal structure of segregation and discrimination, particularly in relation to public accommodation, has virtually collapsed. On the other hand, without making light of the human sacrifices involved in the direct-action tactics (sit-ins, freedom rides, and the rest) that were so instrumental to this achievement, we must recognize that in desegregating public accommodations, we affected institutions which are relatively peripheral both to the American socio-economic order and to the fundamental conditions of life of the Negro people. In a highly industrialized, 20th-century civilization, we hit Jim Crow precisely where it was most anachronistic, dispensable, and vulnerable—in hotels, lunch counters. . . . For in these forms, Jim Crow does impede the flow of commerce . . . it is a nuisance in a society on the move (and on the make). Not surprisingly, therefore, it was the most mobility-conscious and relatively liberated groups in the Negro community—lower middle class college students—who launched the attack that brought down the imposing but hollow structure.

The term "classical" appears especially apt for this phase of the civil rights movement. But in the few years that have passed since the first flush of sit-ins, several developments have taken place that have complicated matters enormously. One is the shifting focus of the movement in the South, symbolized by Birmingham; another is the spread of the revolution to the North; and the third, common to the two, is the expansion of the movement's base in the Negro community. . . .

Thus, the movement in the South began to attack areas of discrimination which were not so remote from the Northern experience as were Jim Crow lunch counters. At the same time, the interrelationship of these apparently distinct areas became increasingly evident. What is the value of winning access to public accommodations for those who lack money to use them? The minute the movement faced this question, it was compelled to expand its vision beyond race relations to economic relations, including the role of education in modern society. And what also became clear is that all these interrelated problems, by their very nature, are not soluble by private, voluntary efforts but require government action—or politics. . . .

The very decade which has witnessed the decline of legal Jim Crow has also seen the rise of *de facto* segregation in our most fundamental socio-economic institutions. . . . And behind this is the continuing growth of racial slums, spreading over our central cities and trapping Negro youth in a milieu which, whatever its legal definition, sows an unimaginable demoralization. Again, legal niceties aside, a resident of a racial ghetto lives in segregated housing, and more Negroes fall into this category than ever before.

These are the facts of life which generate frustration in the Negro community and challenge the civil rights movement. At issue, after all, is not *civil rights*, strictly speaking, but social and economic conditions. Last summer's riots were not race riots; they were outbursts of class aggression in a society where class and color definitions are converging disastrously. . . .

It is precisely this sense of isolation . . . the tendency within the civil rights movement which, despite its militancy, pursues what I call a "no-win" policy. Sharing with many moderates a recognition of the magnitude of the obstacles to freedom, spokesmen for this tendency survey the American scene and find no forces prepared to move toward radical solutions. From this they conclude that the only viable strategy is shock; above all, the hypocrisy of white liberals must be exposed. These spokesmen are often described as the radicals of the movement, but they are really its moralists. They seek to change the white hearts—by traumatizing them. Frequently abetted by white self-flagellants, they may gleefully applaud (though not really agreeing with) Malcolm X because, while they admit he has no program, they think he can frighten white people into doing the right thing. To believe this, of course, you must be convinced, even if unconsciously, that at the core of the white man's heart lies a buried affection for Negroes—a proposition one may be permitted to doubt. But in any case, hearts are not relevant to the issue; neither racial affinities nor racial hostilities are rooted there. It is institutions—social, political, and economic institutions—which are the ultimate molders of collective sentiments. Let these institutions be reconstructed today, and let the ineluctable gradualism of history govern the formation of new psychology.

My quarrel with the "no win" tendency in the civil rights movement . . . parallels my quarrel with the moderates outside the movement. As the latter lack the vision or will for fundamental change, the former lack a realistic strategy for achieving it. For such a strategy they substitute militancy. But militancy is a matter of posture and volume and not effect.

A handful of Negroes, acting alone, could integrate a lunch counter by strategically locating their bodies so as *directly* to interrupt the operation of the proprietor's will; their numbers were relatively unimportant. In politics, however, such a confrontation is difficult because the interests involved are merely *represented*. In the execution of a political decision a direct confrontation may ensue. . . . But in arriving at a political decision, numbers and organizations are crucial, especially for the economically disenfranchised. . . .

Neither that movement [civil rights] nor the country's twenty million black people can win political power alone. We need allies. The future of the Negro struggle depends on whether the contradictions of this society can be resolved by a coalition of progressive forces which becomes the *effective* political majority in the United States. I speak of the coalition which staged the March on Washington, passed the Civil Rights Act, and laid the basis for the Johnson landslide—Negroes, trade unionists, liberals, and religious groups. . . .

The task of molding a political movement . . . is not simple, but no alternatives have been advanced. We need to choose our allies on the basis of common political objectives. It has become fashionable in some no-win Negro circles to decry the white liberal as the main enemy. . . . But the objective fact is that *Eastland and Goldwater* are the main enemies—they are the opponents of civil rights, of the war on poverty, of medicare, of social security, of federal aid to education, of unions, and so forth. The labor movement, despite its obvious faults, has been the largest single organized force in this country. . . . And where the Negro-labor-liberal axis is weak, as in the farm belt, it was the religious groups that were most influential in rallying support for the Civil Rights Bill.

The durability of the coalition was interestingly tested during the election. I do not believe that the Johnson landslide proved the "white backlash" to be a myth. It proved, rather, that economic interests are more fundamental than prejudice. . . . This was a valuable first step in re-educating such people, and it must be kept alive, for the civil rights movement will be advanced only to the degree that social and economic welfare gets to be inextricably entangled with civil rights. . . .

8.8 Staughton Lynd, "Coalition Politics or Nonviolent Revolution?" *Liberation*, Vol. X, no. 4 (1965), pp. 18-21.

Bayard Rustin's "From Protest to Politics" . . . has been widely criticized in radical publications. . . . The gist of the radical critique might be summarized as follows:

1. Rustin writes that "the objective fact is that Eastland and Goldwater are the main enemies." In so doing he exaggerates the liberalism of the Johnson coalition, even asserting that Big Business, forced into the Democratic Party by Goldwater, "does not belong there."

2. Not only does Rustin urge that direct action be abandoned for politics, he argues also that independent political action is only rarely appropriate. The accurate perception that Negroes need white allies leads him to the conclusion that one must choose between existing aggregations of political forces: "The issue is which coalition to join and how to make it responsive to your program."

3. Thus, by exaggerating the Johnson coalition's capacity to solve fundamental social problems and by underestimating the need for independent action by Negroes, Rustin arrives at a stance which . . . "leads to a dissolution of the old Rights movement, as well as assuring that any new Movement will not develop in a more radical fashion." The effect of his advice would be to assimilate Negro protest to the Establishment just as labor protest was coopted at the end of the 1930s, in each case leaving the poorest, least organized parts of the population out in the cold.

I agree with Radosh's analysis, but I think it is not sufficiently fundamental. Fully to appraise Rustin's . . . article, one must see it as the second in a series of three Rustin actions during the past three years. First was his attempt to get the credentials committee offer of token seating accepted by the Mississippi Freedom Democratic Party delegates at Atlantic City. . . . Second was the article. . . . Third was the effort to undermine and stop the March on Washington against the war in Vietnam (March–April, 1965). In this perspective, the most basic criticisms of his article should be these: (1) The coalition he advocates turns out to mean implicit acceptance of Administration foreign policy, to be coalition with the marines; (2) The style of politics he advocates turns out to mean a kind of elitism which Bayard has been fighting all his life, in which the rank-and-file persons would cease to act on their own behalf and be [in Rustin's words] "merely represented." . . .

Coalitionism, then, is pro-Americanism. It is what Sidney Lens has called "two-and-a-half campism." It is a posture which subordinates foreign to domestic politics, which mutes criticism of American imperialism so as to keep open its channels to the White House, which tacitly assumes that no major war will occur. But war is occurring in Vietnam. . . .

Coalitionism is also elitism. Its assumption is that major political decisions are made by deals between the representatives of the interests included in the coalition. Negro protest, according to the Rustin formula, should now take on the role of such an interest. And men like Rustin will become the national spokesman who sell the line agreed-on behind doors to the faithful followers waiting in the street.

This was the meaning of Atlantic City. What was at stake, as it seemed to the SNCC people there, was not so much the question, Should compromise be accepted? as the question, Are plain people from Mississippi competent to decide? Rustin, Martin Luther King and Roy Wilkins answered the latter question: No. The decision, they insisted, involved "national considerations." . . . Hence it should be made wisely, by the leaders, and put over to the delegates from Mississippi. . . .

Direct action is inseparable from the idea that everyone involved in a movement has some ultimate responsibility and initiative. Decentralization was the hallmark of the early *Liberation*, which Bayard helped to found. Participatory democrats, as they move from direct action into politics, insist that direct action must continue along with politics, that there comes into being a new politics which forces the representative back to his people, and politics back to life. . . .

I think the time has come to begin to think of "nonviolent revolution," as the only long-run alternative to coalition with the marines. . . . The events of the past year—the creation of the Mississippi Freedom Democratic Party and the protest against the war in Vietnam—suggest . . . one can now begin to envision a series of nonviolent protests which would from the beginning question the legitimacy of the Administration's authority where it has gone beyond constitutional and moral limits, and might, if its insane foreign policy continues, culminate in the decision of hundreds of thousands of people to recognize the authority of alternative institutions of their own making.

Robert Paris [Moses] has sketched out such a scenario as a possibility in Mississippi. What . . . if Mississippi Freedom Democratic Party voters elected not only legislators but public officials as well? What if the Negroes of Neshoba County, Mississippi began to obey the instructions of the Freedom Sheriff rather than Sheriff Rainey? What if the Freedom Sheriff impaneled a Freedom Grand Jury which indicted Sheriff Rainey for murder? . . .

Suppose (I take this idea from Tom Hayden) there were convened in Washington this summer a new continental congress. The congresses of 1774 and 1775 came about on the initiative of committees of correspondence of the individual colonies. The continental congress of 1965 might stem from the initiative of the community union in a Northern ghetto, or the Freedom Party of a Southern state. Suppose, at any rate, that such a call goes out, saying in effect: This is a desperate situation; our government no longer represents us; let us come together at Washington to consult on what needs to be done. . . . The continental congress of 1965 would seriously and responsibly begin to debate the policies of the United States. The discussions which have failed to take place in the Senate about Vietnam, would take place here. . . .

Six months ago . . . liberals congratulated themselves that America had turned the last corner, integrating the Negro into the happy permanent societal consensus. This was an illusion. America's situation was less secure, Johnson was less rational, the American people were less brainwashed, then they seemed. . . . Now we know: whom the gods would destroy they first make mad; but also; we can overcome. . . .

8.9 James Farmer, *Freedom When?* (New York: Random House, 1965), pp. 25-27, 42-47, and 49.

"But when will the demonstrations end?" The perpetual question. And a serious question. Actually it is several questions, for the meaning of the question differs, depending upon who asks it.

Coming from those whose dominant consideration is peace—public peace and peace of mind—the question means: "When are you going to stop tempting violence and rioting?" Some put it more strongly: "When are you going to stop *sponsoring* violence?" Assumed is the necessary connection between demonstration and violence. . . .

"Isn't the patience of the white majority wearing thin? Why nourish the displeasure of 90 per cent of the population with provocative demonstrations? Remember, you need allies." And the assumption of these Cassandras of the backlash is that freedom and equality are, in the last analysis, wholly gifts in the white man's power to bestow.

And then the question we shall face again and again in this book: "Even granting that there was a time when demonstrations were useful, can we not, now that the Negro civil rights are nearly secure, turn to more familiar techniques of political participation and press for sorely needed economic reforms?'' And the assumptions of those questioners, who include some of the most formidable figures in the civil rights movement, are both that Negro rights are secure and that demonstrations will be ineffective in gaining economic reform. . . .

I must insist that a demonstration is not a riot. On the contrary, rather than leading to riots, demonstrations tend to help prevent them by providing an alternative outlet for frustrations. . . .

What the public must realize is that in a demonstration more things are happening, at more levels of human activity, than meets the eye. Demonstrations in the last few years have provided literally millions of Negroes with their first taste of self-determination and political self-expression. We might think of the demonstration as a rite of initiation through which the black man is mustered into the sacred order of freedom. It is also a rite the entire nation must undergo to exorcise the demons of racial hate. If in a spasm of emancipated exuberance these rites should cause inconvenience or violate the canons of cultivated good taste or trouble the dreams of some good-livers—I think it is forgivable. Enlightened people will understand that exuberance and occasional inconvenience are small prices to pay when a nation is undoing historic wrong. The very least the nation can do is give us room to demonstrate. That is only a small sacrifice, considering the debt. . . .

"Have we not moved now to a stage 'beyond demonstrations'?'' Yes and no. Clearly the rights movement today faces new problems demanding new techniques. . . . If segregation and discrimination were eliminated tomorrow, many, many Negroes would still be ill-equipped to do the work demanded of today's worker. For these problems, traditional demonstrations are not as effective. We will need the financial resources and the concentrated effort of all levels of government, and it will take more money and concentrated effort than is dreamed of in the philosophies of the anti-poverty program. And to persuade the government to undertake needed measures, we will need to engage in forms of political activity other than direct action. But demonstrations will be an indispensable adjunct to almost every new effort.

Demonstrations *alone* did not achieve the civil rights bill either. Without a half century of legal preparation and lobbying by the NAACP and others, the Congress and the President would not have known where to begin in formulating and passing a civil rights law. We have never denied the necessity for expertise and politics-as-usual at one level of the movement's activities. But without a decade's demonstration of deep and legitimate grievances, the law today would still be a dream. . . .

''But when will the demonstrations end?'' I remember the comment of a red-necked young man from St. Augustine, Florida, the leader of a gang of whites who had attacked Negroes trying to swim in the Atlantic Ocean: ''If I thought the niggers would be satisfied with just swimming, I'd let them in. But they won't be. First it's this, and then they'll want more, and before you know it they'll be laying hands on our women. We've got to take a stand now, because the more we let them have, the harder it'll be to draw the line.''

Sometimes, I think that the racists have deeper insight into things than the moderates. The gentleman is right. Nothing short of full equality will stop us. One cannot simply draw up a list of ten or twenty things whose fulfillment would spell equality. . . . The moderate sincerely searches for the concession which will finally satisfy and silence us. He is willing to negotiate and temporarily sacrifice his security to get rid of the problem. The racist knows better how deep the problem is and how long he will need to resist our efforts. But we shall persist, that I promise.

Chapter Nine

BLACK POWER

post watts

The Watts riot and those that followed in the summers of 1966 and 1967 displayed the rage of millions of black Americans for whom the early civil rights movement had little effect, except, perhaps, to raise their expectations. This rage sprouted from a society pervaded by racism and social and economic inequality. The riots themselves were often sparked by an incident or alleged incident involving the police, who routinely violated the rights of blacks. Until Watts exploded, the voice of those who took part in the rioting had largely gone unheard. Even the major civil rights organizations had spoken little on the concerns of the urban ghetto dweller in the North. With the riots, however, a new set of figures and organizations emerged with the goal of articulating the demands of the urban black masses.

The riots and emergence of a strong black nationalist movement represented a new stage in the modern civil rights movement. Activists adopted a more militant tone and constructed a critique of society that called for more than living up to America's ideals. Under the heading "Black Power," this chapter presents a glimpse at some of the different black power advocates and groups of the 1960s. While reading the selections, it is important to consider what produced the renaissance of black nationalism in the second-half of the 1960s. What was the relationship between the early civil rights movement and the latter? Was black power a natural byproduct of the early years? Or did it mark a dramatic change? In addition, the reader should keep in mind that black power was not a monolith. Differences over the relative significance of politics, culture, and economics and over more concrete immediate issues kept black radicals from forging a united movement. Whether a more effective leader, such as Malcolm X had he lived,

*could have overcome these differences cannot be answered conclusively but
deserves some consideration.*

*9.1 Malcolm X was born Malcolm Little in Omaha, Nebraska, in 1925. In
1965, just short of his fortieth birthday, he was assassinated at the Audubon
Ballroom in Harlem. In the interim, he lived a fascinating and turbulent life,
ending up as one of the most prominent black spokesmen in the world. While a
child, his father, Reverend Earl Little, a follower of Marcus Garvey, had been
chased out of Omaha by the KKK. A few years after barely escaping death,
Malcolm X's father was killed by the Black Legionnaires, a white supremacist
group in Michigan. Unable to support him and his seven brothers and sisters,
Malcolm's mother was forced to send him to live in a foster home in East
Lansing, Michigan. When he became a teen, Malcolm left Michigan to live with
his sister Ella, in Boston, where he quickly got hooked on street life, narcotics,
prostitution, and zoot suits. Subsequently, Malcolm moved to Harlem and
rapidly earned a reputation as one of the toughest and craziest blacks around.
Constantly running from the law, at age twenty-one he was arrested and convicted on burglary charges and sent to prison.*

*While in jail Malcolm learned of Elijah Muhammad and shortly thereafter con-
verted to Islam. Following his release from jail he became a minister. Through
the 1950s and early 1960s, Malcolm converted hundreds to Islam and enthralled
thousands more with fiery sermons that attacked whites as the devil. His temple
in Harlem became the largest in all of Elijah Muhammad's church. His voice
grew to be as important as any other black leader. Following a trip to Mecca,
Malcolm broke with Elijah Muhammad, believing that his brand of antiwhite
Islam was incorrect. Nonetheless, as the selection that follows suggests,
Malcolm continued to condemn white institutions and cultural domination and
called for using any means necessary for winning justice and equality.*

9.1 Malcolm X, "Address to a Meeting in New York, 1964."

Friends and enemies, tonight I hope that we can have a little fireside
chat with as few sparks as possible tossed around. Especially because of
the very explosive condition that the world is in today. Sometimes, when
a person's house is on fire and someone comes in yelling fire, instead of
the person who is awakened by the yell being thankful, he makes the mis-
take of charging the one who awakened him with having set the fire. I
hope that this little conversation tonight about the black revolution won't
cause many of you to accuse us of igniting it when you find it at your
doorstep.

I'm still a Muslim, that is, my religion is still Islam. I still believe that
there is no god but Allah and that Mohammed is the apostle of Allah. That
just happens to be my personal religion. But in the capacity which I am
functioning in today, I have no intention of mixing my religion with the
problems of 22,000,000 black people in this country. . . .

I'm still a Muslim, but I'm also a nationalist, meaning that my political philosophy is black nationalism, my economic philosophy is black nationalism, my social philosophy is black nationalism. And when I say that this philosophy is black nationalism, to me this means that the political philosophy for black nationalism is that which is designed to encourage our people, the black people, to gain complete control over the politics and the politicians of our own people.

Our economic philosophy is that we should gain economic control over the economy of our own community, the businesses and the other things which create employment so that we can provide jobs for our own people instead of having to picket and boycott and beg someone else for a job.

And, in short, our social philosophy means that we feel that it is time to get together among our own kind and eliminate the evils that are destroying the moral fiber of our society, like drug addiction, drunkenness, adultery that leads to an abundance of bastard children, welfare problems. We believe that we should lift the level or the standard of our own society to a higher level wherein we will be satisfied and then not inclined toward pushing ourselves into other societies where we are not wanted. . . .

Just as we can see that all over the world one of the main problems facing the West is race, likewise here in America today, most of your Negro leaders as well as the whites agree that 1964 itself appears to be one of the most explosive years yet in the history of America on the racial front, on the racial scene. Not only is the racial explosion probably to take place in America, but all of the ingredients for this racial explosion in America to blossom into a world wide racial explosion present themselves right here in front of us. America's racial powder keg, in short, can actually fuse or ignite a world-wide powder keg.

And whites in this country who are still complacent when they see the possibilities of racial strife getting out of hand and you are complacent simply because you think you outnumber the racial minority in this country, what you have to bear in mind is wherein you might outnumber us in this country, you don't outnumber us all over the earth.

Any kind of racial explosion that takes place in this country today, in 1964, is not a racial explosion that can be confined to the shores of America. It is a racial explosion that can ignite the racial powder keg that exists all over the planet that we call the earth. Now I think that nobody would disagree that the dark masses of Africa and Asia and Latin America are already seething with bitterness, animosity, hostility, unrest, and impatience with the racial intolerance that they themselves have experienced at the hands of the white West.

And just as they themselves have the ingredients of hostility toward the West in general, here we also have 22,000,000 African-Americans, black, brown, red, and yellow people in this country who are also seething with bitterness and impatience and hostility and animosity at the racial intolerance not only of the white West but of white America in particular. . . .

1964 will be America's hottest year; her hottest year yet; a year of much racial violence and much racial bloodshed. But it won't be blood that's going to flow only on one side. The new generation of black people that have grown up in this country during recent years are already forming the opinion, and it's just opinion, that if there is to be bleeding, it should be reciprocal—bleeding on both sides. . . .

So today, when the black man starts reaching out for what America says are his rights, the black man feels that he is within his rights—when he becomes the victim of brutality by those who are depriving him of his rights—to do whatever necessary to protect himself. . . .

There are 22,000,000 African-Americans who are ready to fight for independence right here. When I say fight for independence right here, I don't mean any non-violent fight, or turn-the-other-cheek fight. Those days are gone. Those days are over.

If George Washington didn't get independence for this country non-violently, and if Patrick Henry didn't come up with a non-violent statement, and you taught me to look upon them as patriots and heroes, then it's time for you to realize that I have studied your books well. . . .

Every time a black man gets ready to defend himself some Uncle Tom tries to tell us, how can you win? That's Tom talking. Don't listen to him. This is the first thing we hear: the odds are against you. You're dealing with black people who don't care anything about odds. . . .

Again I go back to the people who founded and secured the independence of this country from the colonial power of England. . . . They didn't care about the odds. . . .

Our people are becoming more politically mature. . . . The Negro can see that he holds the balance of power in this country politically. It is he who puts in office the one who gets in office. Yet when the Negro helps that person get in office the Negro gets nothing in return. . . .

The present administration, the Democratic administration, has been there for four years. Yet no meaningful legislation has been passed by them that proposes to benefit black people in this country, despite the fact that in the House they have 267 Democrats and only 177 Republicans. . . . In the Senate there are 67 Democrats and only 33 Republicans. The Democrats control two thirds of the government and it is the Negroes who put them in a position to control the government. Yet they give the Negroes nothing in return but a few handouts in the form of appointments that are only used as window-dressing to make it appear that the problem is being solved.

No, something is wrong. And when these black people wake up and find out for real the trickery and the treachery that has been heaped upon us you are going to have revolution. And when I say revolution I don't mean that stuff they were talking about last year about "We Shall Overcome." . . .

And the only way without bloodshed that this [revolution] can be brought about is that the black man has to be given full use of the ballot in every one of the 50 states. But if the black man doesn't get the ballot, then you are going to be faced with another man who forgets the ballot and starts using the bullet. . . .

So you have a people today who not only know what they want, but also know what they are supposed to have. And they themselves are clearing the way for another generation that is coming up that not only will know what it wants and know what it should have, but also will be ready and willing to do whatever is necessary to see what they should have materializes immediately. Thank you.

9.2 Even though Malcolm's death came at the height of his popularity, he continued to have an enormous impact on blacks and whites. His Autobiography, *published posthumously with the assistance of Alex Haley, was widely read. So, too, were many of his speeches. Malcolm's influence increased as economic, social, and cultural issues came to take precedence over desegregation. As Julius Lester, a veteran activist and writer explains, Malcolm especially spoke to young blacks because, unlike Martin Luther King, Malcolm was willing to upset white allies, to say what he wanted without regard to whether it met liberal standards of approval.*

9.2 Julius Lester, "The Angry Children of Malcolm X," *Sing Out* (October/November 1966), pp. 120-125.

This is their message: The days of singing freedom songs and the days of combating bullets and billy clubs with love are over. "We Shall Overcome" sounds old, out-dated. "Man, the people are too busy getting ready to fight to bother with singing any more!" The world of the black Americans is different from that of the white American. This difference comes not only from the segregation imposed on the black, but it also comes from the way of life he has evolved for himself under these conditions. Yet, America has always been uneasy with this separate world in its midst. Feeling most comfortable when the black man emulates the ways and manners of white Americans, America has, at the same time, been stolidly unwilling to let the black man be assimilated into the mainstream.

With its goal of assimilation on the basis of equality, the civil rights movement was once the great hope of black men and liberal whites. In 1960 and 1961 Negroes felt that if only Americans knew the wrongs and sufferings they had to endure, these wrongs would be righted and all would be well. If Americans saw well-dressed, well-mannered, clean Negroes on their television screen not retaliating to being beaten by white Southerners, they would not sit back and do nothing. *Amore vincit omnia!* and the Reverend Dr. Martin Luther King, Jr., was the knight going forth to prove to the father that he was worthy of becoming a member of the family. But there was something wrong with this attitude and young Negroes began to feel uneasy. Was this not another form of the bowing and scraping their grandparents had to do to get what they wanted? Were they not acting once again as the white man wanted and expected them to? And why should they have to be brutalized, physically and spiritually, for what every other American had at birth? . . .

More than any other person Malcolm X was responsible for the new militancy that entered The Movement in 1965. Malcolm X said aloud those things which Negroes had been saying among themselves. He even said those things Negroes had been afraid to say to each other. His clear, uncomplicated words cut through the chains of black minds like a giant blow-torch. His words were not spoken for the benfit of the press. He was not concerned with stirring the moral conscience of America, because he knew—America had no moral conscience. He spoke directly and eloquently to black men, analyzing their situation, their predicament, events as they happened, explaining what it all meant for a black man in America.

America's reaction to what the Negro considered just demands was a disillusioning experience. Where whites could try to attain the Dream, Negroes always had to dream themselves attaining The Dream. But The Dream was beginning to look like a nightmare. They'd been living one a long time. They had hopes that America would respond to their needs and America had equivocated. Integration had once been the unquestioned goal that would be the proudest moment for Negro America. Now it was beginning to be questioned.

The New York school boycotts of 1964 pointed this up. Integration to the New York City Board of Education meant busing Negro children to white schools. This merely said to Negroes that whites were saying Negroes had nothing to offer. Integration has always been presented as a Godsend for Negroes and something to be endured for whites. When the Board of Ed decided to bus white children to Negro schools the following

year, the reaction was strangely similar to that of New Orleans and Little Rock. Today, whites in Chicago and New York chat at Negro demonstrators, "I wish I was an Alabama deputy, so I could kill a nigger legally."

When it became more and more apparent that integration was only designed to uplift Negroes and improve their lot, Negroes began wondering whose lot actually needed improving. Maybe the white folks weren't as well-educated and cultured as they thought they were. Thus, Negroes began cutting a path toward learning who they were. . . .

Now the Negro is beginning to study his past, to learn those things that have been lost, to recreate what the white man destroyed in him and to destroy that which the white man put instead. He has stopped being a Negro and has become a black man in recognition of his new identity, his real identity. "Negro" is an American invention which shut him off from those of the same color in Africa. He recognizes now that part of himself is in Africa. . . .

Many things that have happened in the past six years have had little or no meaning for most whites, but have had vital meaning for Negroes. Wasn't it only a month after the March on Washington that four children were killed in a church bombing in Birmingham? Whites could feel morally outraged, but they couldn't feel the futility, despair and anger that swept through The Nation within a nation—Black America. There were limits to how much one people could endure and Birmingham Sunday possibly marked that limit. . . .

What was needed that Sunday was ol' John Brown to come riding into Birmingham as he had ridden into Lawrence, Kansas, burning every building that stood and killing every man, woman and child that ran from his onslaught. Killing, killing, killing, turning men into fountains of blood, spouting until Heaven itself drew back before the frothing red ocean.

But the Liberal and his Negro sycophants would've cried, Vengeance accomplishes nothing. You are only acting like your oppressor and such an act makes you no better than him. John Brown, his hands and wrists slick with blood, would've said, oh so softly and so quietly, Mere Vengeance is folly. Purgation is necessity.

Now it is over. America has had chance after chance to show that it really meant "that all men are endowed with certain inalienable rights." America has had precious chances in this decade to make it come true. Now it is over. The days of singing freedom songs and the days of combating bullets and billy clubs with Love. We Shall Overcome (and we have overcome our blindness) sounds old, out-dated and can enter the pantheon of the greats along with the IWW songs and the union songs. As one SNCC veteran put it after the Mississippi March, "Man, the people are too busy getting ready to fight to bother with singing anymore." And as for Love? That's always been better done in bed than on the picket line and marches. Love is fragile and gentle and seeks a like response. They used to sing "I Love Everybody" as they ducked bricks and bottles. Now they sing:

> Too much love,
> Too much love,
> Nothing kills a nigger like
> Too much love. . . .

9.3 Stokely Carmichael first popularized the term "black power" during the 1966 "Meredith" march—a march that joined SCLC, CORE, and SNCC in Mississippi. While delivering a speech at a rally in Greenwood, Mississippi, Carmichael repeatedly chanted "Black Power!" instead of the usual slogan, "Freedom Now!" The media broadcast Carmichael's rallying cry around the country and shortly thereafter demanded an explanation. On several occasions Carmichael sought to give meaning to the term, including the following piece.

9.3 Stokely Carmichael, "What We Want," *New York Review of Books*, September 26, 1966.

One of the tragedies of the struggle against racism is that up to now there has been no national organization which could speak to the growing militancy of young black people in the urban ghetto. There has been only a civil rights movement, whose tone of voice was adapted to an audience of liberal whites. It served as a sort of buffer zone between them and angry young blacks. None of its so-called leaders could go into a rioting community and be listened to. In a sense, I blame ourselves—together with the mass media—for what has happened in Watts, Harlem, Chicago, Cleveland and Omaha. Each time the people in those cities saw Martin Luther King get slapped, they became angry; when they saw four little black girls bombed to death, they were angrier; and when nothing happened, they were steaming. We had nothing to offer that they could see, except to go out and be beaten again. We helped to build their frustration. . . .

An organization which claims to speak for the needs of a community—as does the Student Nonviolent Coordinating Committee—must speak in the tone of that community, not as somebody else's buffer zone. This is the significance of black power as a slogan. For once, black people are going to use the words they want to use—not just the words whites want to hear. And they will do this no matter how often the press tries to stop the use of the slogan by equating it with racism or separatism. . . .

Black power can be clearly defined for those who do not attach the fears of white America to their questions about it. We should begin with the basic fact that black Americans have two problems: they are poor and they are black. All other problems arise from this two-sided reality: lack of education, the so-called apathy of black men. Any program to end racism must address itself to that double reality. . . .

The concept of "black power" is not a recent or isolated phenomenon: It has grown out of the ferment of agitation and activity by different people and organizations in many black communities over the years. Our last year of work in Alabama added a new concrete possibility. In Lowndes county, for example, black power will mean that if a Negro is elected sheriff, he can end police brutality. If a black man is elected tax assessor, he can collect and channel funds for the building of better roads and schools serving black people—thus advancing the move from political power into the economic arena. In such areas as Lowndes, where black men have a majority, they will attempt to exercise control. This is what they seek: control. Where Negroes lack a majority, black power means proper representation and sharing of control. It means the creation of power bases from which black people can work to change statewide or nationwide patterns of oppression through pressure from strength—instead of weakness. Politically, black power means what it has always meant to SNCC: the coming-together of black people to elect representatives and *to force those representatives to speak to their needs*. It does not mean merely putting black faces into office. A man or woman who is black and from the slums cannot be automatically expected to speak to the needs of black people. Most of the black politicians we see around the country today are not what SNCC means by black power. The power must be that of a community, and emanate from there. . . .

Ultimately, the economic foundations of this country must be shaken if black people are to control their lives. The colonies of the United States—and this includes the black ghettos within its borders, north and south—must be liberated. For a century, this nation has been like an octopus of exploitation, its tentacles stretching from Mississippi and Harlem to South America, the Middle East, southern Africa, and Vietnam; the form of exploitation varies from area to area but the essential result has been the same—a powerful few have been maintained and enriched at the expense of the poor and voiceless colored masses. This pattern must be broken. As its grip loosens here and there around the world, the hopes of black Americans become more realistic. For racism to die, a totally different America must be born.

This is what the white society does not wish to face; this is why the society prefers to talk about integration. But integration speaks not at all to the problem of poverty, only to the problem of blackness. Integration today means the man who "makes it," leaving his black brothers behind in the ghetto as fast as his new sports car will take him. It has no relevance to the Harlem wino or to the cotton-picker making three dollars a day. As a lady I know in Alabama once said, "The food that Ralph Bunche eats doesn't fill my stomach."

Integration, moreover, speaks to the problem of blackness in a despicable way. As a goal, it has been based on complete acceptance of the fact that *in order to have* a decent house or education, blacks must move into a white neighborhood or send their children to a white school. This reinforces, among both black and white, the idea that "white" is automatically better and "black" is by definition inferior. This is why integration is a subterfuge for the maintenance of white supremacy. It allows the nation to focus on a handful of Southern children who get into white schools, at great price, and to ignore the 94 per cent who are left behind in unimproved all-black schools. Such situations will not change until black people have power—to control their own school boards, in this case. Then Negroes become equal in a way that means something, and integration ceases to be a one-way street. Then integration doesn't mean draining skills and energies from the ghetto into white neighborhoods; then it can mean white people moving from Beverly Hills into Watts, white people joining the Lowndes County Freedom organization. Then integration becomes relevant. . . .

To most whites, black power seems to mean that the Mau Mau are coming to the suburbs at night. The Mau Mau are coming, and whites must stop them. Articles appear about plots to "get Whitey," creating an atmosphere in which "law and order must be maintained." Once again, responsibility is shifted from the oppressor to the oppressed. Other whites chide, "Don't forget—you're only 10 per cent of the population: if you get too smart, we'll wipe you out." If they are liberals, they complain, "What about me?—don't you want my help any more?" These are people supposedly concerned about black Americans, but today they think first of themselves, of their feelings of rejection. Or they admonish, "You can't get anywhere without coalitions," when there is in fact no group at present with whom to form a coalition in which black will not be absorbed or betrayed. Or they accuse us of "polarizing the races" by our calls for black unity, when the true responsibility for polarization lies with whites who will not accept their responsibility as the majority power for making the democratic process work.

White America will not face the problem of color, the reality of it. The well-intended say: "We're all human, everybody is really decent, we must forget color." But color cannot be "forgotten" until its weight is recognized and dealt with. White America will not acknowledge that the ways in which this country sees itself are contradicted by being black—and always have been. Whereas most of the people who settled this country came here for freedom or for economic opportunity, blacks were brought here to be slaves. When the Lowndes County Freedom Organization chose the black panther as its symbol, it was christened by the press "the Black Panther Party—but the Alabama Democratic Party, whose symbol is a rooster, has never been called the White Cock Party. No one ever talked about "white power" because power in this country *is* white. All this adds up to more than merely identifying a group phenomenon by some catchy name or adjective. The furor over the black panther reveals the problems that white America has with color and sex; the furor over "black power" reveals how deep racism runs and the great fear which is attached to it. . . .

From birth, black people are told a set of lies about themselves. We are told that we are lazy—yet I drive through the Delta area of Mississippi and watch black people picking cotton in the hot sun for fourteen hours. We are told, "If you work hard, you'll succeed"—but if that were true, black people would own this country. We are oppressed because we are black—not because we are ignorant, not because we are lazy, not because we're stupid (and got good rhythm), but because we're black. . . .

The need for psychological equality is the reason why SNCC today believes that blacks must organize in the black community. Only black people can convey the revolutionary idea that black people are able to do things themselves. Only they can help create in the community an aroused and continuing black consciousness that will provide the basis for political strength. In the past, white allies have furthered white supremacy without the whites involved realizing it—or wanting it, I think. Black people must do things for themselves; they must get poverty money they will control and spend themselves, they must conduct tutorial programs themselves so that black children can identify with black people. This is one reason Africa has such importance. The reality of black men ruling their own nations gives blacks elsewhere a sense of possibility, of power, which they do not now have.

This does not mean we don't welcome help, or friends. But we want the right to decide whether anyone is, in fact, our friend. In the past, black

Americans have been almost the only people whom everybody and his momma could jump up and call their friends. We have been tokens, symbols, objects—as I was in high school to many young whites, who liked having "a Negro friend." We want to decide who is our friend. . . . We will not be isolated from any group or nation except by our own choice. We cannot have the oppressor telling the oppressed how to rid themselves of the oppressor. . . .

We hope to see, eventually, a coalition between poor blacks and poor whites. That is the only coalition which seems acceptable to us, and we see such a coalition as the major internal instrument of change in American society. . . . It is purely academic today to talk about bringing poor blacks and whites together, but the job of creating a poor-white community power block must be attempted. The main responsibility for it falls upon whites. . . .

9.4 Carmichael's essay defined black power in relatively moderate terms. On other occasions, Carmichael used much more combative language. For example, at a "Free Huey" rally in Oakland, California, Carmichael rejected any alliance with whites. Such rejection of integration combined with the emergence of new radical black organizations, most importantly the Black Panther Party of Oakland, California, led many whites to be terrified by the new rallying cry. Huey Newton and Bobby Seale founded the Black Panthers in the fall of 1966. They recruited a number of streetwise and energetic blacks and quickly gained notoriety by organizing armed street patrols that followed the police into the black community. The Panthers meshed fiery rhetoric with down-to-earth programs, such as a free breakfast program for black children. Though the latter won the hearts of many in the ghetto, it was the former that won the attention of the national media. The Panther's augmented their militant image by staging a press conference on the steps of the California capitol building adorned with shotguns, straps of bullets, and black leather jackets and caps. In the following essay, Newton expands on the right and necessity of taking up arms. Newton, himself, got into several confrontations with police in the Bay Area, including a shoot-out in which a policeman was killed and for which Newton was arrested for murder—Newton and much of the New Left claimed that he had fired in self-defense.

9.4 Huey P. Newton, "In Defense of Self Defense," *The Black Panther*, June 20, 1967.

Laws and rules have always been made to serve the people. Rules of society are set up by people so that they will be able to function in a harmonious way. In other words, in order to promote the general welfare of society, rules and laws are established by men. Rules should serve men, and not men serve rules. Much of the time, the laws and rules which officials attempt to inflict upon poor people are non-functional in relation to the status of the poor in society.

These officials are blind to the fact that people should not respect rules that are not serving them. It is the duty of the poor to write and construct rules and laws that are in their better interests. This is one of the basic human rights of all men.

Before 1776, white people were colonized by the English. The English government had certain laws and rules that the colonized Americans viewed as not in their best interests. . . . At the time the English government felt that the colonized Americans had no right to establish laws to promote the general welfare of the people living here in America. The colonized American felt he had no choice but to raise the gun in defense of the welfare of the colonized people. At this time, he made certain laws insuring his protection from external and internal aggressions from government and agencies. One such form of protection was the Declaration of Independence, which states ". . . . whenever any government becomes destructive to these ends, it is the right of the people to alter or to abolish it, and to institute a new government, laying its foundations on such principles and organizing its powers in such forms as to them shall seem most likely to effect their safety and happiness."

Now these same colonized white people, these ex-slaves, robbers, and thieves, have denied the colonized black man the right to even speak of abolishing this oppressive system which the white colonized American created. They have carried their madness to the four corners of the earth, and now there is universal rebellion against their continued rule and power. . . .

Penned up in the ghettos of America, surrounded by his . . . factories and all the physical components of his economic system, we have been made into the "wretched of the earth," who are relegated to the position of spectators while the white racists run their international con game on the suffering people. . . .

The people must repudiate the channels established as tricks and deceitful snares by the exploiting oppressors. The people must oppose everything the oppressor supports and support everything he opposes. . . .

The oppressor must be harassed until his doom. He must have no peace by day or by night. The slaves have always outnumbered the slavemasters. The power of the oppressor rests upon the submission of the people. When Black people really unite and rise up in all their splendid millions, they will have the strength to smash injustice. We do not understand the power in our numbers. We are millions and millions of Black people scattered across the continent and throughout the Western hemisphere. . . .

The racist dog oppressor fears the armed people; they fear most of all black people armed with weapons and the ideology of the Black Panther Party for Self Defense. An unarmed people are slaves or are subject to slavery at any given moment. . . . There is a world of difference between thirty million unarmed, submissive Black people and thirty million Black people armed with freedom and defense guns and the strategic methods of liberation.

When a mechanic wants to fix a broken-down car engine, he must have the necessary tools to do the job. When the people move for liberation, they must have the basic tool of liberation: the gun. Only with the power of the gun can the Black masses halt the terror and brutality perpetuated against them by the armed racist power structure; and in one sense only by the power of the gun can the whole world be transformed. . . . One successful practitioner of the art and science of national liberation and self defense, Brother Mao Tse-Tung, put it this way: "We are advocates of the abolition of war, we do not want war; but war can only be abolished through war, and in order to get rid of the gun it is necessary to take up the gun." . . .

9.5 and 9.6   Several black intellectuals and activists contended that blacks had to undergo a cultural transformation if they were to achieve equality. Art and literature and history were just as much the keys to liberation as were politics or economics. Not until blacks came to accept themselves, to repudiate the belief that white European culture and history were superior to black African-American culture and history could they be free. The following two pieces, the first by Amiri Baraka (LeRoi Jones) and the second by Eldridge Cleaver, reflect this theme. Baraka was a prominent poet and playwright whose works exuded racial pride and a sharp critique of white culture and institutions. Cleaver was the minister of culture for the Black Panthers.

9.5 LeRoi Jones, "State/Meant," in *Home: Social Essays* (New York: William Morrow, 1966).

The Black Artist's role in America is to aid in the destruction of America as he knows it. His role is to report and reflect so precisely the nature of the society, and of himself in that society, that other men will be moved by the exactness of his rendering and, if they are black men, grow strong through this moving, having seen their own strength, and weakness; and if they are white men, tremble, curse, and go mad, because they will be drenched with the filth of their evil.

The Black Artist must draw out of his soul the correct image of the world. He must use this image to band his brothers and sisters together in common understanding of the nature of the human soul.

The Black Artist must see life, how it differs from the deathly grip of the White Eyes. The Black Artist must teach the White Eyes their deaths, and teach the black man how to bring these deaths about.

> We are unfair, and unfair,
> We are black magicians, black arts
> we make in black labs of the heart.
> The fair are
> fair, and death
> ly white.
> The day will not save them
> and we own
> the night.

9.6 Eldridge Cleaver, "On Watts," in *Soul on Ice* (New York: Dell, 1968), pp. 26-27.

As we left the Mess Hall Sunday morning and milled around in the prison yard, after four days of abortive uprising in Watts, a group of low riders from Watts assembled on the basketball court. They were wearing jubilant, triumphant smiles, animated by a vicarious spirit by which they, too, were in the thick of the uprising taking place hundreds of miles away to the south in the Watts ghetto.

"Man," said one, "what they doing out there? Break it down for me, Baby."

They slapped each other's outstretched palms in a cool salute and burst out laughing with joy.

"Home boy, them Brothers is taking care of Business!" shrieked another ecstatically.

Then one low rider, stepping into the center of the circle formed by the others, reared back on his legs and swaggered, hunching his belt up with his forearms as he'd seen James Cagney and George Raft do in too many gangster movies. I joined the circle. Sensing a creative moment in the offing, we all got very quiet, very still, and others passing by joined the circle and did likewise.

"Baby," he said, "They walking in fours and kicking in doors, dropping Reds and busting heads; drinking wine and committing crime, shooting and looting; high-siding and low-riding, setting fires and slashing tires; turning over cars and burning down bars; making Parker mad and making me glad; putting an end to that 'go slow' crap and putting sweet

Watts on the map—my black ass is in Folsom this morning but my black heart is in Watts!'' Tears of joy were rolling from his eyes.

It was a cleansing, revolutionary laugh we all shared, something we have not often had occasion for.

Watts was a place of shame. We used to use Watts as an epithet in much the same way as city boys used "country" as a term of derision. To deride one as a "lame," who did not know what was happening (a rustic bumpkin), the "in-crowd" of the time from L.A. would bring a cat down by saying that he had just left Watts, that he ought to go back to Watts until he had learned what was happening, or that he had just stolen enough money to move out of Watts and was already trying to play a cool part. But now, blacks are seen in Folsom saying, "I'm from Watts, Baby!''—whether true or no, but I think their meaning is clear. Confession: I too, have participated in this game, saying, I'm from Watts. In fact, I did live there for a time, and I'm *proud* of it, the tired lamentations of Whitney Young, Roy Wilkins, and The Preacher notwithstanding.

9.7 The latter half of the 1960s witnessed the rise of a wide variety of black militant groups, many which advocated black power, others which shared black power's rhetoric and style if not its ideas. For example, in Detroit, Michigan, black autoworkers at Dodge's Hamtramck plant formed the Dodge Revolutionary Union Movement (DRUM). Along with several other radical black worker caucuses, DRUM established the League of Revolutionary Black Workers. DRUM and the league protested against the racism of the big three automakers and the United Automobile Workers (UAW) previously considered a staunch ally of the civil rights movement. (UAW President Walter Reuther had delivered a keynote address at the March on Washington and the UAW had supported numerous civil rights protests in the first half of the decade.) The league emphasized that the UAW participated in the exploitation of black workers, and if the UAW stood accused, by inference, the entire labor movement was suspect.

9.7 Dodge Revolutionary Union Movement, "Dare to Fight! Dare to Win!" 1968.

I. Preamble

We the super-exploited black workers of Chrysler's Hamtramck Assembly Plant recognize the historic role that we must play and the grave responsibility that is ours in the struggle for the liberation of black people in racist U.S.A. and people of color around the world from the yoke of oppression that hold all of us in the chains of slavery to this country's racist exploitative system. Because we recognize the magnitude of the problem and the dire predicament of our people, we do here proclaim our solemn duty to take this the first step on the road to final victory over the great common enemy of humanity; i.e. the monstrous U.S.A. and the aforementioned system of exploitation and degradation.

We fully understand after 5 centuries under this fiendish system and the heinous savages that it serves, namely the white racist owners and operators of the means of production. We further understand that there have been previous attempts by our people in this country to throw off the degrading yoke of brutal oppression, which have ended in failure. Throughout our history, black workers, first slaves and later as pseudo-freedmen, have been in the vanguard of potentially successful revolutionary struggles both in all black movements as well as in integrated efforts. As examples of these we would cite: Toussaint L'Ouverture and the beautiful Haitian Revolution; the slave revolts led by Nat Turner; Denmark Vesey and Gabriel Prosser; the Populist Movement, and the labor movement of the 30's in this country. Common to all of these movements were two things, their failure and the reason why they failed. These movements failed because they were betrayed from within or in the case of the integrated movements by the white leadership exploiting the racist nature of the white workers they led. We of course, must avoid this pitfall and purge our ranks of any traitors and lackeys that may succeed in penetrating this organization. At this point we loudly proclaim that we have learned our lesson from history and we shall not fail. So it is that we who are the hope of the black people and oppressed people everywhere dedicate ourselves to the cause of liberation to build the world anew, realizing that only a struggle by black workers can triumph over our powerful reactionary enemy.

II. Purpose and Objective

Our purpose is to come together as black workers to relieve the long suffering of our people under the demon system of racist exploitation. Our sole objective is to break the bonds of white racist control over the lives and destiny of black workers with the full understanding that when we successfully carry out this mammoth task, relief will be brought to people all over the world oppressed by our common enemy. With stakes so high the enemy will undoubtedly resist with great ferocity, this tide of change that will sweep over him and his system like a mighty storm.

We must gear ourselves in the days ahead toward getting rid of the racist, tyrannical and unrepresentative UAW . . . so that with this enemy out of the way we can deal directly with our main adversary, the white racist management of Chrysler Corporation. In this way we will be able to overcome the obstacle that the enemy has erected between himself and black workers that denies us the necessary confrontation in order to bring down this racist exploitative system. . . .

9.8 Unions were not the only liberal institutions to come under attack. Universities, both black and white, were condemned for perpetuating white supremacy (see chapter ten). Organized religion, including churches which had supported the early civil rights movement, became a target of black power invective. James Forman's "Black Manifesto," excerpted below, for instance, demanded that religious institutions, as representatives of white America, pay reparations to black America. The fact that Forman, longtime executive secretary of SNCC, would make such a demand showed the distance that many blacks had traveled in a decade's time, from advocates of Christian nonviolence to inquisitors of the church itself. Some churches raised money for a variety of black causes, but, by and large, most did not.

9.8 James Forman, "The Black Manifesto," address given on April 26, 1969, in *Black Viewpoints*, ed. by Arthur Littleton and Mary W. Burger (New York: Mentor, 1971), pp. 394-400.

We the black people . . . are fully aware that we have been forced to come together because racist white America has exploited our resources, our minds, our bodies, our labor. For centuries we have been forced to live as colonized people inside the United States, victimized by the most vicious, racist system in the world. We have helped to build the most industrialized country in the world.

We are therefore demanding of the white Christian churches and Jewish synagogues, which are part and parcel of the system of capitalism, that they begin to pay reparations to black people in this country. We are demanding $500,000,000 from the Christian white churches and the Jewish synagogues. This total comes to fifteen dollars per nigger. This is a low estimate, for we maintain there are probably more than 30,000,000 black people in this country. Fifteen dollars a nigger is not a large sum of money, and we know that the churches and synagogues have tremendous wealth and its membership, white America, has profited and still exploits black people. We are also not unaware that the exploitation of colored people around the world is aided and abetted by the white Christian churches and synagogues. This demand for $500,000,000 is not an idle resolution or empty words. Fifteen dollars for every black brother and sister in the United States is only a beginning of the reparations due us as people who have been exploited and degraded, brutalized, killed and persecuted. Underneath all this exploitation, the racism of this country has produced a psychological effect upon us that we are beginning to shake off. We are no longer afraid to demand our full rights as a people in this decadent society. . . .

Brothers and sisters, we are no longer shuffling our feet and scratching our heads. We are tall, black and proud.

And we say to the white Christian churches and Jewish synagogues, to the government of this country and to all the white racist imperialists who compose it, there is only one thing left that you can do to further degrade black people and that is to kill us. But we have been dying too long for this country. . . .

The new black man wants to live, and to live means that we must not become static or merely believe in self-defense. We must boldly go out and attack the white Western world at its power centers. . . . But to win our demands from the church . . . we must not forget that it will ultimately be by force and power that we will win. . . .

9.9 The final piece in this chapter, the "Report of the National Advisory Commission on Civil Disorders," ironically confirmed many of the claims made by advocates of black power. Established by President Johnson following the Newark and Detroit riots of 1967, the commission, which was headed by Illinois Governor Otto Kerner and staffed by many other prominent national figures, including New York Mayor John Lindsay, concluded that America was dividing into two separate societies, one white and one black and that white racism was largely responsible for the riots. The report's tone was alarmist, yet President Johnson did not follow its recommendations, except to pass a Fair Housing Law. Moreover, most Republican politicians harshly criticized both its recommendations and findings, countering that by blaming whites for the riots the report was sanctioning criminal behavior. Richard Nixon and Ronald Reagan, for example, proclaimed that the federal government had spent enough money. They added that the government needed to coddle the militants less and to enforce the law more.

9.9 "Report of the National Advisory Commission on Civil Disorders" (Washington, D.C.: GPO, 1968).

The summer of 1967 again brought racial disorders to American cities, and with them shock, fear and bewilderment to the nation.

The worst came during a two-week period in July, first in Newark and then in Detroit. Each set off a chain reaction in neighboring communities.

On July 28, 1967, the President of the United States established this Commission and directed us to answer three basic questions: What happened? Why did it happen? What can be done to prevent it from happening again?

To respond to these questions, we have undertaken a broad range of studies and investigations. We have visited the riot cities; we have heard many witnesses; we have sought counsel of experts across the country.

This is our basic conclusion: *Our nation is moving toward two societies, one black, one white—separate and unequal.*

Reaction to last summer's disorders has quickened the movement and deepened the division. Discrimination and segregation have long permeated much of American life; they now threaten the future of every American. The deepening racial division is not inevitable. The movement apart can be reversed. Choice is still possible. Our principle task is to define that choice and to press for a national resolution.

To pursue the present course will involve the continuing polarization of the American community and, ultimately, the destruction of basic democratic values. The alternative is not blind repression or capitulation to lawlessness. It is the realization of common opportunities for all within a single society.

This alternative will require a commitment to national action—compassionate, massive and sustained, backed by the resources of the most powerful and the richest nation on this earth. From every American it will require new attitudes, new understanding, and, above all, new will.

The vital needs of the nation must be met; hard choices must be made, and, if necessary, new taxes enacted.

Violence cannot build a better society. Disruption and disorder nourish repression, not justice. They strike at the freedom of every citizen. The community cannot—it will not—tolerate coercion and mob rule. Violence and destruction must be ended—in the streets of the ghetto and in the lives of people.

Segregation and poverty have created in the racial ghetto a destructive environment totally unknown to most white Americans.

What white Americans have never fully understood—but what the Negro can never forget—is that the white society is deeply implicated in the ghetto. White institutions created it, white institutions maintain it, and white society condones it. . . .

It is time to make good the promises of American democracy to all citizens—urban and rural, black and white, Spanish-surname, American Indian, and every minority group. . . .

Chapter Ten

THE CIVIL RIGHTS MOVEMENT AND OTHER SOCIAL MOVEMENTS

As the 1950s drew to a close numerous commentators bemoaned the placidity of the times. Society seemed self-absorbed, complacent, even bored. Students swallowed goldfish and prepared themselves for jobs on the corporate ladder (or, in the case of women, for raising children). Old Left and pacifist organizations dwindled in size and significance. Unions stagnated and worker militancy became a thing of the past. Social critics dubbed youths the "silent generation" and announced that we had entered an era in which ideological differences mattered little.

The sit-ins served notice that much of this commentary had been groundless. Students flocked to the civil rights movement; radical organizations emerged and the counterculture flourished. By the end of the decade, one Gallup Poll revealed that Americans considered student unrest to be the nation's number one problem, more so than inflation, unemployment, crime, or taxes. Vietnam became synonymous with a nightmare abroad and never-ending demonstrations at home. Women, Chicanos, Puerto Ricans, Native Americans, gay men and women formed their own liberation movements.

This chapter contains documents written by activists representing different facets of "the movement," as the collection of social protests came to be known. One theme that stands out is the link between the civil rights movement and the many other movements of the decade. The specter of black men and women risking their lives for freedom inspired others to do the same. As Bernice Reagon observed, the challenging of one boundary or barrier led to the challenging of others. In addition, many activists moved from the struggles against white supremacy in the South in the early 1960s to other liberation movements in the latter half of the decade, armed with the organizing skills they had learned as part of the former. Female civil rights activists and students who participated in Freedom Summer returned to their campuses to lead student rebellions, antiwar campaigns, and/or other personal liberation movements.

In turn, these new movements both added to the strength of the civil rights movement and threatened to tear it apart. By inspiring others to fight for their own rights the civil rights movement broadened its base of potential allies. Yet, at the same time, these new movements diverted attention away from the cause of civil rights and contributed to the growing resistance to reform in general. For example, black student activists, even though they often acted separately and in a more disciplined manner than their fellow white student activists, were often held responsible for the irresponsible behavior of student activism in general. While black students often inspired white students to protest, in many cases they had little control over the latter's actions in the name of the student movement, black and white.

10.1 Mario Savio's speech, "An End to History," delivered in December 1964 at the University of California at Berkeley in the early days of the Free Speech Movement, signified the beginning of the student movement. Prior to that time, a small radical student culture had emerged at Berkeley and at several other campuses. With the Free Speech Movement, these small movements spread. Savio, himself, was a member of CORE and had participated in Freedom Summer. He was one of the first individuals to suggest that, just like blacks, relatively affluent white students were oppressed. Other civil rights activists who were part of the Free Speech Movement made the same argument.

10.1 Mario Savio, "An End to History," address on December 2, 1964, *The Berkeley Student Revolt*, ed. by Seymour Martin Lipset and Sheldon S. Wolin (New York: Anchor, 1965), pp. 216-219.

Last summer I went to Mississippi to join the struggle there for civil rights. This fall I am engaged in another phase of the same struggle, this time in Berkeley. The two battlefields may seem quite different to some observers, but this is not the case. The same rights are at stake in both places—the right to participate as citizens in democratic society and the right to due process of law. Further, it is a struggle against the same enemy. In Mississippi an autocratic and powerful minority rules, through organized violence, to suppress the vast, virtually powerless, majority. In California, the privileged minority manipulates the University bureaucracy to suppress the students' political expression. That "respectable" bureaucracy masks the financial plutocrats; that impersonal bureaucracy is the efficient enemy in a "Brave New World." . . .

The most crucial problems facing the United States today are the problem of automation and the problem of racial injustice. Most people who will be put out of jobs by machines will not accept an end to events, this historical plateau, as the point beyond which no change occurs. Negroes will not accept an end to history here. All of us must refuse to accept history's final judgment that in America there is no place for people whose skin is dark. On campus, students are not about to accept it as fact that the university has ceased evolving and is in its final state of perfection. . . .

The things we are asking for in our civil rights protests have a deceptively quaint ring. We are asking for the due process of law. We are asking that regulations ought to be considered as arrived at legitimately only from the consensus of the governed. These phrases are all pretty old, but they are not being taken seriously in America today, nor are they taken seriously on the Berkeley campus. . . .

The free speech fight points up a fascinating aspect of contemporary campus life. Students are permitted to talk all they want so long as their speech has no consequences. . . . Someone may advocate radical change in all aspects of American society, and this I am sure he can do with impunity. But if someone advocates sit-ins to bring about changes in discriminatory hiring practices, this can not be permitted because it goes against the status quo of which the university is part. And that is how the fight began here. . . .

The most exciting thing going on in America today are movements to change America. America is becoming ever more the utopia of sterilized, automated contentment. The "futures" and "careers" for which American students now prepare are for the most part intellectual and moral wastelands. This chrome-plated consumers' paradise would have us grow up to be well-behaved children. But an important minority of men and women coming to the front today have shown that they will die rather than be standardized, replaceable, and irrelevant.

10.2 Many student protests were led by black students who, with other minority students and the support of white student activists, demanded the hiring of black professors, development of black studies courses and departments, and admission of more minority students. At San Francisco State, the Third World Liberation Front, a coalition of radical white and nonwhite students, closed the school down. At Columbia, Cornell, Harvard, and other Ivy League campuses, black student groups struck out both on their own and in concert with white radicals to demand immediate change. Black students even protested against the education they were receiving at black colleges, such as Howard University.

Black student activism along with the increasing militancy of the civil rights movement itself tended to inspire white student activists to take increasingly radical stances. For instance, Students for a Democratic Society (SDS)—a

*highly idealistic and somewhat liberal organization in the early 1960s—began to
call for a revolution in the latter part of the 1960s, as is revealed by the following
piece by the Weathermen—one of the militant factions to inherit SDS's mantle in
the later 1960s. The Weathermen based their manifesto, in part, on the belief
that blacks wanted a revolution and that to work within the system was to bow to
white chauvinism. A number of the group's members had been active in the civil
rights movement and the organization considered itself an ally of the Black
Panther Party.*

10.2 Weathermen, "You Don't Need a Weatherman to Know Which Way the Wind Blows," June 1969, SDS Papers.

. . . The vanguard role of the Vietnamese and other Third World countries in defeating U.S. imperialism has been clear to our movement for
some time. What has not been so clear is the vanguard role black people
have played, and continue to play, in the development of revolutionary
consciousness and struggle within the United States. Criticisms of the
black liberation struggle as being "reactionary" or of black organizations
on campus as being conservative or "racist" very often express this lack
of understanding. These ideas are incorrect and must be defeated if a
revolutionary movement is going to be built among whites.

The black colony, due to its particular nature as a slave colony, never
adopted a chauvinistic identification with America as an imperialist power,
either politically or culturally. Moreover, the history of black people in
America has consistently been one of the greatest overall repudiation of and
struggle against the state. From the slave ships from Africa to the slave
revolts, the Civil War, etc., black people have been waging a struggle for
survival and liberation. In the history of our own movement this has also
been the case: the civil rights struggles, initiated and led by blacks in the
South; the rebellions beginning with Harlem in 1964 and Watts in 1965
through Detroit and Newark in 1967; the campus struggles at all-black
schools in the South and struggles led by blacks on campuses all across the
country. As it is the blacks—along with the Vietnamese and other Third
World people—who are most oppressed by U.S. imperialism, their class
interests are most solidly and resolutely committed to waging revolutionary
struggle through to its completion. Therefore it is no surprise that time and
time again, in both political content and level of consciousness and
militancy, it has been the black liberation movement that has upped the ante
and defined the terms of the struggle. . . .

The spread of black caucuses in the shops and other workplaces
throughout the country is an extension of the black liberation struggle.
These groups have raised and will continue to raise anti-racist issues to
white workers in a sharper fashion than any whites have or could raise

them. Blacks leading struggles against racism have made the issue un-avoidable, as the black students movement leadership did for white students. At the same time these black groups have led fights which tradi-tional union leaders have consistently refused to lead. . . . As white mother country radicals we should try to be in shops, hospitals, and com-panies where there are black caucuses, perhaps organizing solidarity groups, but at any rate pushing the importance of the black liberation struggle to whites, handing out Free Huey literature, bring guys out to Panther rallies, and so on. . . .

10.3 Drawing on their experiences within the civil rights movement, SNCC activists Casey Hayden and Mary King broached the idea that women were oppressed. In the following memo which was addressed to both SNCC and SDS, they argued that gender, like race, was a category or caste in which women were thrown and restricted. Initially, Hayden's and King's ideas were not well received. Some blacks saw them as divisive and many males felt that the two exaggerated their claims. Yet, by the late 1960s, Hayden's and King's concerns would seem moderate.

10.3 Casey Hayden and Mary King, "A Kind of Memo . . . to a Number of Other Women in the Peace and Freedom Movements," reprinted in Mary King, *Freedom Song* (New York: William Morrow, 1987).

. . . Sex and caste: There seem to be many parallels that can be drawn between treatment of Negroes and treatment of women in our society as a whole. But in particular, women we've talked to who work in the move-ment seem to be caught up in a common-law caste system that operates, sometimes subtly, forcing them to work around or outside hierarchical structures of power which may exclude them. Women seem to be placed in the same position of assumed subordination in personal situations too. It is a caste system which, at its worst, uses and exploits women.

This is complicated by several facts, among them: (1) The caste system is not institutionalized by law (women have the right to vote, to sue for divorce, etc.); (2) Women can't withdraw from the situation (à la nationalism) or overthrow it; (3) There are biological differences (even though these biological differences are usually discussed or accepted with-out taking present and future technology into account so we probably can't be sure what these differences mean). Many people who are very hip to the implications of the racial caste system, even people in the move-ment, don't seem to be able to see the sexual-caste system and if the question is raised they respond with: "That's the way it's supposed to be. There are biological differences." Or with other statements which recall a white segregationist confronted with integration.

Women and problems of work: The caste-system perspective dictates the roles assigned to women in the movement, and certainly even more to women outside the movement. Within the movement, questions arise in situations ranging from relationships of women organizers to men in the community, to who cleans the freedom house, to who holds leadership positions, to who does secretarial work and to who acts as spokesman for groups. Other problems arise between women with varying degrees of awareness of themselves as being capable as men but are held back from full participation, or between women who see themselves as needing more control of their work than other women demand. And there are problems with relationships between white women and black women.

Women and personal relations with men: Having learned from the movement to think radically about the personal worth and abilities of people whose role in society had gone unchallenged before, a lot of women in the movement have begun trying to apply those lessons to their own relations with men. Each of us probably has her own story of the various results, and of the internal struggle occasioned by trying to break out of very deeply learned fears, needs, and self-perceptions, and of what happens when we try to replace them with concepts of people and freedom learned from the movement and organizing.

Institutions: Nearly everyone has real questions about those institutions which shape perspectives on men and women: marriage, child-rearing patterns, women's (and men's) magazines, etc. People are beginning to think about and even to experiment with new forms in these areas. . . .

Lack of community for discussion: Nobody is writing, or organizing or talking publicly about women in any way that reflects the problems that various women in the movement come across and which we've tried to touch above. . . .

Objectively, the chances seem nil that we could start a movement based on anything as distant to general American thought as a sex-caste system. Therefore, most of us will probably want to work full time on problems such as war, poverty, race. The very fact that the country can't face, much less deal with, the questions we're raising means that the movement is one place to look for some relief. Real efforts at dialogue within the movement and with whatever liberal groups, community women, or students might listen are justified. That is, all the problems between men and women and all the problems of women functioning in society as equal human beings are among the most basic that people face. We've talked in the movement about trying to build a society which would see basic human problems (which are now seen as private troubles), as public problems and would try to shape institutions to meet human needs rather than shaping people to meet the needs of those with power. To raise questions like those above illustrates very directly that society hasn't dealt with some of its deepest problems and opens discussion of why that is so. . . . The second objective reason we'd like to see discussion begin is that we've learned a great deal in the movement and perhaps this is one area where a determined attempt to apply ideas we've learned there can produce some new alternatives.

10.4 Michele Wallace's piece on the place, or lack thereof, of black women in the women's movement, hints at some of the more difficult issues raised by the near-simultaneous development of the civil rights and women's movement. Black women seemed to face the double dilemma of both racial and sexual discrimination. Yet neither the civil rights nor the women's movement, largely white and middle class, seemed willing to speak to their concerns.

10.4 Michele Wallace, "A Black Feminist's Search for Sisterhood," *Village Voice*, 1975.

When I was in the third grade I wanted to be president. I can still remember the stricken look on my teacher's face when I announced it in class. By the time I was in the fourth grade I had decided to be the president's wife instead. It never occurred to me that I could be neither because I was Black. Growing up in a dreamy state of mind not uncommon to the offspring of the Black middle class, I was convinced that hatred was an insubstantial emotion and would certainly vanish before it could affect me. I had the world to choose from in planning a life.

On rainy days my sister and I used to tie the short end of a scarf around our scrawny braids and let the rest of its silken mass trail to our waists. We'd pretend it was hair and that we were some lovely heroine we'd seen in the movies. There was a time when I would have called that wanting to be white, yet the real point of the game was being feminine. Being feminine *meant* being white to us. . . .

In 1968, when I was sixteen and the term Black consciousness was becoming popular, I started wearing my hair natural again. This time I ignored my "elders," I was too busy reshaping my life. Blackness, I reasoned, meant that I could finally be myself. Besides recognizing my history of slavery and my African roots, I began a general house-cleaning. All my old values, gathered from "playing house" in nursery school to *Glamour* Magazine's beauty tips, were discarded. . . .

It took me three years to fully understand that Stokely was serious when he'd said my position in the movement was "prone"; three years to understand that the countless speeches that all began "the Black man . . ." did not include me. . . . No I wasn't to go to the beauty parlor but yes I was to spend hours controlling my hair. No I wasn't to flirt with or take shit from white men but yes I was to sleep with and take unending shit from Black men. . . .

Enough was enough. . . . I discovered my voice when brothers talked to me. I talked back. This had its hazards. Almost got my eye blackened several times. My social life was like guerrilla warfare. Here was the logic behind our grandmothers' saying, "A nigga man ain't shit." It was shorthand for "The Black man has learned to hate himself and to hate you even more. Be careful. He will hurt you." . . .

Whenever I raised the question of a black woman's humanity in conversation with a Black man, I got a similar reaction. Black men, at least the ones I knew, seemed totally confronted when it came to treating Black women like people. Trying to be what we were told to be by the brothers of the "nation"—sweet and smiling. . . . Young Black female friends of mine were dropping out of school because their boyfriends had convinced them that it was "not correct" and "counterrevolutionary" to strive to do anything but have babies and clean house. . . .

The most popular justification Black women had for not becoming feminists was their hatred of white women. They often repeated this for approving Black male ears. . . . But what I figured out was that the same Black men who trembled with hatred for white men found white women irresistible. . . .

When I first became a feminist, my Black friends used to cast pitying eyes upon me and say, "That's whitey's thing." I used to laugh it off, thinking, yes there are some slight problems, a few things white women don't completely understand, but we can work them out. In *Ebony*, *Jet* and *Encore* and even in the *New York Times*, various Black writers cautioned Black women to be wary of smiling white feminists. The women's movement enlists the support of Black women only to lend credibility to an essentially middle-class, irrelevant movement, they asserted. . . . Today when many white feminists think of Black women, they too often think of faceless masses of welfare mothers and rape victims to flesh out their statistical studies of woman's plight. . . .

Despite a sizable number of Black feminists who have contributed much to the leadership of the women's movement, there is still no Black women's movement, and it appears there won't be for some time to come. It is conceivable that the level of consciousness feminism would demand in Black women wouldn't lead to any sort of separatist movement, anyway—despite our very separate problems. Perhaps a multicultural movement is somewhere in the future. But for now, Black feminists, of necessity it seems, exist as individuals—some well known, like Eleanor Holmes Norton, Florence Kennedy, Faith Reingold, Shirley Chisholm, Alice Walker, and some unknown, like me. We exist as women who are Black who are feminists, each stranded for the moment, working independently because there is not yet an environment in this society remotely congenial to our struggle—because, being on the bottom, we would have to do what no one else has done; we would have to fight the world.

10.5 Coretta Scott King's speech to striking health and hospital workers in Charleston, South Carolina, in the spring of 1969 provides a taste of another dimension of the women's and civil rights movements. The two movements inspired women and black workers, especially when they were one in the same, to challenge the conditions under which they had traditionally labored. When aided by progressive unions, such as Local 1199 of the Health and Hospital Workers, the results could be dramatic. In the case of the Charleston strike, black women workers, historically one of the most exploited segments of the population, stood up in unison to demand a living wage and dignity. Coming shortly after the strike of Memphis' sanitation workers, during which Martin Luther King, Jr., was assassinated, the Charleston strike served as a potential focus for all of the movements that were involved.

10.5 Coretta Scott King, "Address to Local 1199 Rally," 1969.

I am happy to be back in Charleston.

On the plane in this morning, I was reading a magazine article with the title, "South Carolina Is Charming." It went on and on about Charleston's "soft and pervasive charm, its lovely gardens and colonial homes," and so on.

You know, I just couldn't find one word about some of Charleston's other attractions—the national guard, the tanks, the state police, the curfew and those terribly awful people, those outside agitators and foreign agents. You know who I mean. I'm referring to those remarkable women—the heroines of 1969—the hospital strikers.

I spent several hours with these women this afternoon over at the headquarters on East Bay Street. And I can really understand why the city and state officials are so worried about them. I was impressed by their determination and their dedication to continue this struggle no matter how long it takes. One of the strikers put it this way. She said, "Mrs. King, you know if this strike had never taken place I guess nobody would ever have heard of us. We would have lived out our lives as nurses aides, dietary and housekeeping workers. But now the whole world seems to know what we're trying to do here. We never knew too much about demonstrations and picketing, about going to jail and having to suffer for what's right. But we do now. And, we also know a great deal more about ourselves.''

''And Mrs. King, we're grateful to all the thousands of people from all over America who are helping us. Please tell them tonight, because the television people will be there. Tell them for us that we know how important this fight is—not only for ourselves and our families—but for people everywhere. Please tell them for us that we are going to keep on marching and we're going to keep on fighting until we win.'' So I want to say to you that these remarkable women just ain't gonna let anybody turn them around. And Charleston and the state of South Carolina had better believe it.

After talking to the strikers today I had a feeling that in addition to such phrases as soul power, black power and green power, we're going to have to add another one—and that's woman power. For these women and their leaders are displaying the kind of quiet determination that can move mountains. . . .

The hospitals of our nation are staffed by hundreds of thousands of women—black women, white women, Mexican women and Puerto Rican women. They have one thing in common. All of them are poor. Most of them earn as little as $50 and $60 a week. They are sick and tired of working full-time jobs at part-time pay. And as Mary Moultrie has put it, they are simply sick of being sick and tired. . . .

Personally, I feel a bond of true friendship with the members of Local 1199B. . . . For ours is a common struggle. A struggle to make it possible for all of God's children to walk on earth in dignity and self-respect. Everywhere I go people ask me about this strike. For what began as a little known strike by hospital workers has captured the imagination and touched the conscience of millions of Americans.

The truth is that you are making history here in Charleston. You have won the active support of every major civil rights organization in the nation. You have won the full support of the organized labor movement. . . . You have won the support of all major religious groups. . . . Every day, every week, more organizations add their voices to your struggle. . . .

I know that if my husband were alive today he would be at your side. He would be marching with Rev. Abernathy, with the hospital strikers, with the students, with the clergy, with the labor movement, demonstrating to this city and to the nation that Charleston can become that moment in our history when the unity of black and white, of the civil rights movement with organized labor may be recaptured. For that unity was my husband's dream. That dream will never die.

And if we will continue to work together, to march together and to fight together we will win this historic fight and bring into being that day when America will no longer be two nations, but one nation, indivisible with liberty and justice for all.

10.6 and 10.7 Among those to be inspired by the civil rights movement were other nonwhite Americans across the country; Puerto Ricans, Mexican Americans (or Chicanos), Hispanic Americans, and Native American formed their own liberation movements. The United Farm Workers, more than any other group, by marrying the struggle against racial prejudice with the fight for economic equality, became a cause célèbre. Although much less known than the Farm Workers Union, Native American activists led by Dennis Banks, heightened the nation's awareness of their continued oppression. Most of these organizations explicitly and implicitly noted their debt to and solidarity with the civil rights movement. For instance, the Young Lords, a radical Puerto Rican group, drafted a set of demands modeled on the Black Panther Party's ten-point platform. And Reies Tijerina, co-founder of a militant Chicano organization, wrote a letter from the Santa Fe Jail that imitated King's "Letter from Birmingham Jail."

10.6 Young Lords Party, "13 Point Program and Platform," reprinted in *Palante*, ed. by F. Abramson (New York: McGraw-Hill, 1971), pp. 8-13.

The Young Lords Party is a Revolutionary Political Party Fighting for the Liberation of All Oppressed People

1. We want self determination for Puerto Ricans, liberation on the island and inside the United States. . . .

2. We want self determination for all Latinos. . . .

3. We want liberation of all third world people. . . .

4. We are revolutionary nationalists and oppose racism. . . .

5. We want equality for women. Down with machismo and male chauvinism. . . .

6. We want community control of our institutions and land. . . .

7. We want a true education of our Afro-Indo culture and Spanish language. . . .

8. We oppose capitalists and alliances with traitors. . . .

9. We oppose the Amerikan military. . . .

10. We want freedom for all political prisoners and prisoners of war. . . .

11. We are internationalists. . . .

12. We believe armed self-defense and armed struggle are the only means to liberation. . . .

13. We want a socialist society. . . .

Hasta La Victoria Siempre!

10.7 Reies Tijerina, "Letter from the Santa Fe Jail," reprinted in *A Documentary History of the Mexican Americans*, ed. by Wayne Moquin (New York: Praeger, 1971).

From my cell block in this jail I am writing these reflections. I write them to my people, the Indo-Hispanos, to my friends among the Anglos, to the agents of the federal government, the state of New Mexico. . . .

I write to you as one of the clearest victims of the madness and racism in the hearts of our present-day politicians and rulers. At this time, August 17, I have been in jail for 65 days—since June 11, 1969, when my appeal for bond from another case was revoked by a federal judge. I am here today because I resisted an assassination attempt led by an agent of the federal government—an agent of all those who do not want Reies Lopez Tijerina to stand out for the poor, all those who do not want Reies Lopez Tijerina to stand in their way as they continue to rob the poor people, all those many rich people from outside the state with their summer homes and ranches here whose pursuit of happiness depends on thievery, all those who have robbed the people of their land and culture for 120 years. . . .

What is my real crime? As I and the poor people see it, especially the Indo-Hispanos, my only real crime is UPHOLDING OUR RIGHTS AS PROTECTED BY THE TREATY OF GUADALUPE HIDALGO which ended the so-called Mexican-American War of 1846-48. My only crime is demanding the respect and protection of our property, which has been confiscated illegally by the federal government. Ever since the treaty was signed in 1848, our people have been asking every elected president of the United States for a redress of grievances. Like the Black people, we too have been criminally ignored. Our right to the Spanish land grant pueblos is the real reason why I am in prison at this moment. . . .

This truth is denied by the conspirators against the poor and by the press which they control. There are also the Silent Contributors. The Jewish people accused the Pope of Rome for keeping silent while Hitler and his machines persecuted the Jews in Germany and other countries. I support the Jews. . . . By the same token, I denounce those in New

Mexico who have never opened their mouths at any time to defend or support the thousands who have been killed, robbed, raped of their culture. I don't know of any church or Establishment organization or group of elite intellectuals that has stood up for the Treaty of Guadalupe-Hidalgo. We condemn the silence of these groups. . . .

As I sit in my jail cell in Santa Fe, capital of New Mexico, I pray that all the poor people will unite to bring justice to New Mexico. My cell block has no day light, no ventilation of any kind, no light of any kind. After 9 P.M. we are left in a dungeon of total darkness. Visiting rules allow only 15 minutes per week. . . . But these uncomfortable conditions do not bother me, for I have a divine dream to give me strength: the happiness of my people. . . .

10.8 The Vietnam War had a significant impact on the civil rights movement and vice versa. As early as the summer of 1964, COFO workers in Mississippi questioned President Johnson's willingness to fight for democracy in South Vietnam but unwillingness to protect civil rights workers. Robert Moses delivered one of the keynote addresses at one of the first antiwar protests, sponsored by SDS in the early spring of 1965. Shortly after being pummeled by an Alabama state trooper in Selma, John Lewis rhetorically badgered the president for sending troops to the Congo, the Dominican Republic and Indochina, but not to Alabama. Another SNCC veteran, Julian Bond, became one of the first candidates for public office to denounce the war, a decision that did not hurt him amongst Atlanta's black voters but led the state legislature to strip him of his seat. In early 1966, following the murder of Sammy Young, Jr., one of its members and a Navy veteran, SNCC formally declared its opposition to the war. SNCC even suggested that blacks should refuse to cooperate with the draft.

10.8 SNCC, "Statement on Vietnam," January 6, 1966.

The Student Nonviolent Coordinating Committee assumes the right to dissent with the United States foreign policy on any issue, and states its opposition to United States involvement in the war in Vietnam on these grounds:

We believe the United States government has been deceptive in claims of concern for the freedom of the Vietnamese people, just as the government has been deceptive in claiming concern for the freedom of the colored people in such other countries as the Dominican Republic, the Congo, South Africa, Rhodesia and in the United States itself.

We of the Student Nonviolent Coordinating Committee have been involved in the black people's struggle for liberation and self-determination in this country for the past five years. Our work, particularly in the

South, taught us that the United States government has never guaranteed the freedom of oppressed citizens and is not yet truly determined to end the ruse of terror and oppression within its own borders.

We ourselves have often been victims of violence and confinement executed by U.S. government officials. We recall the numerous persons who have been murdered in the South because of their efforts to secure their civil and human rights, and whose murderers have been allowed to escape penalty for their crimes. The murder of Samuel Young in Tuskegee, Alabama is no different from the murder of people in Vietnam, for both Young and the Vietnamese sought and are seeking to secure the rights guaranteed them by law. In each case, the U.S. government bears a great part of the responsibility for these deaths.

Samuel Young was murdered because U.S. law is not being enforced. Vietnamese are being murdered because the United States is pursuing an aggressive policy in violation of international law. The U.S. is no respecter of persons or law when such persons or laws run counter to its needs, and desires. We recall the indifference, suspicion and outright hostility with which our reports of violence have been met in the past by government officials.

We know for the most part that elections in this country, in the North as well as the South, are not free. We have seen that the 1965 Voting Rights Act and the 1964 Civil Rights Act have not yet been implemented with full federal power and concern. We question then the ability and even the desire of the U.S. government to guarantee free elections abroad. We maintain that our country's cry of "Preserve freedom in the world" is a hypocritical mask behind which it squashes liberation movements which are not bound and refuse to be bound by the expediency of the U.S. cold war policy.

We are in sympathy with and support the men in this country who are unwilling to respond to the military draft which would compel them to contribute their lives to U.S. aggression in the name of the "freedom" we find so false in this country. We recoil with horror at the inconsistency of this supposedly free society where responsibility to freedom is equated with responsibility to lend oneself to military aggression. We take note of the fact that 16% of the draftees from this country are Negro, called on to stifle liberation of Vietnam, to preserve a "democracy" which does not exist for them at home.

We ask: Where is the draft for the Freedom fight in the United States?

We therefore encourage those Americans who prefer to use their energy in building democratic forms within the country. We believe that work in the civil rights movement and other human relations organizations is a valid alternative to the draft. We urge all Americans to seek this alternative knowing full well that it may cost them their lives, as painfully as in Vietnam.

10.9 Unlike SNCC, CORE, MFDP, and the Black Panther Party, all of which announced their opposition to the war shortly after LBJ sent troops to Vietnam, Martin Luther King, Jr., initially did not align himself with the antiwar movement. King refused to comment publicly on Vietnam through 1966 because he feared it would divert attention away from the needs of blacks at home and would estrange President Johnson. But by early 1967 he could no longer reign-in his long-standing personal disagreement with Johnson's policy. In a speech which he delivered first at a fund-raising dinner for the Nation *and then even more emphatically at Riverside Church in New York City, King publicly pronounced his opposition to the war. While his speech reflected the black populace's disagreement with Johnson's foreign policy, it put him at odds with many previous allies. The NAACP, National Urban League, Senator Edward Brooke (the only black senator), Bayard Rustin, the* New York Times, *and others lambasted King for breaking with the president. Prominent black* Washington Post *columnist, Carl Rowan, decried King's action: "Many who have listened to him with respect will never accord him the same confidence. He has diminished his usefulness to his cause, to his country and to his people." Yet, at the same time, King's Riverside church address energized an already-vibrant antiwar movement and may have legitimized further criticism of Johnson's policy, especially among liberals who had allied with King in the early 1960s.*

10.9 Martin Luther King, Jr., "Beyond Vietnam," 1967.

Over the past two years, as I have moved to break the betrayal of my own silences and to speak from the burnings of my own heart, as I have called for radical departures from the destruction of Vietnam, many persons have questioned me about the wisdom of my path. At the heart of their concerns this query has often loomed large and loud: Why are *you* speaking about the war, Dr. King? Why are *you* joining the voices of dissent? Peace and civil rights don't mix, they say. Aren't you hurting the cause of your people, they ask. And when I hear them, though I often understand the source of their concern, I am nevertheless greatly saddened, for such questions mean that the inquirers have not really known me, my commitment or my calling. Indeed, their questions suggest that they do not know the world in which they live. . . .

Since I am a preacher by trade, I suppose it is not surprising that I have seven major reasons for bringing Vietnam into the field of my moral vision. There is at the onset a very obvious and almost facile connection between the war in Vietnam and the struggle I, and others, have been waging in America. A few years ago there was a shining moment in that struggle. It seemed as if there was a real promise of hope for the poor—both black and white—through the Poverty Program. Then came the build-up in Vietnam, and I watched the program broken and eviscerated as if it were some idle political plaything of a society gone mad on war, and I knew that America would never invest the necessary funds or energies in rehabilitation of its poor so long as Vietnam continued to draw men and skills and money like some demonic, destructive suction tube. So I was increasingly compelled to see the war as an enemy of the poor and to attack it as such.

Perhaps the more tragic recognition of reality took place when it became clear to me that the war was doing far more than devastating the hopes of the poor at home. It was sending their sons and their brothers and their husbands to fight and to die in extraordinarily high proportions relative to the rest of the population. We were taking the young black men who had been crippled by our society and sending them 8000 miles away to guarantee liberties in Southeast Asia which they had not found in Southwest Georgia and East Harlem. So we have been repeatedly faced with the cruel irony of watching Negro and white boys on TV screens as they kill and die together for a nation that has been unable to seat them together in the same schools. So we watch them in brutal solidarity burning the huts of a poor village, but we realize that they would never live in the same neighborhoods in Detroit. I could not be silent in the face of such cruel manipulation of the poor.

My third reason grows out of my experience in the ghettos of the North over the last three years—especially the last three summers. As I have walked among the desperate, rejected and angry young men, I have told them that molotov cocktails and rifles would not solve their problems. I have tried to offer them my deepest compassion while maintaining my conviction that social change comes most meaningfully through non-violent action. But, they asked, what about Vietnam? They asked if our own nation wasn't using massive doses of violence to solve its problems, to bring about the changes it wanted. Their questions hit home, and I knew that I could never again raise my voice against the violence of the oppressed in the ghettos without having first spoken clearly to the greatest purveyor of violence in the world today—my own government.

For those who ask the question, "Aren't you a Civil Rights leader? and thereby mean to exclude me from the movement for peace, I have this further answer. In 1957 when a group of us formed the Southern Christian Leadership Conference, we chose as our motto: "To save the soul of

America.'' We were convinced that we could not limit our vision to certain rights for black people, but instead affirmed the conviction that America would never be free or saved from itself unless the descendants of its slaves were loosened from the shackles they still wear.

Now, it should be incandescently clear that no one who has any concern for the integrity and life of America today can ignore the present war. If America's soul becomes totally poisoned, part of the autopsy must read ''Vietnam.'' It can never be saved so long as it destroys the deepest hopes of men and the world over.

As if the weight of such a commitment to the life and health of America were not enough, another burden of responsibility was placed upon me in 1964; and I cannot forget that the Nobel Prize for Peace was also a commission—a commission to work harder than I had ever worked before for the ''brotherhood of man.'' This is a calling that takes me beyond allegiances, but even if it were not present I would yet have to live with the meaning of my commitment to the ministry of Jesus Christ. To me the relationship of this ministry to the making of peace is so obvious that I sometimes marvel at those who ask me why I am speaking against the war. Could it be that they do not know that the good news was meant for all men—for communist and capitalist, for their children and ours, for black and white, for revolutionary and conservative? Have they forgotten that my ministry is in obedience to the One who loved His enemies so fully that He died for them? What then can I say to the Viet Cong or to Castro or to Mao as a faithful minister of this One? Can I threaten them with death, or must I not share with them my life.

As I ponder the madness of Vietnam, my mind goes constantly to the people of that peninsula. . . . They must see Americans as strange liberators. . . . Even though they quoted the American Declaration of Independence in their own document of freedom, we refused to recognize them. Instead, we decided to support France in its re-conquest of her former colony. . . .

Now they languish under our bombs and consider us—not their fellow Vietnamese—the real enemy. . . . They watch as we poison their water, as we kill a million acres of their crops. . . .

At this point, I should make it clear that while I have tried to give a voice to the voiceless of Vietnam and to understand the arguments of those who are called enemy, I am as deeply concerned about our troops there as anything else. For it occurs to me that what we are submitting them to in Vietnam is not simply the brutalizing process that goes on in any war where armies face each other and seek to destroy. We are adding cynicism to the process of death, for our troops must know after a short period there that none of the things we claim to be fighting for are really involved. . . .

Somehow this madness must cease. I speak as a child of God and brother of the suffering poor of Vietnam and the poor of America who are paying the double price of smashed hopes at home and death and corruption in Vietnam. I speak as a citizen of the world, for the world as it stands aghast at the path we have taken. I speak as an American to the leaders of my own nation. The great initiative in this war is ours. The initiative to stop it must be ours. . . .

The war in Vietnam is but a symptom of a far deeper malady within the American spirit, and if we ignore this sobering reality we will find ourselves organizing clergy- and laymen-concerned committees for the next generation. We will be marching and attending rallies without end unless there is a significant and profound change in American life and policy. . . . This business of burning human beings with napalm, of filling our nation's homes with orphans and widows, of injecting poisonous drugs of hate into the veins of peoples normally humane, of sending men home from dark and bloody battlefields physically handicapped and psychologically deranged, cannot be reconciled with wisdom, justice, and love. A nation that continues to spend more money on military defense than on programs of social uplift is approaching spiritual death. . . .

These are revolutionary times. All over the globe men are revolting against old systems of exploitation and oppression, and out of the wombs of a frail world, new systems of justice and equality are being born. . . . We in the West must support these revolutions. It is a sad fact that, because of comfort, complacency, a morbid fear of communism . . . the Western nations that initiated so much of the revolutionary spirit of the modern world have now become the arch anti-revolutionaries. . . . Our only hope today lies in our ability to recapture the revolutionary spirit and go out into a sometimes hostile world declaring eternal hostility to poverty, racism, and militarism.

We must move past indecision to action. We must find new ways to speak for peace in Vietnam and justice throughout the developing world— a world that borders on our doors. If we do not act we shall surely be dragged down the long, dark and shameful corridors of time reserved for those who possess power without compassion, might without morality, and strength without sight. . . .

Chapter Eleven

WHITE RESISTANCE

At each stage of the civil rights movement, blacks encountered stiff white resistance. J. W. Milam and Roy Bryant murdered Emmett Till in the summer following the Brown *edict. White Citizens Councils, comprised of leading members of the white community, which took as their goal the defense of the "Southern way of life," sprung up in Mississippi and other states in the latter half of the 1950s. The Ku Klux Klan enjoyed a renaissance. "Progressive" southern statesmen, such as Alabama Governor Jim Folsom, watched their political bases evaporate. Moderate leaders, such as Arkansas Governor Orval Faubus, shifted to the right. And reactionary politicians, who prior to* Brown *had enjoyed little success, such as Ross Barnett, were elected to office including the top posts in their states.*

The North's reaction to the civil rights movement was more complex and ambiguous. While surveys showed that white Northerners favored the Brown *decision, most initially disapproved of the tactics of nonviolent direct action. As late as the summer of 1963, one poll revealed that the majority of whites felt that the March on Washington would harm blacks more than it would help them. From 1963 through 1965 white northern support for civil rights increased precipitously. Moreover, white Northerners condemned the actions of southern white supremacists. Yet, following the passage of the Voting Rights Act, as white Northerners themselves were asked to integrate their schools and were faced with urban disorders, resistance developed that was comparable to that which the civil rights movement had faced in the South. Martin Luther King asserted that the worst hatred he ever faced was in Cicero, Illinois, an all-white working-class suburb of Chicago. In New York and Boston, heretofore bastions of white support for the civil rights movement, whites and blacks violently feuded over how to deal with school desegregation. In New York, the American Federation of Teachers, a liberal union which had supported the early civil rights movement, called a massive strike to protest against an experimental program in Ocean Hill–Brownsville, which gave local blacks control over the district. Whites in South Boston exploded with anger when blacks were bused into their districts. Many Northerners condemned such overtly bigoted behavior. Nonetheless, they too practiced a more subtle form of resistance. For example, moderate whites fled from the central cities to white suburbs.*

Just as importantly, by adopting strong law-and-order positions and criticizing liberal welfare programs, conservative politicians adeptly courted the votes of white Southerners and northern urban ethnics, in other words the base of the Democratic Party. Conservative and neoconservative writers argued that such appeals were not racist, insisting, instead, that they favored the original goals of the civil rights movement, creating a color-blind society. Conservatives added that their criticisms of the abuses of the courts and the federal government grew out of their desire to protect individual liberties. Yet, many others saw such claims as a ruse and countered that conservatives were consciously courting the racist vote, but through more subtle means than those traditionally employed by white supremacists.

11.1 The following selection, "The Southern Manifesto," provides a sense of the breadth of white southern resistance to reform. Largely the work of Senator Sam J. Ervin, Jr., of North Carolina, it was endorsed by the South's leading citizens, including one hundred congressmen from eleven states of the Old Confederacy. Although the sentiment of the manifesto was not new, the document was significant because it put elected officials on record in opposition to Brown, *and, arguably, legitimated other forms of resistance.*

11.1 "The Southern Manifesto: Declaration of Constitutional Principles," in the *Congressional Record*, 84th Congress, 2nd Session, March 12, 1956, pp. 4460-4461, 4515-4516.

The unwarranted decision of the Supreme Court in the public school cases is now bearing the fruit always produced when men substitute naked power for established law.

The Founding Fathers gave us a Constitution of checks and balances because they realized the inescapable lesson of history that no man or group of men can be safely entrusted with unlimited power. They framed this Constitution with its provisions for change by amendment in order to secure the fundamentals of government against the dangers of temporary popular passion or the personal predilections of public office-holders.

We regard the decision of the Supreme Court in the school cases as a clear abuse of judicial power. It climaxes a trend in the Federal Judiciary undertaking to legislate, in derogation of the authority of Congress, and to encroach upon the reserved rights of the States and the people.

The original Constitution does not mention education. Neither does the 14th amendment nor any other amendment. The debates preceding the submission of the 14th amendment clearly show that there was no intent that it should affect the system of education maintained by the States. . . .

In the case *Plessy v. Ferguson* in 1896 the Supreme Court expressly declared that under the 14th amendment no person was denied any of his rights if the States provided separate but equal public facilities. This decision has been followed in many other cases. It is notable that the Supreme Court, speaking through Chief Justice Taft, a former President of the United States, unanimously declared in 1927 in *Lum v. Rice* that the "separate but equal" principle is "within the discretion of the State in regulating its public schools and does not conflict with the 14th amendment."

This interpretation, restated time and again, became a part of the life of the people of many of the States and confirmed their habits, customs, traditions, and way of life. It is founded on elemental humanity and common sense, for parents should not be deprived by Government of the right to direct the lives and education of their own children. . . .

This unwarranted exercise of power by the Court, contrary to the Constitution, is creating chaos and confusion in the States principally affected. It is destroying the amicable relations between the white and Negro races that have been created through 90 years of patient effort by the good people of both races. It has planted hatred and suspicion where there has been heretofore friendship and understanding.

Without regard to the consent of the governed, outside agitators are threatening immediate and revolutionary changes in our public-school systems. If done, this is certain to destroy the system of public education in some of the States.

With the gravest concern for the explosive and dangerous condition created by this decision and inflamed by outside meddlers:

We reaffirm our reliance on the Constitution as the fundamental law of the land.

We decry the Supreme Court's encroachments on the rights reserved to the States and to the people, contrary to established law, and to the Constitution.

We commend the motives of those States which have declared the intention to resist forced integration by any lawful means.

We appeal to the States and people who are not directly affected by these decisions to consider the constitutional principles involved against the time when they too, on issues vital to them, may be victims of judicial encroachment.

Even though we constitute a minority in the present Congress, we have full faith that a majority of the American people believe in the dual system of government which has enabled us to achieve our greatness and will in time demand that the reserved rights of the States and of the people be made secure against judicial usurpation.

We pledge ourselves to use all lawful means to bring about a reversal of this decision which is contrary to the Constitution and to prevent the use of force in its implementation.

In this trying period, as we all seek to right this wrong, we appeal to our people not to be provoked by the agitators and troublemakers invading our States and to scrupulously refrain from disorder and lawless acts. . . .

11.2 and 11.3 The White Citizens' Council was born in Greenwood, Mississippi, shortly after the Brown decision was rendered and sister branches rapidly surfaced throughout Mississippi and other southern states. Many of Mississippi's leading citizens joined with the expressed goal of maintaining a segregated society. The council used economic and political pressure to achieve its ends. The election of Ross Barnett as governor of the Magnolia State, on the promise of defending Mississippi's traditions, which meant white supremacy, was just one display of the success of the White Citizens' Council. Barnett became one of the South's best-known spokespersons, putting forth the argument that blacks in the South were content and that outside agitators were responsible for stirring up trouble in the region. Moreover, Barnett contended that Northerners should examine their own treatment of blacks before they started casting stones at the South.

11.2 Association of Citizens' Councils, "Why Does Your Community Need a Citizens' Council?" [pamphlet], n.d.

Maybe your community has had no racial problems! This may be true; however, you may not have a fire, yet you maintain a fire department. You can depend on one thing: The NAACP (National Association for the Agitation of Colored People), aided by alien influences, bloc vote seeking politicians and left-wing do-gooders, will see that you have a problem in the near future.

The Citizens' Council is the South's answer to the mongrelizers. *We will not be integrated!* We are proud of our white blood and our white heritage of sixty centuries.

People with racial pride are attacked by the NAACP and its affiliates as being bigoted, prejudiced, immoral, un-American, etc. These hysterical smear words are used in lieu of any logical reason why a person can no longer be loyal to his white blood, his church, his state, and his nation above all else.

In other words, the right to *esprit de corps* which has won every war we have fought is no longer in style. The idea now is seemingly to pride ourselves in the fact that everybody in the world should be made equal by law, regardless of aptitude or heritage. The "have nots" must share equally with the "have gots" in this new world order.

If we are bigoted, prejudiced, un-American, etc., so were George Washington, Thomas Jefferson, Abraham Lincoln and our other illustrious forebears who believed in segregation. We choose the old paths of our founding fathers and refuse to destroy their ancient landmarks to appease anyone, even the internationalists. This integration scheme ties right in with the new, one world, one creed, one race philosophy fostered by the ultra-idealists and international left-wingers.

The fate of our great nation may well rest in the hands of the Southern white people today. If we submit to this unconstitutional, judge-made integration law, the malignant powers of atheism, communism and mongrelization will surely follow, not only in our Southland but throughout our nation. To falter would be tragic; to fail would be fatal. The white people of the South will again stand fast and preserve an unsullied race as our forefathers did eighty years ago. We will not be integrated, either suddenly or gradually.

Mississippi is considered a poor state in cash values. Yet we have only one known communist, the best record of any state in the union. This year a Mississippi boy was elected President of Boy's Nation and a Mississippi girl was elected President of Girl's Nation at the national convention in Washington. Our youth, then, of both races is our wealth and our proven defense against the sinister forces that would destroy our nation. We are certainly not ashamed of our traditions, our conservative beliefs, nor our segregated way of life.

11.3 Ross Barnett, "Raps Yankee Salons for Attacks on Mississippi," *White Sentinel* (April 1963), pp. 6-7.

Senator Jacob K. Javits, R-N.Y. was quoted in a United Press International release in Friday's newspapers as saying: "the situation in Mississippi is a national disgrace. The country cannot tolerate lawlessness. It must find a way to deal with it."

I say, without reservation, that Senator Javits is either sadly misinformed about the situation in Mississippi or is deliberately slandering our state for his own selfish political gains with the Negro minorities of New York.

When he says that "the country cannot tolerate lawlessness," I fully agree with him. But he will not find lawlessness in Mississippi as he infers, but rather in Washington, D.C., in New York, in Detroit, in Chicago, in Los Angeles and in the other beautiful examples of "show case" mixing by bleeding heart groups of one-worlders dedicated to destroying every single thing that helped make this nation what it is today.

I challenge Senator Javits to tell the American people what he intends to do about so-called discrimination in New York, in New Jersey, in Washington, D.C., and in all of the fifty states. Will he cut off all federal grant-in-aid programs to all the American states?

Mississippi stands today as one of the few places in the world where law and order prevail, where the crime rate is among the lowest in the nation, where people can walk our streets, day or night, without fear of bodily harm, and where two races, each representing about one-half of the total population, are working and living peacefully in a segregated society that for one hundred years has been tried, tested and found to be the best for both races.

Mississippi citizens, white and Negro, would not trade our peace, our tranquility, our law-and-order, our opportunities for honest improvement and advancement for a deed to all of Senator Javits' crime-ridden Washington, D.C., and New York City combined.

Before Senator Javits infers that "the country cannot tolerate lawlessness" in Mississippi I challenge him to tell the American people when he is going to eliminate the gangs of Negro hoodlums that roam the streets of Chicago, Washington, and New York and, endanger the lives of all law-abiding citizens including the police force of these cities? These are the things that Americans cannot tolerate unless we want all of our cities to become blackboard jungles of crime and disgrace.

It is evident to all thinking Americans that Senator Javits has a very sizeable job on his hands to restore law-and-order in his home state of New York and in the nation's capitol city, Washington, D.C., without sticking his nose into the internal affairs of Mississippi or any of the other sovereign states of this nation.

It is a shocking example of political trickery and shameful un-American foul play to see northern senators open a drive to cut off federal funds for Mississippi "or any state that refuses to lower the color line." These men know full well that segregation is the order of the day in private schools, in housing, in restricted residential areas and in all areas of social activity in their states just as it is in Mississippi.

The big difference is that we are honest about segregation in Missisippi and we intend to remain honest, law abiding and segregated—federal hand-outs and northern senators notwithstanding.

11.4 By 1964 Alabama Governor George Wallace had become the most notorious white supremacist in the nation. In the 1950s Wallace had run for governor as a populist/moderate. He lost and vowed "never to be out-niggered again." A fiery orator and a masterful politician, Wallace not only defended the southern way of life, he reached out to whites in the North with subtle and not-so-subtle racist appeals. In 1964 he entered several presidential primaries and did remarkably well in a handful of border and northern states. In 1968, running as an independent candidate for president, he won a larger percentage of the vote than any third-party candidate for president since Theodore Roosevelt. Four years later, running as a Democrat, he strung together a series of primary victories, only to have his campaign cut short by a bullet from an intended assassin, which left him paralyzed and unable to complete his run for the White House. His most famous speech, his first "Inaugural Address," is excerpted below. Note his defiant defense of segregation and populist tone.

11.4 Governor George C. Wallace, "Inaugural Address," January 14, 1963.

Governor Patterson, Governor Barnett . . . fellow Alabamians:

. . . This is the day of my Inauguration as Governor of the State of Alabama. And on this day I feel a deep obligation to renew my pledges, my covenants with you . . . the people of this great state.

General Robert E. Lee said that "duty" is the sublimest word in the English language and I have come, increasingly, to realize what he meant. I SHALL do my duty to you, God helping . . . to every man, to every woman . . . yes, and to every child in this State. . . .

Today I have stood, where once Jefferson Davis stood, and took an oath to my people. It is very appropriate then that from this Cradle of the Confederacy, this very Heart of the Great Anglo-Saxon Southland, that today we sound the drum for freedom as have our generations of forebearers before us done, time and again down through history. Let us rise to the call of freedom-loving blood that is in us and send our answer to the tyranny that clanks its chains upon the South. In the name of the greatest people that ever trod the earth, I draw the line in the dust and toss the gauntlet before the feet of tyranny . . . and I say . . . segregation now . . . segregation tomorrow . . . segregation forever.

The Washington, D.C. school riot report is disgusting and revealing. We will not sacrifice our children to any such type of school system—and you can write that down. The federal troops in Mississippi could better be used guarding the safety of the citizens of Washington D.C., where it is even unsafe to walk or go to a ball game—and that is the nation's capitol. I was safer in a B-29 bomber over Japan during the war in an air raid, than the people of Washington are walking in the White House neighborhood.

A closer example is Atlanta. The city officials fawn for political reasons over school integration and THEN build barricades to stop residential integration—what hypocrisy!

Let us send this message back to Washington . . . that from this day we are standing up, and the heel of tyranny does not fit the neck of an upright man . . . that we intend to take the offensive and carry our fight for freedom across the nation, wielding the balance of power we know we possess in the Southland. . . . that WE, not the insipid bloc voters of some sections will determine in the next election who shall sit in the White House . . . that from this day, from this minute, we give the word of a race of honor that we will not tolerate their boot in our face no longer. . . .

Hear me, Southerners! You sons and daughters who have moved north and west throughout this nation. We call on you from your native soil to join with us in national support and vote and we know wherever you are, away from the hearths of the Southland, that you will respond, for though you may live in the farthest reaches of this vast country, your heart has never left Dixieland.

And you native sons and daughters of old New England's rock-ribbed patriotism, and you sturdy natives of the great Mid-West, and you descendants of the far West flaming spirit of pioneer freedom, we invite you to come and be with us, for you are of the Southern mind, and the Southern spirit, and the Southern philosophy. You are Southerners too and brothers with us in our fight. . . .

To realize our ambitions and to bring to fruition our dreams, we as Alabamians must take cognizance of the world about us. We must re-define our heritage, re-school our thoughts in the lessons our forefathers knew so well, first hand, in order to function and to grow and to prosper. We can no longer hide our head in the sand and tell ourselves that the ideology of our free fathers is not being attacked and is not being threatened by another idea, for it is. We are faced with an idea that if centralized government assumes enough authority, enough power over its people that it can provide a utopian life, that if given the power to dictate, to forbid, to require, to demand, to distribute, to edict and to judge what is best and enforce that will of judgment upon its citizens from unimpeachable authority, then it will produce only "good" and it shall be our father and our God. It is an idea of government that encourages our fears and destroys our faith, for where there is faith, there is no fear, and where there is fear, there is no faith. . . .

Not so long ago men stood in marvel and awe at the cities, the buildings, the schools, the autobahns that the government of Hitler's Germany had built . . . but it could not stand, for the system that built it had rotted the souls of the builders and in turn rotted the foundation of what God meant that God should be. Today that same system on an international scale is sweeping the world. It is the "changing world" of which we are told. It is now called "new" and "liberal." It is as old as the oldest dictator. It is degenerate and decadent. As the national racism of Hitler's Germany persecuted a national minority to the whim of a national majority so the international racism of liberals seek to persecute the international white minority to the whim of the international colored majority, so that we are footballed about according to the favor of the Afro-Asian bloc. But the Belgian survivors of the Congo cannot present their case to the war crimes commission . . . nor the survivors of Castro, nor the citizens of Oxford, Mississippi.

It is this theory of international power politic that led a group of men on the Supreme Court for the first time in American history to issue an edict, based not on legal precedent, but upon a volume, the editor of which has said our Constitution is outdated and must be changed and the writers of which, some had admittedly belonged to as many as half a hundred communist front organizations. It is this theory that led this same group of men to briefly bare the ungodly core of the philosophy in forbidding little school children to say a prayer. . . .

This nation was never meant to be a unit of one but a unit of the many, that is the exact reason our freedom loving forefathers established the states, so as to divide the rights and powers among the many states, insuring that no central power could gain master control.

In united effort we were meant to live under this government, whether Baptist, Methodist . . . or whatever one's denomination or religious belief, each respecting the others right to a separate denomination. And so it was meant in our political lives . . . each . . . respecting the rights of others to be separate and work from within the political framework. . . .

And so it was meant in our racial lives, each race, within its own framework has the freedom to teach, to instruct, to develop, to ask for and receive deserved help from others of separate racial stations. This is the great freedom of our American founding fathers. But if we amalgamate into the one unit as advocated by the communist philosophers, then the enrichment of our lives, the freedom for our development, is gone forever. We become, therefore, a mongrel unit of one under a single all powerful government and we stand for everything and for nothing.

The true brotherhood of America, of respecting separateness of others and uniting in effort, has been so twisted and distorted from its original concept that there is small wonder that communism is winning the world.

We invite the negro citizens of Alabama to work with us from his separate racial station, as we will work with him, to develop, to grow. . . . But we warn those, of any group, who would follow the false doctrine of communistic amalgamation that we will not surrender our system of government, our freedom of race and religion, that freedom was won at a hard price and if it requires a hard price to retain it, we are able and quite willing to pay it. . . .

We remind all within hearing of the Southland that . . . Southerners played a most magnificent part in erecting this great divinely inspired system of freedom, and as God is our witness, Southerners will save it.

Let us, as Alabamians, grasp the hand of destiny and walk out of the shadow of fear and fill our divine destiny. Let us not simply defend but let us assume the leadership of the fight and carry our leadership across the nation. God has placed us here in this crisis. Let us not fail in this our most historical moment. . . .

11.5 While Presidents Kennedy and Johnson supported civil rights measures and provided moral support for the civil rights movement, they also allowed the Federal Bureau of Investigation (FBI), under the command of J. Edgar Hoover, to conduct intensive surveillance and ultimately harassment of various civil rights figures and organizations. Under President Nixon these programs were continued and in some instances expanded. The "Final Report" of the "Church" Committee, excerpted below, provides an official assessment of the FBI's "counterintelligence" operations. The Bureau treated King as if he were a foreign spy, tapping his phones and seeking to discredit him in the press. Lesser-known blacks faced at least as much harassment. In addition, other law enforcement agencies working with and independently of the FBI conducted their own "counterintelligence" programs, which added to the obstacles that the civil rights movement had to overcome.

11.5 U.S. Senate, "Final Report of the Select Committee to Study Governmental Operations with Respect to Intelligence Activities," 94th Congress, 2nd Session, pp. 3, 20-23, 81-87, and 188-195.

COINTELPRO began in 1956, in part because of frustration with Supreme Court rulings limiting Government's power to proceed overtly against dissident groups; it ended in 1971 with the threat of public exposure. In the intervening 15 years, the Bureau [FBI] conducted a sophisticated vigilante operation aimed squarely at preventing the exercise of First Amendment rights of speech and association, on the theory that preventing the growth of dangerous groups and the propagation of dangerous ideas would protect the national security and deter violence.

Many of the techniques used would be intolerable in a democratic society even if all of the targets had been involved in violent activity, but COINTELPRO went far beyond that. The unexpressed major premise of the program was that a law enforcement agency has the duty to do whatever is necessary to combat perceived threats to the existing social and political order. . . .

In marked contrast to prior COINTELPRO, which grew out of years of intensive intelligence investigation, the Black Nationalist COINTELPRO and the racial intelligence investigation section were set up at about the same time in 1967.

Prior to that time, the Division's investigations of "Negro matters" was limited to instances of alleged Communist infiltration of civil rights groups and to monitoring civil rights protest activity. However, the long, hot summer of 1967 led to intense pressure on the Bureau to do something to contain the problem, and once again, the Bureau heeded the call.

The originating letter was sent out to twenty-three field offices on August 25, 1967, describing the program's purpose as: ". . . to expose, disrupt, misdirect, discredit, or otherwise neutralize the activities of black nationalist, hate-type organizations and groupings, their leadership, spokesman . . . and to counter their propensity for violence and civil disorder. . . . Efforts of the various groups to consolidate their forces or to recruit new or youthful adherents must be frustrated."

Initial group targets for "intensified attention" were the Southern Christian Leadership Conference, the Student Nonviolent Coordinating Committee, Revolutionary Action Movement, Deacons for Defense and Justice, Congress of Racial Equality, and the Nation of Islam. Individuals named as targets were Stokely Carmichael, H. "Rap" Brown, Elijah Muhammad, and Maxwell Stanford. . . .

On March 4, 1968, the program was expanded . . . "to prevent the 'coalition of militant black nationalist groups,' which might be the first step toward a real 'Mau Mau' in America; to prevent the rise of a 'messiah' who could 'unify, and electrify,' the movement, naming specifically Martin Luther King, Stokely Carmichael, and Elijah Muhammad. . . . To prevent groups and leaders from gaining 'respectability' by discrediting them to the 'responsible' Negro community, to the white community . . . and to Negro radicals. . . ."

From December 1963 until his death in 1968, Martin Luther King, Jr. was the target of an intensive campaign by the Federal Bureau of Investigation to "neutralize" him as an effective civil rights leader. In the words of the man in charge of FBI's "war" against Dr. King: "No holds were barred. We have used [similar] techniques against Soviet agents. [The same methods were] brought home against any organization which we targeted. We did not differentiate. This is a rough, tough business.'' . . .

Wire-taps, which were initially approved by Attorney General Robert F. Kennedy, were maintained on Dr. King's home telephone from October 1963 until mid-1965; the SCLC headquarters's telephones were covered by wiretaps for an even longer period. . . .

The FBI campaign to discredit and destroy Dr. King was marked by extreme personal vindictiveness. As early as 1962, Director Hoover penned . . . ''King is no good.'' At the August 1963 March on Washington, Dr. King told the country of his dream. . . . The FBI's Domestic Intelligence Division described this ''demagogic speech'' as yet more evidence that Dr. King was ''the most dangerous and effective Negro leader in the country.'' . . . The depth of Director Hoover's bitterness toward Dr. King, a bitterness which he had effectively communicated to his subordinates in the FBI, was apparent from the FBI's attempts to sully Dr. King's reputation long after his death. . . . In 1970, Director Hoover told reporters that Dr. King was the ''last one in the world who should ever have received'' the Nobel Peace Prize. . . .

By July 1969, the Black Panthers had become the primary focus of the program, and was ultimately the target of 233 of the total 295 authorized ''Black Nationalist'' COINTELPRO actions.

Although the claimed purpose of the Bureau's . . . tactics was to prevent violence, some of the FBI's tactics against the BPP were clearly intended to foster violence, and many others could reasonably have been expected to cause violence. For example, the FBI's efforts to ''intensify the degree of animosity'' between the BPP and the Blackstone Rangers, a Chicago street gang, included sending an anonymous letter to the gang's leader falsely informing him that the Chicago Panther's had ''a hit out'' on him. The stated intent of the letter was to induce the Ranger leader to ''take reprisals against'' the Panther leadership. . . .

11.6 David Brudnoy's essay on South Boston's resistance to busing allows the reader to assess white attitudes and behavior in the North on two different levels. On one level Brudnoy's description of the antibusing views of Irish-Americans in South Boston accurately conveys one form of resistance—crude, unsophisticated, and straightforward, that of a substantial number of working-class whites in urban neighborhoods throughout the North. On another level, Brudnoy's interpretation of the reasons behind their behavior offers the reader insight into the more sophisticated and less blatant defense of the racial status quo—that of conservative intellectuals and politicians who rationalized resistance to the law by portraying working- and middle-class whites, North and South, as victims of an abusive judicial system and an overgrown liberal government. Brudnoy's article appeared in National Review. *In the early 1960s this arch-conservative magazine reached a limited audience and carried little weight. But like the argument that Brudnoy made, its influence grew rapidly in the latter half of the 1960s and it became a major political and intellectual force in the 1970s and 1980s.*

11.6 David Brudnoy, "Fear and Loathing in Boston," *National Review*, October 25, 1974, pp. 1228-1231.

The first day of busing: only ten of 525 whites assigned to Roxbury High, the black school, showed up; and buses carrying 56 Negro kids (500 had been expected) from Roxbury to South Boston were stoned. Policemen suffered injuries, adults and kids threw bottles at Negro children, whites set off a chant of "Die, Niggers, Die!" Six white teen-age boys were in custody, apprehended for disorderly conduct, assault and battery, resisting arrest. Thomas Atkins—head of Boston's NAACP, who had worked his way through graduate school at Harvard by serving as a Boston city councilor, failed in a mayoral race, and then won appointment to Republican Governor Francis Sargent's cabinet—warned on September 7 of legal action against any official who failed to enforce school attendance laws and any parent who kept his kid out of school. The first day of busing, September 1, Atkins urged *Negro* parents to keep *their* kids out of school in Southie because of violence. The irony was lost on the Boston media; at least they didn't notice Atkins' turnabout. The next day, the morning after a day of violence unparalleled in modern Boston history, a day of hatred against outsiders not witnessed here in decades, the *Boston Globe* flashed its front page headline: "Boston Schools Desegregate, Opening Day Generally Peaceful."

It's been that sort of month; massive fear, loathing, hysteria, bitter and vengeful frustration, an experience worse even than foreseen, coupled with an effort to accentuate the affirmative and minimize the negative, to salvage even at the price of distorted media coverage some value from a gruesome experience. . . .

When law 'n' order in the form of hundreds of cops came to South Boston, to protect bused-in-students and forbid gatherings by whites, this community, so boastful of its law-abiding tradition, so insulated from the contemporary social advances and perversions alike, screamed bloody murder. "Southie Is My Home Town," they sing, and "town" is what they call this district, cut off from the rest of Boston, by railroad tracks, bridges, dead spaces, sticking out into Boston's Harbor like a pimple on

Boston's cheek. Southie is the home to former House Speaker John McCormack and to Louise Day Hicks; Southie is one of the most fiercely proud Irish-American communities in this country. . . .

Busing came to Boston in a day and took nine years to do so. In 1965, Massachusetts passed its landmark Racial Imbalance Act requiring that no school in the Commonwealth contain more than 50 per cent minority students. For nine years Boston and Springfield school authorities pretended the law didn't exist. The Boston School Committee built several new schools, all erected within, rather than on, the frontiers of racially discrete areas, thus ensuring that the composition of those schools would remain uniracial. While voluntary busing was initiated from Negro neighborhoods (in token numbers) into certain of the tonier suburbs—an exotic a day keeps white guilt at bay—nothing official happened. . . .

Kevin White faithfully promised never to countenance busing in Boston. "It's a lousy, rotten law," he declared; but then: "We fought the thing. We lost. Now we have to go along with it." . . .

Southie considers itself a self-contained unit, and it is. Its mentality is provincial, it's suspicious of all outsiders. . . . "The colored's aren't getting an equal education, right?" asks a Southie mother, then answers: "Yet they want to put our children in these schools where they're not getting an equal education, so then our children aren't getting an equal education. Forget it."

Southie can't forget it. And won't let the polls forget it either. When Ted Kennedy tried in early September to address an antibusing rally in downtown Boston, the crowd jeered and shouted him down. "Why don't you put your one-legged son on the bus for Roxbury!" "Yeah, let your daughter get bused there so she can get raped." . . . Rape, mugging, murder: these are themes recurrent in the speech of South Bostonians. . . . One lady, a refugee from Hitler's Germany, said to me that the scene of Southie mothers screaming in terror and fainting on the streets as children were bused off to Roxbury evoked a familiar image, an image of German Jewish mothers similarly terrified during the 1930s. . . .

Boston would not have busing now, and a daily expenditure of $90,000 for police overtime pay, and special rifle teams of cops perched on rooftops of buildings in housing projects which have experienced shooting incidents, and searches of hundreds of housing units which alienate hundreds of families, had the philosophy of legislation by judicial directive not replaced the notion of judicial directive arising out of the will of the citizenry. Boston would not have busing now had government not become something the Founders never intended: they intended that government protect the citizens against violence domestic and foreign, ensure the domestic tranquillity, and provide for the common welfare by providing for the common safety. The nature of the American government now is one of intrusion, tampering with the fabric of society, denigration of the communal ethic. . . .

There are bigots, there are racists, there are vicious people in Southies, as everywhere; there are also bigots so blinded to the realities of social cohesiveness that they focus only on their ideological fixations. They will see—they are now seeing—the fruit of busng, but they will not alter their action.

Chapter Twelve

THE STRUGGLE CONTINUES

As the 1960s drew to a close, civil rights activists recognized that blacks had made tremendous strides. Yet they equally noted that great inequalities persisted. As the economy stagnated and the nation's mood became more conservative, many blacks remained trapped in large ghettos and some studies suggested that they were falling further and further behind the white and black middle class. Perhaps Gerald David Jaynes and Robin M. Williams (eds.) in A Common Destiny: Blacks and American Society *(Washington, D.C.: National Academy Press, 1989) put it best:*

> *Just five decades ago, most black Americans could not work, live, shop, eat, seek entertainment or travel where they chose. Even a quarter a century ago—100 years after the Emancipation Proclamation of 1863— most blacks were effectively denied the right to vote. A large majority of blacks lived in poverty, and very few black children had the opportunity to receive basic education. . . . Today the situation is very different. . . . Yet, the great gulf that existed between black and white . . . has only been narrowed. It has not been closed. One of three blacks still live in . . . poverty. Even more blacks live in areas where ineffective schools, high rates of dependence on public assistance, severe problems of crime and drug use, and law and declining employment prevail. (p. 3)*

The selections in this chapter review the achievements of the civil rights movement and make recommendations for further courses of action. A number of the pieces raise themes that were raised on the eve of the civil rights movement.

Jesse Jackson, like Gunnar Myrdal, emphasizes that the Negro problem is a moral one. Even if social and economic inequalities are Jackson's immediate concerns, he feels that one has to appeal to America's ideals, to her conscience, to right America's wrongs. William Julius Wilson and to a lesser extent Benjamin Hooks adopt a more hard-headed or pragmatic approach. Like A. Philip Randolph, they tend to focus on economic concerns and political solutions. Julian Bond's reflection on the life and philosophy of W.E.B. DuBois, reminds us of the international context of the civil rights struggle, in the 1940s and 1950s and today. Although all of the authors recognize that blacks have made tremendous strides, they tend to speak in a less-optimistic tone of voice than their predecessors. Perhaps this is only to be expected. Myrdal, Randolph, DuBois, and Robeson wrote their pieces as the modern civil rights movement was being born, or was gaining momentum. In contrast, the later works were written on the downward swing. They seek to "keep hope alive," as Jesse Jackson put it, until such a time as the conditions for a reborn freedom movement improved.

12.1 Shortly before he was assassinated, Martin Luther King, Jr., discussed what blacks and their allies needed to do next. His prescription depicted his increasing radicalism. While maintaining his faith in nonviolence, King called for economic and political power. He also echoed the black nationalist celebration of African-American heritage and culture and sharply criticized American capitalism and imperialism.

12.1 Martin Luther King, Jr., "Where Do We Go from Here?" *Worldview* (April 1972).

Now, in order to answer the question, "Where do we go from here?" which is our theme, we must first honestly recognize where we are now. When the Constitution was written, a strange formula to determine taxes and representation declared that the Negro was sixty percent of a person. Today another curious formula seems to declare that he is fifty percent of a person. Of the good things in life, the Negro has approximately one half those of whites. Of the bad things in life, he has twice as those of whites. Thus half of all Negroes live in substandard housing. And Negroes have half the income of whites. When we view the negative experiences of life, the Negro has a double share. There are twice as many unemployed. The rate of infant mortality among Negroes is double that of whites and there are twice as many Negroes dying in Vietnam as whites in proportion to their size in the population.

. . . This is where we are. Where do we go from here? First, we must massively assert our dignity and worth. We must stand up amidst a system that still oppresses us and develop an unassailable and majestic sense of values. We must no longer be ashamed of being black. The job of arousing manhood within a people that have been taught for so many centuries that they are nobody is not easy. . . .

The tendency to ignore the Negro's contribution to American life and to strip him of his personhood is as old as the earliest history books and as contemporary as the morning's newspaper. To upset this cultural homicide, the Negro must rise up with an affirmation of his own Olympian manhood. Any movement for the Negro's freedom that overlooks this necessity is only waiting to be buried. As long as the mind is enslaved, the body can never be free. . . . No Lincolnian emancipation proclamation or Johnsonian civil rights bill can totally bring this kind of freedom. The Negro will only be free when he reaches down to the inner depths of his own being and signs with the pen and ink of assertive manhood his own emancipation proclamation. And, with a spirit straining toward true self-esteem, the Negro must boldy throw off the manacles of self-abnegation and say to himself and to the world, "I am somebody. I am a person. I am a man with dignity and honor. I have a rich and noble history. How painful and exploited that history has been. Yes, I was a slave through my foreparents and I am not ashamed of that. I'm ashamed of the people who were so sinful to make me a slave." Yes, we must stand up and say, "I'm black and I'm beautiful," and this self-affirmation is the black man's need, made compelling by the white man's crimes against him.

Another basic challenge is to discover how to organize our strength in terms of economic and political power. No one can deny that the Negro is in dire need of this kind of legitimate power. Indeed, one of the great problems that the Negro confronts is the lack of power. From old plantations of the South to newer ghettos of the North, the Negro has been confined to a life of voicelessness and powerlessness. Stripped of the right to make decisions concerning his life and destiny he has been subject to the authoritarian and sometimes whimsical decisions of this white power structure. The plantation and ghetto were created by those who had power, both to confine those who had no power and to perpetuate their powerlessness. The problem of transforming the ghetto, therefore, is a problem of power—confrontation of the forces of power demanding change and the forces of power dedicated to the preserving of the status quo. Now power properly understood is nothing but the ability to achieve purpose. It is the strength required to bring about social, politial and economic change. Walter Reuther defined power one day. He said, "Power is the ability of a labor union like the UAW to make the most powerful corporation in the world, General Motors, say, 'Yes' when it wants to say 'No.' That's power."

Now, let me say briefly that we must reaffirm our commitment to non-violence. I want to stress this. The futility of violence in the struggle for racial justices has been tragically etched in all the recent Negro riots. . . .

Occasionally Negroes contend that the 1965 Watts riot and the other riots in various cities represented effective civil rights action. But those who express this view always end up with stumbling words when asked what concrete gains have been won as a result. At best, the riots have produced a little additional antipoverty money allotted by frightened government officials. . . . Nowhere have the riots won any concrete improvement. . . .

It is perfectly clear that a violent revolution on the part of American blacks would find no sympathy and support from the white population and very little from the majority of the Negroes themselves. This is no time for romantic illusions. . . . And the other thing is that I'm concerned about brotherhood. I'm concerned about truth. And when one is concerned about these, he can never advocate violence. . . .

I want to say to you as I move to my conclusion, as we talk about "Where do we go from here," that we honestly face the fact that the movement must address itself to the question of restructuring the whole of American society. There are forty million poor people here. And one day we must ask the question, "Why are there forty million poor people in America?" And when you begin to ask that question, you are raising questions about the economic system, about a broader distribution of wealth. When you ask the question, you begin to question the capitalistic economy. And I'm simply saying that more and more, we've got to begin to ask questions about the whole society. . . .

Now, don't think that you have me in a "bind" today. I'm not talking about communism. What I'm saying to you this morning is that communism forgets that life is individual. Capitalism forgets that life is social, and the kingdom of brotherhood is found in neither the thesis of communism nor the antithesis of capitalism but a higher synthesis. . . .

If you will let me be a preacher just a little bit—One night, a juror came to Jesus and he wanted to know what he could do to be saved. Jesus didn't get bogged down in the kind of isolated approach of what he shouldn't do. Jesus didn't say, "Now Nicodemus, you must stop lying." He didn't say, "Nicodemus, you must stop cheating if you are doing that." . . . He said something altogether different . . . "Nicodemus, you must be born again."

He said, in other words, "Your whole structure must be changed." A nation that will keep people in slavery for 244 years will "thingify" them—make them things. Therefore they will exploit them, and poor people generally, economically. And a nation that will exploit economically will have to have foreign investments and everything else, and will have to use its military might to protect them. All of these problems are tied together. What I am saying today is that we must go from this convention and say, "America you must be born again!" . . .

I must confess, my friends, the road ahead will not always be smooth. . . . [But] let us realize that William Cullen Bryant is right: "Truth crushed to earth will rise again." Let us go out realizing that the Bible is right: "Be not deceived, God is not mocked. Whatsoever a man soweth, that shall he also reap." This is for hope for the future, and with this faith we will be able to sing in some not too distant tomorrow with a cosmic past tense, "We have overcome, we have overcome, deep in my heart, I did believe we would overcome."

12.2 Julian Bond, one of the founders of SNCC, an early opponent of the Vietnam War, and an articulate spokesman for the civil rights movement well after its zenith in the mid-1960s, like King, presented a radical critique of America. Turning the law-and-order argument on its head, Bond contended that the perpetuation of racial inequality was an act of violence against the poor, disproportionately black. Bond also called for reviving W.E.B. DuBois' goal of eradicating prejudice, celebrating the beauty of the black race, and eliminating colonial and imperial control of nonwhites by whites.

12.2 Julian Bond, *A Time to Speak a Time to Act* (New York: Simon & Schuster, 1972), pp. 22-24.

W.E.B. DuBois correctly predicted that the problem of the twentieth century would be the problem of the color line.

With those words, he summed up the crisis that has primarily occupied men and nations and has become the first order of business for millions of oppressed peoples. Racism, the root of the crisis, is as old as the world itself. Internationally, the world's white minority has consistently exploited the resources of the colored majority of the world's population, and has continued to refuse to share the wealth and power it has gained in this way.

Here in the United States the struggle has been taken to the streets of most cities in the country, both violently and nonviolently. It broke out, for a time, on almost every college campus.

It was one part of the struggle that inspired Cuban cane cutters to overthrow a dictator and Vietnamese peasants to resist . . . through the bitter years, the attempts to dominate their homeland. It is also part of the struggle that inspires Alabama sharecroppers to risk their lives in order to have a chance at controlling their destiny, a chance to vote, to find a decent job, to secure a good education for their children.

Dr. DuBois believed that scientific and rational study of the problem of race and class would yield rational and logical solutions; civilized men, or educated men, are supposed to solve their problems in a civilized manner.
. . .

But the problems of the twentieth century are so vast, and the resistance to change has been so great, that many have quite naturally been tempted to seek uncivilized solutions. . . .

This revolutionary nation—revolutionary two hundred years ago—has become counterrevolutionary. This country, which has visited death on hundreds of thousands of Indochinese, has also found the arrogance to ignore the centuries of pleading for justice from her own domestic colony, the blacks. While these pleadings are dismissed, the central and final issue of the twentieth century comes to the fore, the violence is done to the notion that men can solve their problems without . . . violence. We need to discover just who is and who isn't violent in America.

Violence is black children going to school for twelve years and receiving six years' worth of education. Violence is almost thirty million hungry stomachs in the most affluent nation in the world. Violence is having black men represent a disproportionate share of the inductees and casualties in Vietnam. Violence is a country where property counts for more than people. Violence is an economy that believes in socialism for the rich and capitalism for the poor. . . .

Yet an antidote to *that* violence exists, an antidote that began with Denmark Vesey . . . was given impetus by DuBois . . . and was spurred on by Martin Luther King, Jr., plus thousands of nameless fighters for freedom.

However, movements are not built on the helpful motions of a few, but by the determined actions of the mass. The chance at power comes in this country not in seizing a dean, but in seizing a welfare office; from organizing a strike of domestic workers; from beginning the arduous process of transferring strength and power from those who have it to those who do not.

This is not easy work. . . . It means more than just the commitment of summer soldiers, although any soldiers are welcome in an understaffed army. . . .

DuBois later enlarged his remark . . . to include the problems of the have-nots pitted against the haves.

Sixty-five years ago, he wrote a personal credo that if adopted by those in power would be the beginning in the struggle to eliminate the problem:

''I believe in God who made of one blood all races that dwell on earth. I believe that all men, black and brown and white, are brothers, varying, through Time and Opportunity, in form and gift and feature, but differing in no essential particular, and alike in soul and in the possibility of infinite development.

"Especially do I believe in the Negro race; in the beauty of its genius, the sweetness of its soul, its strength in the meekness which shall inherit this turbulent earth. . . .

"I believe in the Prince of Peace. I believe that War is Murder . . . and I believe that the wicked conquest of weaker and darker nations by nations white and stronger but foreshadows the death of that strength." . . .

12.3 Benjamin L. Hooks, head of the NAACP, adopted a much more militant tone than his predecessor Roy Wilkins. In the following address to the NAACP, Hooks urged blacks to maintain their efforts to attain economic, social, and political equality for all blacks in the face of the mounting obstacles of the Reagan years. Echoing the words of Paul Robeson and Septima Clark, Hooks told blacks to remember that they had a history of struggle. Blacks had overcome tremendous obstacles in the past and they would be able to overcome insurmountable barriers to full equality in the near future.

12.3 Benjamin L. Hooks, "Struggle On!" *Crisis* (August/September 1983), pp. 22-24.

I come humbled by the knowledge that as we assemble in this convention center, we stand on the shoulders of many giants who put their lives on the line in order that the racial progress we now enjoy could be made. We pay tribute to our own martyred Medgar Evers who, 20 years ago on June 12, was cut down by an assassin's bullet. Medgar realized better than most that to stand up for justice in Mississippi was a dangerous and potentially fatal endeavor. Yet he stood boldly and tall, declaring to the world that it is better to die in dignity for a just cause than to live on one's knees as a supplicant. . . . Let us not forget other martyrs who gave their lives—Harry T. Moore, Vernon Dahmer, George Lee and others.

Today there are more elected black public officials in the State of Mississippi than in any state in the nation. Today, the face of race relations has been drastically altered by the surgical knife of self-denial and self-sacrifice by the thousands of men and women who met in churches off lonely roads assembled around dining-room tables of shacks and shanties and who marched until the Ross Barnetts gave way to elected officials who helped bring this state into the twentieth century. *Life is a struggle.* . . .

So it should come as no surprise that even though slavery has been officially over for more than 118 years, we still find ourselves struggling against slavery under new guises: racial discrimination in this country,

apartheid and colonialism abroad. But as far back as we can read recorded history, life for every group of people has been a struggle. . . .

Here in America, from the *Mayflower* at Plymouth Rock to the men of
war at Jamestown, life for the earliest settlers and their first slaves has
been a struggle.

Today as our 74th Annual Convention assembles in this historic city, a
city where blacks fought alongside Andrew Jackson . . . we find ourselves in a race in the struggle for survival.

• One out of every three blacks in the country is officially listed below
the poverty line.

• One out of every three blacks lives in substandard housing.

• One out of five black adults is unemployed. . . .

• Black infant mortality is twice as high as that of whites. . . .

I cite these figures to highlight the fact that although we have made tremendous progress in the area of race relations, we still have a long way to
go; and contrary to the glib assertions of the present Administration,
much remains to be done if blacks are to share in the economic wealth and
prosperity of this nation.

Yes, my friends, we are in the midst of a fierce struggle, one that
becomes more difficult with the passing of each day. . . .

Anyone who has an appreciation for history should be cognizant of the
fact that nations and great civilizations were not destroyed from without,
but from within. When hopes are blasted, when expectations are doomed,
when respect for government is shattered by the disparate treatment of
groups of individuals; when people are left out—then a social order is
doomed to destruction. Yes, social and economic destruction from within,
not foreign aggressors, constitutes the greatest threat to our system of
government. . . .

Fortunately for us, and for our nation I might add, there is the NAACP,
strong and vibrant. Although we are put upon as ineffective and out-
moded by the nattering nabobs of negativism, ostracized, vilified by
cynics from both inside and outside, nonetheless, the NAACP stands
today as it stood for the past 74 years as a bastion of hope for black
Americans. . . .

My brothers and sisters, as I close tonight, I want you to know that the
struggle that we will face through the remaining period of the '80s and on
through the twenty-first century will not be an easy one. It is fraught with
pitfalls and plagued with setbacks, but we as people have developed a
resiliency which has made it possible for us to survive slavery and various
discrimination. We must never tire nor become frustrated. . . . We must

transform stumbling blocks into stepping stones and march on with the determination that we will make America a better nation for all. . . .

12.4 In 1984 and 1988, Reverend Jesse L. Jackson, a protégé of Martin Luther King, Jr., mounted strong campaigns for the Democratic nomination for the presidency of the United States. In both efforts he won the lion's share of the black vote and in 1988 won a substantial number of white votes. Though he did not win the nomination, his attempt to become the first black man to be president captured America's attention like few others in American history. In the following address, delivered at the 1988 Democratic convention in Atlanta, Jackson paid homage to the black freedom fighters of the 1950s and 1960s who had made his campaign possible. At the same time, Jackson beseeched America not to forget that not all Americans had achieved the American Dream.

12.4 Jesse Jackson, "Common Ground and Common Sense," address on July 20, 1988, *Vital Speeches*, Vol. LIV, no. 21 (August 15, 1988), pp. 649-653.

Tonight we pause and give praise and honor to God for being good enough to allow us to be at this place at this time. . . . We're really standing on someone's shoulders. Ladies and gentlemen. Mrs. Rosa Parks. . . .

Twenty-four years ago, the late Fannie Lou Hamer and Aaron Henry—who sits here tonight from Mississippi—were locked out on the streets of Atlantic City, the head of the Mississippi Freedom Democratic Party. But tonight, a black and white delegation from Mississippi is headed by Ed Cole, a black man, from Mississippi.

. . . Many were lost in the struggle for the right to vote. Jimmy Lee Jackson, a young student, gave his life. Viola Liuzzo, a white mother from Detroit, called nigger lover, had her brains blown out at point blank range. Schwerner, Goodman and Chaney—two Jews and a black—found in a common grave, bodies riddled with bullets in Mississippi. The four little girls in the church in Birmingham, Alabama. They died that we might have a right to live.

Dr. Martin Luther King, Jr. lies only a few miles from us tonight. Tonight he must feel good as he looks down upon us. We sit here together, a rainbow, a coalition—the sons and daughters of slave masters and the sons and daughters of slaves sitting together around a common table, to decide the direction of our party and our country. His heart would be full tonight.

As a testament to the struggles of those who have gone before; as a legacy for those who will come after . . . their work has not been in vain, and hope is eternal; tomorrow night my name will go into nomination for the presidency of the United States of America.

We meet tonight at a crossroads, a point of decision. Shall we expand, be inclusive, find unity and power; or suffer division and impotence.

We come to Atlanta, the cradle of the old south, the crucible of the new South. Tonight there is a sense of celebration because we are moved, fundamentally moved, from racial battlegrounds by law, to economic common ground, tomorrow we will challenge to move to higher ground.

Common ground! . . .

Many people, many cultures, many languages—with one thing in common, the yearning to be free.

Common ground! . . .

The good of our nation is at stake—its commitment to working men and women, to the poor and vulnerable, to the many in the world. With so many guided missiles, and so much misguided leadership, the stakes are exceedingly high. Our choice, full participation in a Democratic government, or more abandonment and neglect. And so this night, we choose not a false sense of independence, not our capacity to act and unite for the greater good. The common good is finding commitment to new priorities, to expansion and inclusion. A commitment to expanded participation in the Democratic Party at every level. . . .

Common ground. Easier said than done. Where do you find common ground at the point of challenge? . . .

We find common ground at the plant gate that closes on workers without notice. We find common ground at the farm auction where a good farmer loses his or her land to bad loans or diminishing markets. Common ground at the schoolyard where teachers cannot get adequate pay, and students cannot get a scholarship and can't make a loan. Common ground at the hospital admitting room where somebody tonight is dying because they cannot afford to go upstairs to a bed that's empty, waiting for someone with insurance to get sick. We are a better nation than that. We must do better. . . .

America's not a blanket woven from one thread, one color, one cloth. When I was a child growing up in Greenville, S.C., and grandmother could not afford a blanket, she didn't complain and we did not freeze. Instead, she took pieces of old cloth—patches, wool, silk, gabardine, crockersak on the patches—barely good enough to wipe off your shoes with.

But they didn't stay that way very long. With sturdy hands and a strong cord, she sewed them together into a quilt, a thing of beauty and power and culture. Now, Democrats, we must build such a quilt. Farmers you seek fair prices and you are right, but you cannot stand alone. Your patch is not big enough. Workers, you fight for fair wages. You are right. But your patch labor is not big enough. Women you seek comparable worth and pay equality. You are right. But your patch is not big enough. Women, mothers, who seek Head Start and day care and pre-natal care on the front side of life, rather than jail care and welfare on the back side of life, you are right, but your patch is not big enough. . . .

But don't despair. Be as wise as my grandma. Pool the patches and the pieces together, bound by a common thread. When we form a great quilt of unity and common ground we'll have the power to bring about health care and housing and jobs and education and hope to our nation.

We the people can win. We stand at the end of a long dark night of reaction. We stand tonight united in a commitment to a new direction. For almost eight years, we've been led by those who view social good coming from private interest, who view public life as a means to increase private wealth. They have been prepared to sacrifice the common good of the many to satisfy the private interest and the wealth of a few. We believe in a government that's a tool of our democracy in service to the public, not an instrument of the aristocracy. . . .

Wherever you are tonight, I challenge you to hope and to dream. Don't submerge your dreams . . . dream of things as they ought to be. Dream. Face pain, but love, hope, faith, and dreams will help you rise above the pain. . . . Don't surrender and don't give up. Why can I challenge you this way? Jesse Jackson, you don't understand my situation. . . . I understand. . . . I wasn't always on television. Writers were not always outside my door. When I was born late one afternoon, October 8th, in Greenville, S.C., no writers asked my mother her name. Nobody chose to write down our address. My mama was not supposed to make it. And I was not supposed to make it. You see, I was born to a teen-age mother who was born to a teen-age mother.

I understand. I know abandonment. . . . I wasn't born in the hospital. . . . I was not born with a silver spoon in my mouth. I had a shovel programmed for my hand. My mother, a working woman. . . . I was born in the slum, but the slum was not born in me. And it wasn't born in you, and you can make it. . . .

You must not surrender. You may or may not get there, but just know that you're qualified and you hold on and hold out. We must never surrender. America will get better and better. Keep hope alive. . . . On tomorrow night and beyond, keep hope alive. . . .

12.5 William Julius Wilson, a black sociologist at the University of Chicago, has produced some of the most insightful studies on race relations in recent times. Wilson argues that "race" has declined in significance since the 1960s. He does not contend, as do conservatives, that blacks have achieved equality with whites, rather that class or economics best explain the persistence of inequality. In the following piece, Wilson tackles the issue of how to build a coalition that can win the presidential election in 1992. Wilson insists that the politics of race will continue to drive white voters away from the Democratic Party, that only a politics of class can succeed.

12.5 William Julius Wilson, "How the Democrats Can Harness Whites and Blacks in '92," *New York Times*, March 24, 1989, p. 31.

The election of Ronald Brown as the first black chairman of the Democratic National Committee has set off a new round of soul-searching. Is the party committing political suicide by becoming strongly identified with the aspirations of black and minority voters? Is America in the 1980s so lost in a new round of racism that whites will desert the Democrats at the slightest hint that blacks might be running things?

The answer to both questions is an emphatic no. Many white Americans have turned not against blacks but against a strategy that emphasizes programs perceived to benefit only minorities.

The party needs to develop new policies to fight inequality that goes beyond court ordered busing, affirmative action programs and anti-discrimination lawsuits. By stressing coalition politics and race-blind programs, such as full-employment policies, job skills training, comprehensive health care legislation, education reform in the public schools, child-care legislation and crime and drug abuse prevention programs, the Democrats could be in a strong position for the 1992 election. . . .

Such a change of emphasis is long overdue. In the 1960s, efforts to raise public consciousness about the plight of black Americans helped to create civil rights legislation and affirmative action programs. By 1980, however, the habit of many black intellectuals and civil rights leaders of dramatizing blacks' disadvantages was backfiring. It played easily into the hands of conservative critics of government efforts to reduce racial inequality, simply reinforcing the erroneous impression that Federal anti-discrimination efforts had been largely unsuccessful.

As we entered the 1980s, the accomplishments of the civil rights struggle could be seen, for example, in the rising number of blacks in professional, technical, managerial and administrative positions. Progress was evident also in the increasing enrollment of blacks in colleges and universities, and the growing number of black homeowners—increases that were proportionately greater than for whites.

It was also apparent, however, that some problems among the more disadvantaged segments of the black population, especially the ghetto underclass, appeared to be getting worse. These included the concentration of poverty in the inner city, joblessness, family breakup, educational retardation in the inner-city public schools, crime and drug abuse.

By 1980, a new political strategy was needed, one that combined discussion of blacks' persistent disadvantages with reminders about the accomplishments of the civil rights movement—one that acknowledged the need to move beyond programs aimed at one race or groups to address many of the problems that originated from racial practices.

When I presented these arguments to academic audiences in 1980, I was told that any new solutions would be opposed on two grounds. First, they would be too costly. Second, they would be unpopular with many whites, who had become disenchanted with the black movement's pessimistic themes and calls for affirmative action during periods of economic stagnation.

But if this approach was arguably wrong for 1980, when America's top priority was rebuilding military defenses and talk of a kinder and gentler nation was unthinkable, it might be right today. Recent opinion surveys show consistently that Americans across racial and class boundaries are concerned about unemployment and job security, declining real wages, escalating medical and hospital costs, child care, the sharp decline in public education, crime and drug trafficking.

Programs that address these concerns could be introduced today not as ways to help poor minorities, even though they would disproportionately benefit from them, but as strategies to help all groups regardless of race or economic background.

All minority leaders—not just Ronald Brown—should begin to recognize and publicly emphasize the importance of universal policies. These policies appeal to wide segments of the population, not just a specific race or group.

Black voters who doubt this approach ought to think of the success of the Rev. Jesse Jackson's Presidential campaign. Mr. Jackson, who put forth universal themes that highlighted and proposed solutions to the social problems plaguing all racial groups in America, drew far more support from white working and middle class voters than most political observers thought possible.

To call for a Democratic coalition organized around universal social policy themes does not mean that all programs targeted exclusively to blacks (or other minorities) would or should be sacrificed. Anti-discrimination and affirmative action programs will be needed as long as racial minorities are restricted in where they can live and work and are disproportionately concentrated in low-paying positions. But such strategies have to be backed by other programs to improve opportunities for all members of racial minorities.

STATISTICAL PROFILE OF BLACK AMERICA

Through the use of charts and graphs this appendix presents an overview of the state of black America, its size, distribution, health, economic circumstances, education, and political standing in modern times. Three themes deserve emphasis. First, the figures reveal a silent revolution in the state of black America in the twentieth century. This revolution was demographic in nature. In 1930, over 75 percent of all blacks lived in the South and most of them lived in rural areas. By the 1980s only about one-half of all blacks lived in the South and the majority of blacks, nationwide, lived in urban areas. Second, the figures demonstrate that while blacks improved their material circumstances they remained unequal to whites. Blacks still lived shorter lives, were more likely to be unemployed and poor, earned less money, were less likely to own a home, and achieved fewer years of education than whites. Third, the figures show that while de jure segregation or Jim Crow laws were abolished, schools, neighborhoods, and other facets of American life remain de facto segregated. Many blacks still live in all-black neighborhoods and attend all-black schools; many white still grow up in all-white suburbs and attend all-white schools. While black voter registration and the number of black elected officials have increased dramatically, blacks are more likely to vote for a white candidate than vice versa. Even if blatant forms of prejudice and bigotry have diminished, such realities about American life demonstrate the depth of racism and its legacy in America. The problems that plague millions of black Americans may not be intractable, but it is unlikely that piecemeal reforms will produce genuine equality. Only a mass movement, driven by ordinary men and women, can do that.

Exhibit I
Total Black Population, 1890-1990

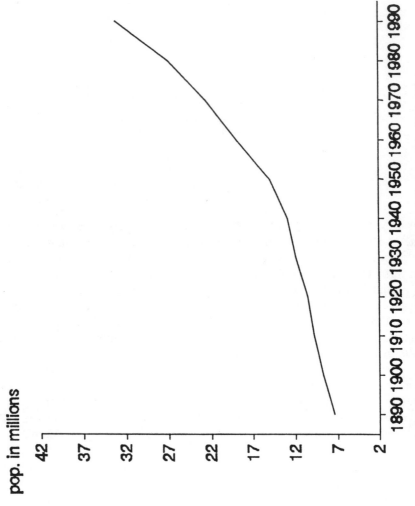

pop. in millions

Source: *Historical Statistics of the United States; Statistical Abstract of the United States.*

Exhibit II
Black Population as Percent of Total, 1890-1990

Percent

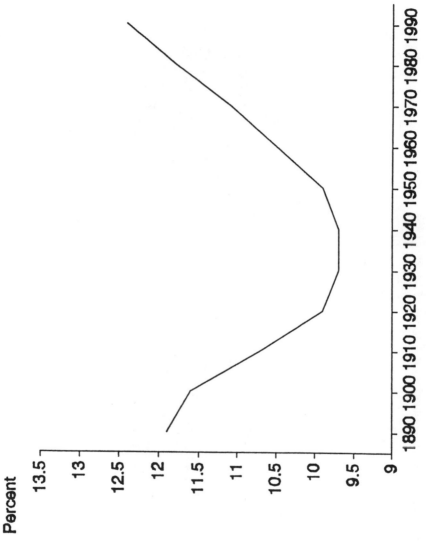

13.5
13
12.5
12
11.5
11
10.5
10
9.5
9

1890 1900 1910 1920 1930 1940 1950 1960 1970 1980 1990

Source: *Historical Statistics of the United States; Statistical Abstract of the United States.*

Exhibit III
Distribution of Black Population, in Percent, 1930 and 1950

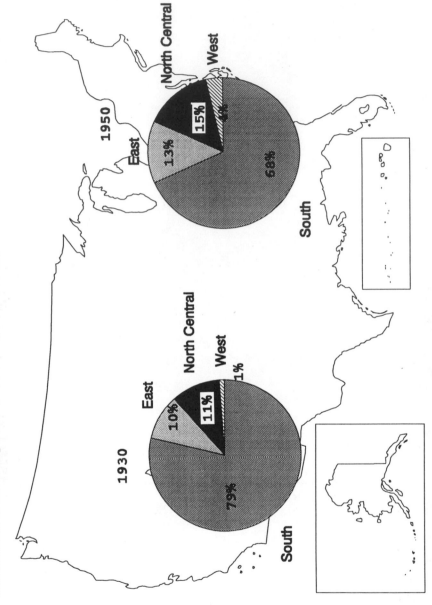

Source: *Historical Statistics of the United States; Statistical Abstract of the United States.*

Exhibit IV
Distribution of Black Population, in Percent, 1970 and 1990

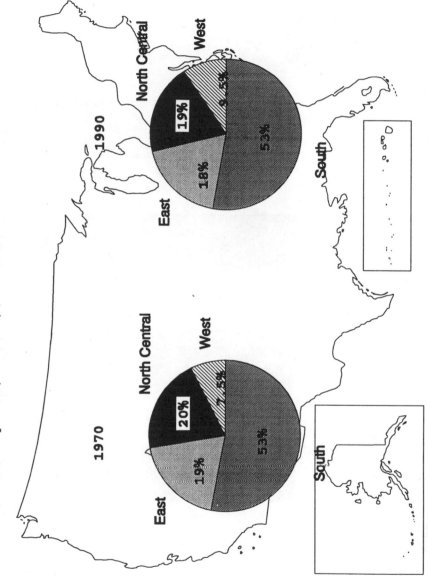

Source: *Historical Statistics of the United States; Statistical Abstract of the United States.*

Exhibit V
Black Population, Urban/Rural, 1930-1987

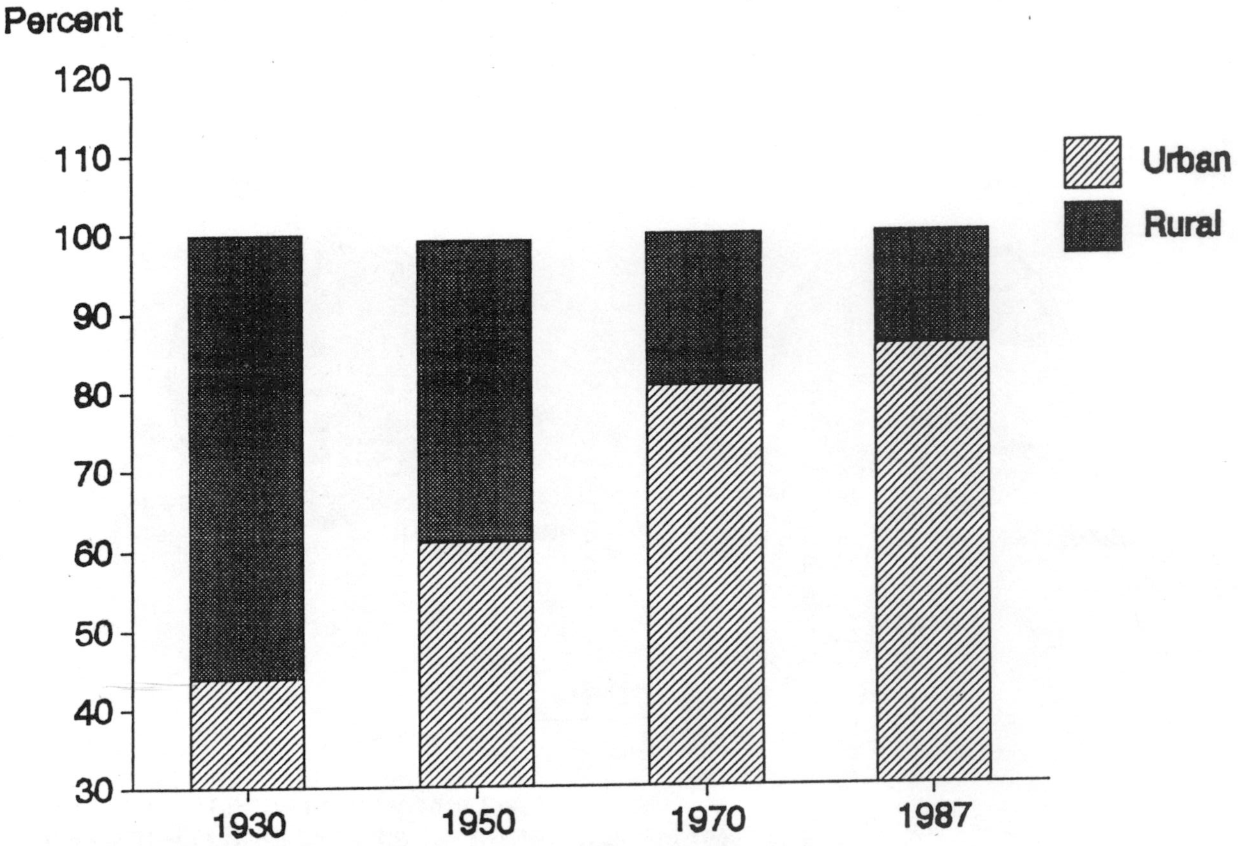

Percent

Urban

Rural

120
110
100
90
80
70
60
50
40
30

1930   1950   1970   1987

Source: *Historical Statistics of the United States; Statistical Abstract of the United States.*

Exhibit VI
Life Expectancy at Birth, by Race, 1920-1985

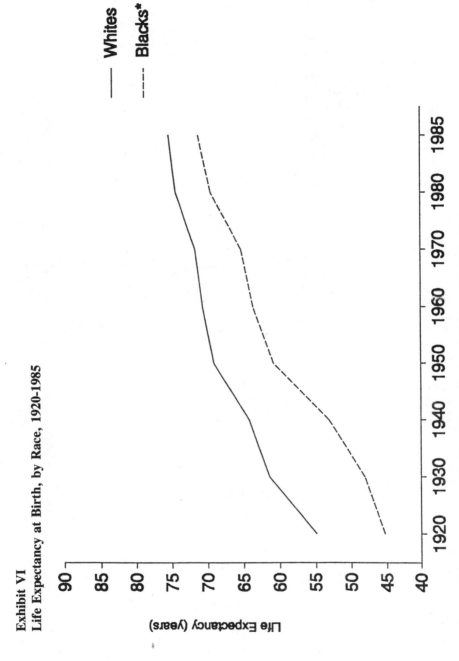

Source: *Historical Statistics of the United States; Statistical Abstract of the United States.*

Exhibit VII
Infant Mortality Rates, by Race, 1940-1985

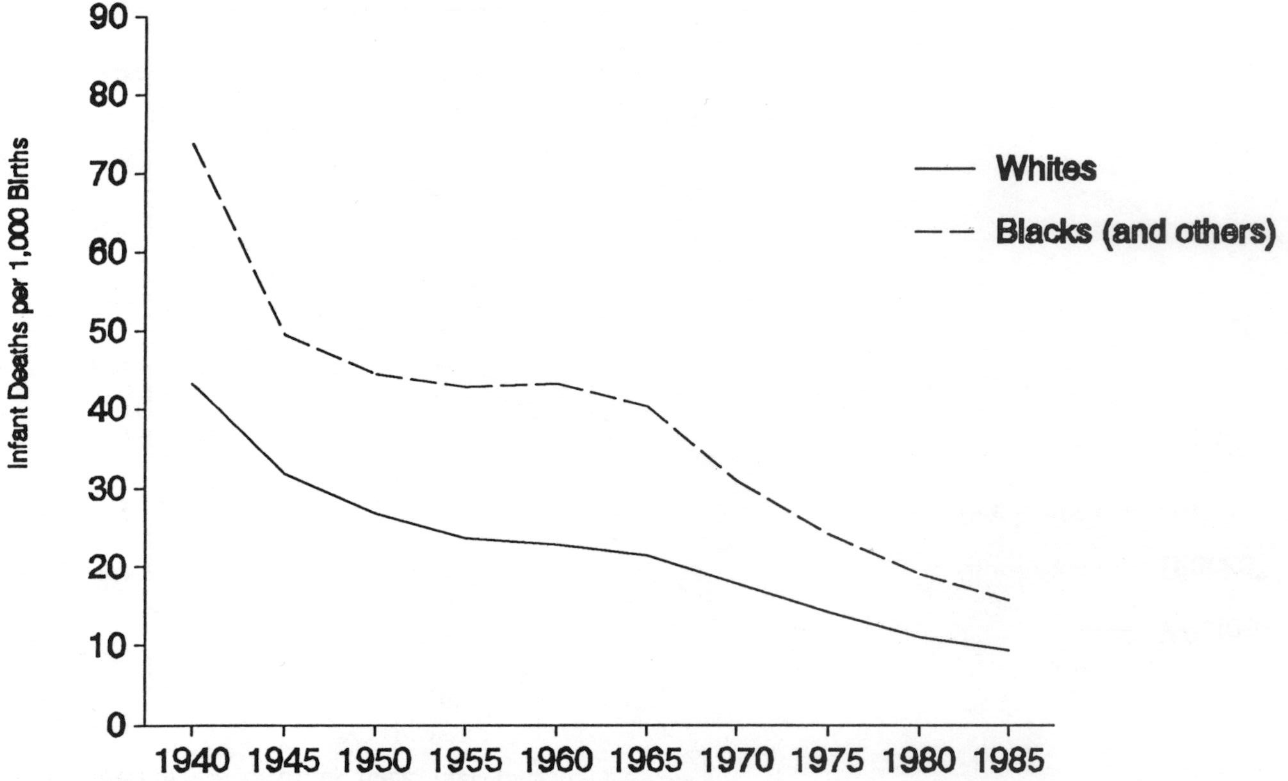

Source: *Historical Statistics of the United States; Statistical Abstract of the United States.*

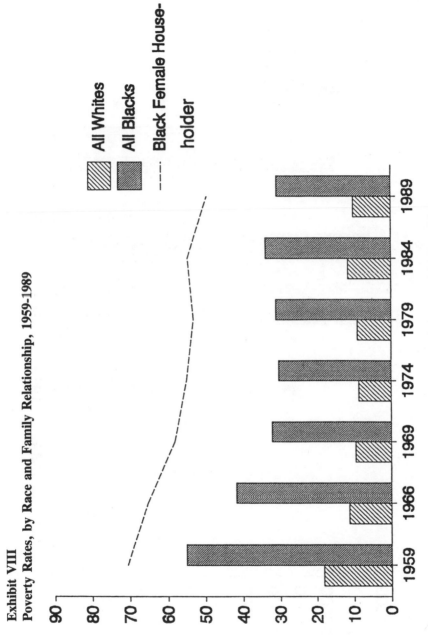

Exhibit VIII
Poverty Rates, by Race and Family Relationship, 1959-1989

All Whites
All Blacks
Black Female House-
holder

Source: *Historical Statistics of the United States; Statistical Abstract of the United States.*

249

Exhibit IX
Mean Income, by Race and Sex, 1941-1984

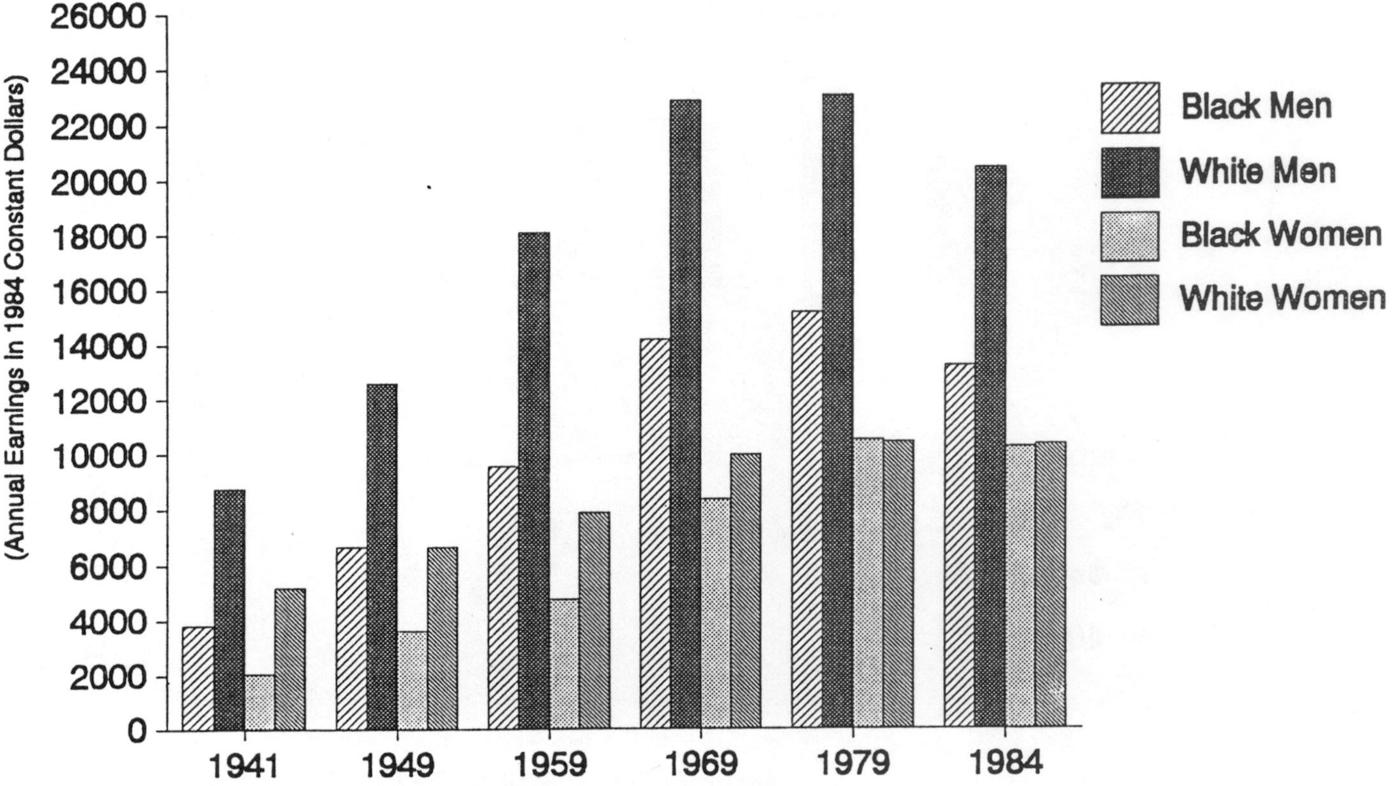
26000
24000
22000
20000
18000
16000
14000
12000
10000
8000
6000
4000
2000
0
(Annual Earnings In 1984 Constant Dollars)
1941
1949
1959
1969
1979
1984
Black Men
White Men
Black Women
White Women

Source: *Historical Statistics of the United States*; *Statistical Abstract of the United States*.

Exhibit X
Unemployment Rates, by Race, 1950-1985

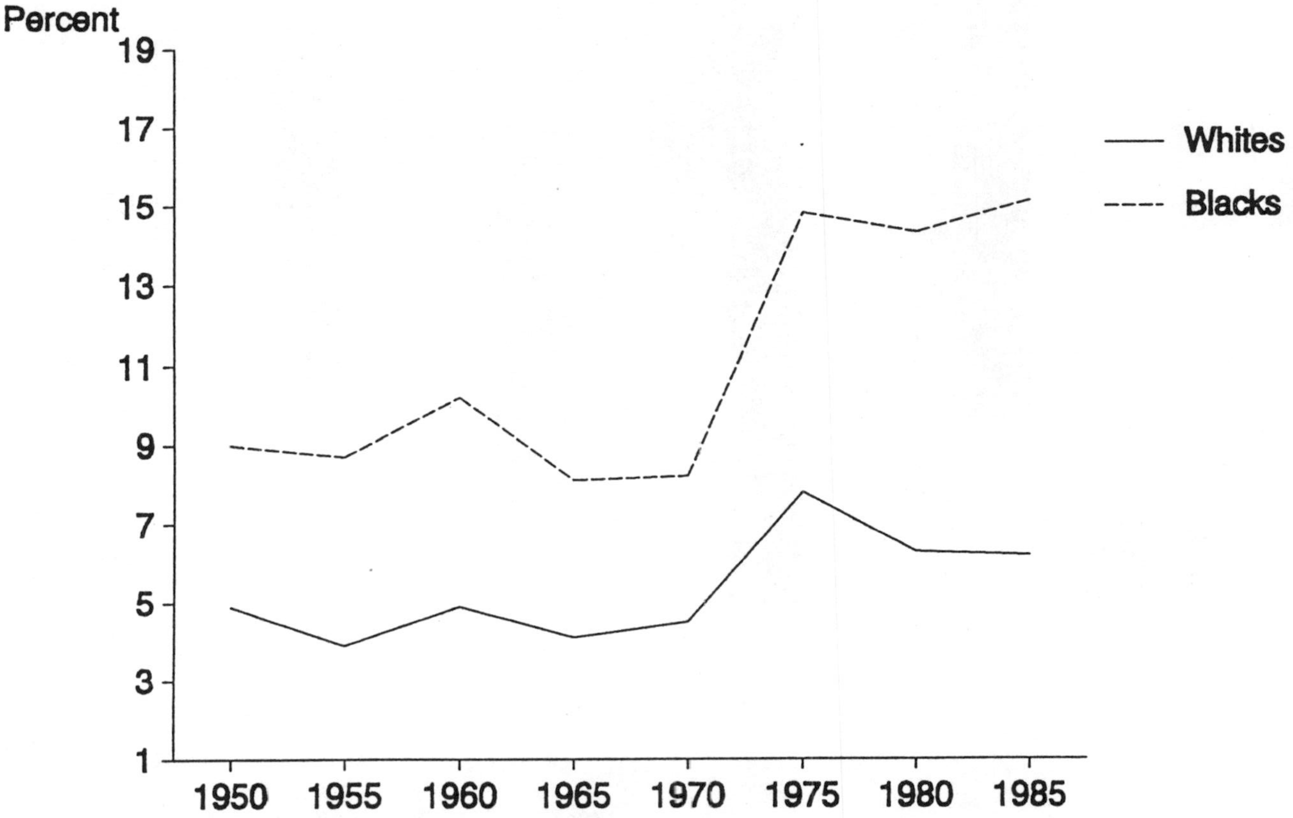

Percent

— Whites

---- Blacks

19
17
15
13
11
9
7
5
3
1

1950 1955 1960 1965 1970 1975 1980 1985

Source: Historical Statistics of the United States; Statistical Abstract of the United States.

251

Exhibit XI
Youth Unemployment Rates, by Race, 1972-1987

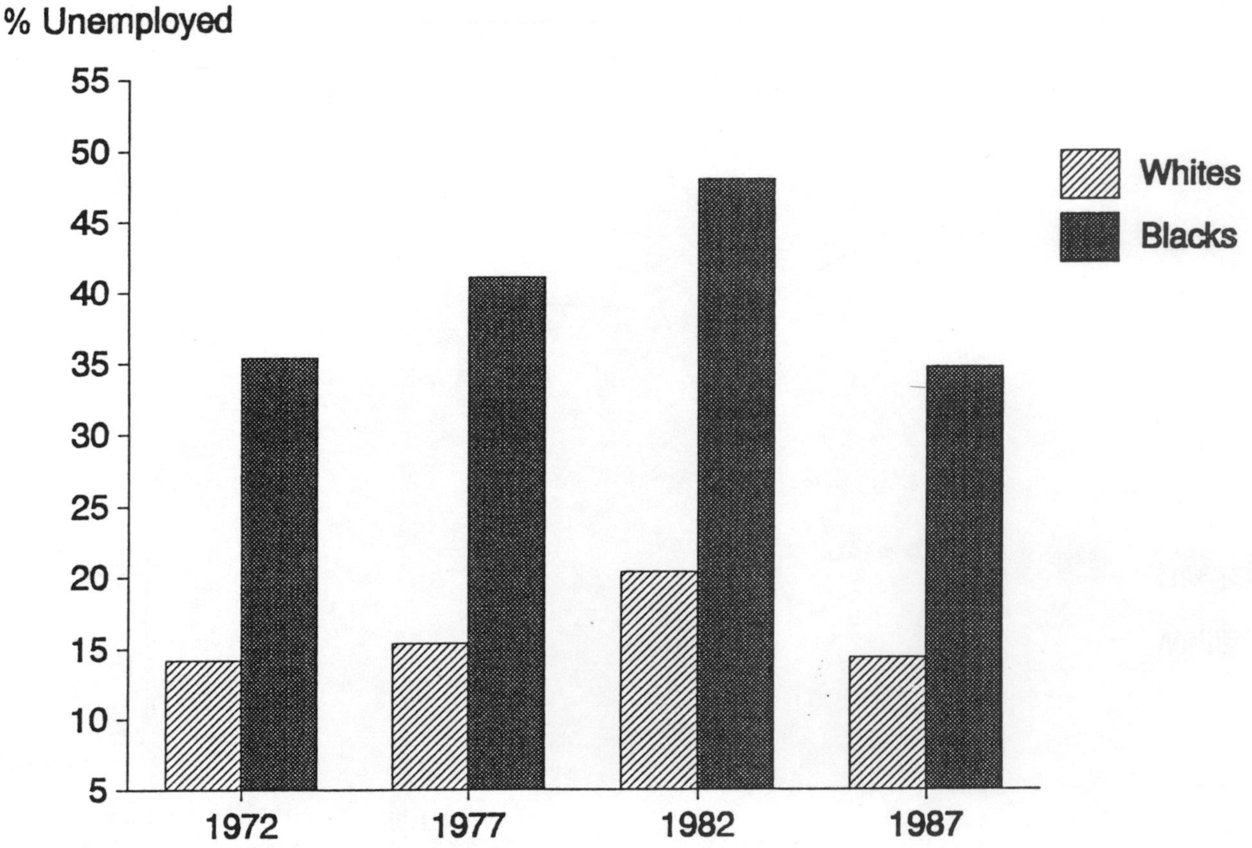

% Unemployed

Whites

Blacks

55
50
45
40
35
30
25
20
15
10
5

1972   1977   1982   1987

Source: *Historical Statistics of the United States; Statistical Abstract of the United States.*

Exhibit XII
Homeownership, by Race, 1940-1975

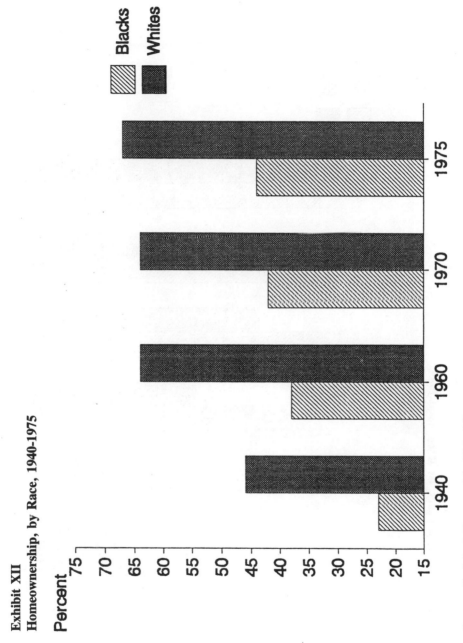

Source: *Statistical Abstract of the United States.*

Exhibit XIII
Median School Years, by Race, 1940-1988

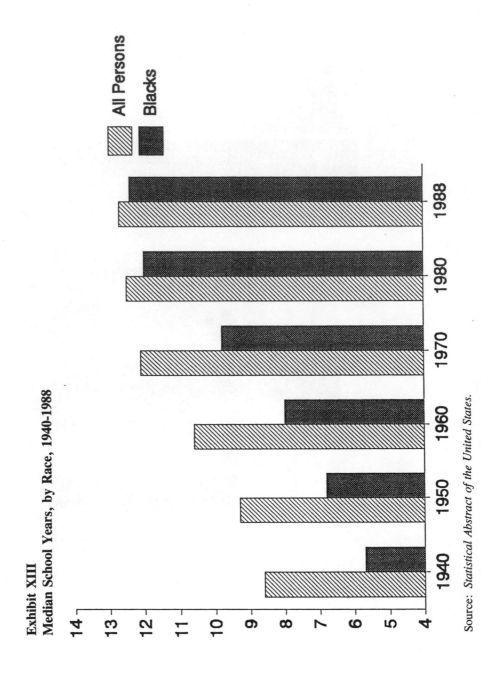

Source: *Statistical Abstract of the United States.*

Exhibit XIV
**Voter Registration in Eleven Southern States,
1964, 1980, and 1986***

Percent

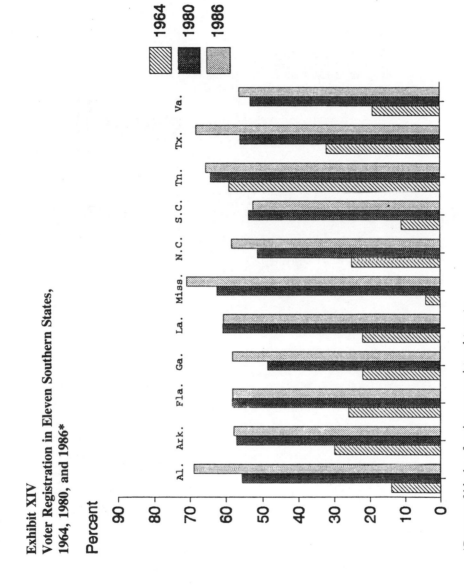

1964
1980
1986

*Percent of blacks of voting age registered to vote.

Source: *The Common Destiny; Statistical Abstract of the United States.*

Exhibit XV
Black Elected Officials, by Region, 1941-1985

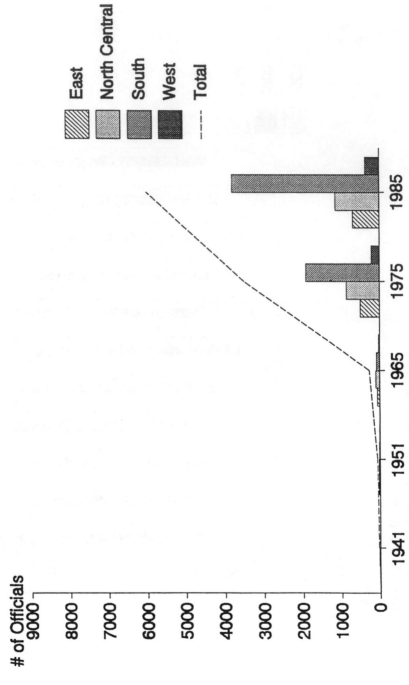

Source: *The Common Destiny; Statistical Abstract of the United States.*

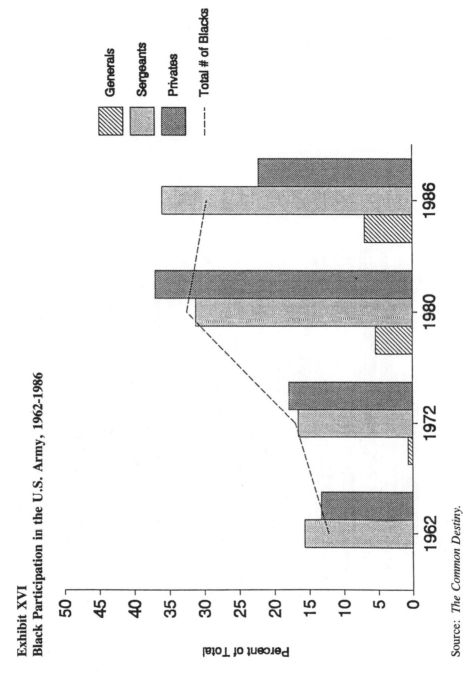

Exhibit XVI
Black Participation in the U.S. Army, 1962-1986

Generals
Sergeants
Privates
Total # of Blacks

Percent of Total

1962   1972   1980   1986

Source: *The Common Destiny*.

257

Exhibit XVII
Residential Segregation in Major Metropolitan Areas, 1960, 1970, and 1980

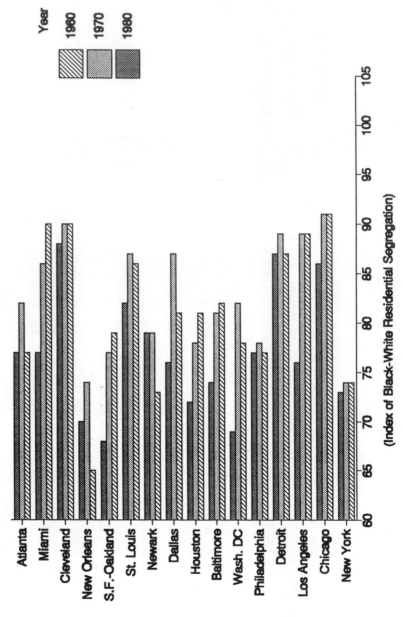

(Index of Black-White Residential Segregation)

Source: *The Common Destiny.*

258

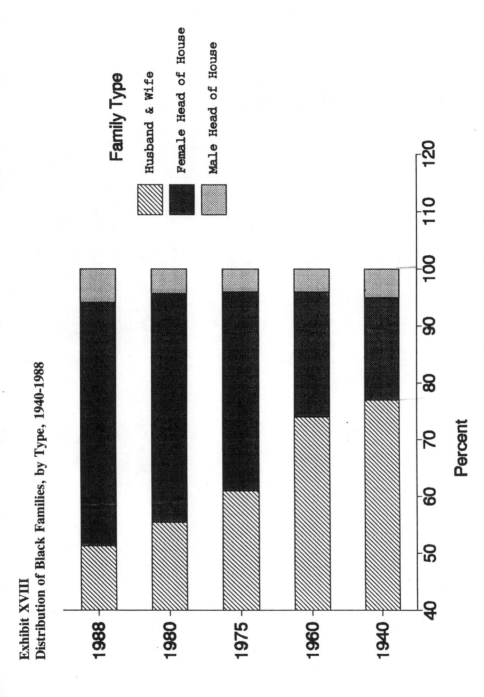

Exhibit XVIII
Distribution of Black Families, by Type, 1940-1988

Family Type

Husband & Wife

Female Head of House

Male Head of House

Percent

Source: U.S. Department of Commerce; *Current Population Reports*, Series P-23, no. 80.

Exhibit XIX

Homicide Rates, by Race and Sex, 1960-1987

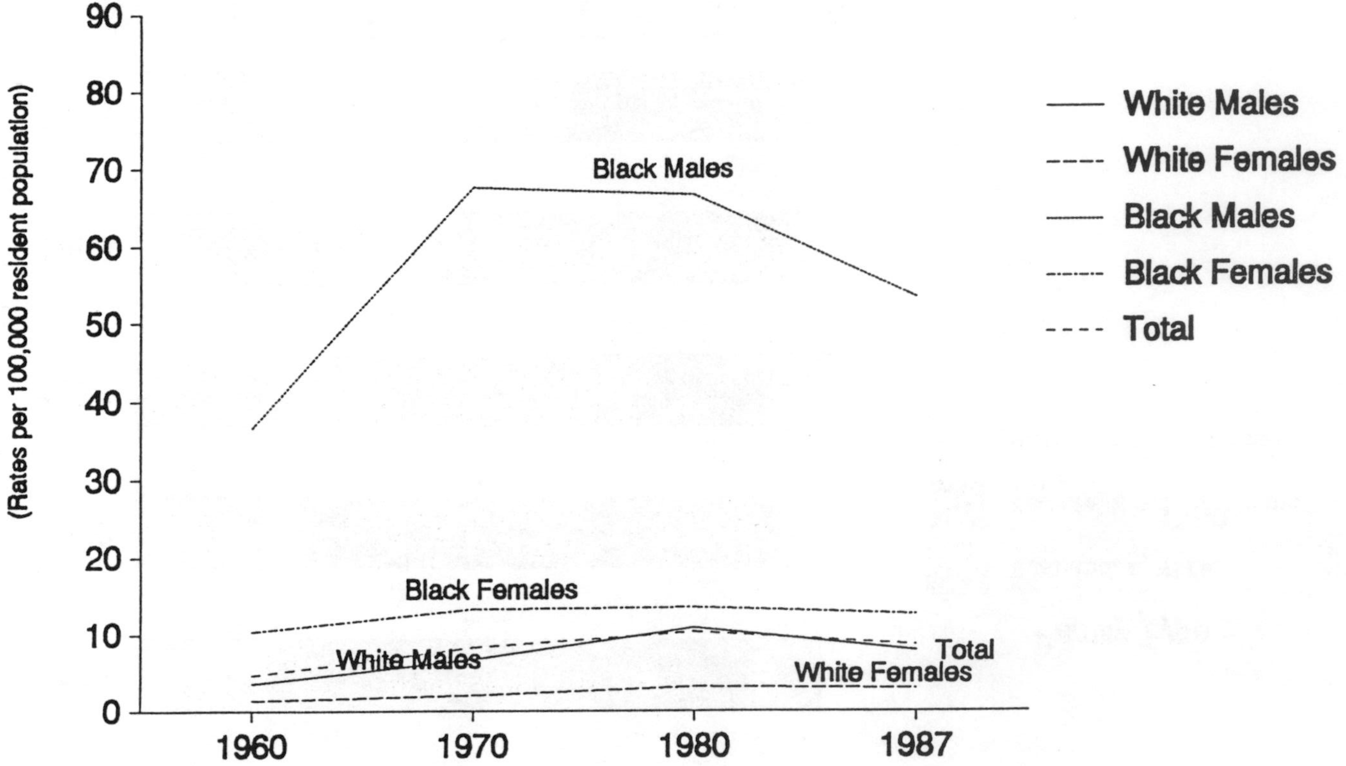

Legend:
— White Males
--- White Females
— Black Males
-·- Black Females
--- Total

(Rates per 100,000 resident population)

1960   1970   1980   1987

90 80 70 60 50 40 30 20 10 0

Black Males

Black Females

White Males

Total

White Females

Source: *Statistical Abstract of the United States; Current Population Reports*, Series P-23, no. 159.

Exhibit XX

School Segregation: Percentage of Blacks in Minority Schools, 1968 and 1980

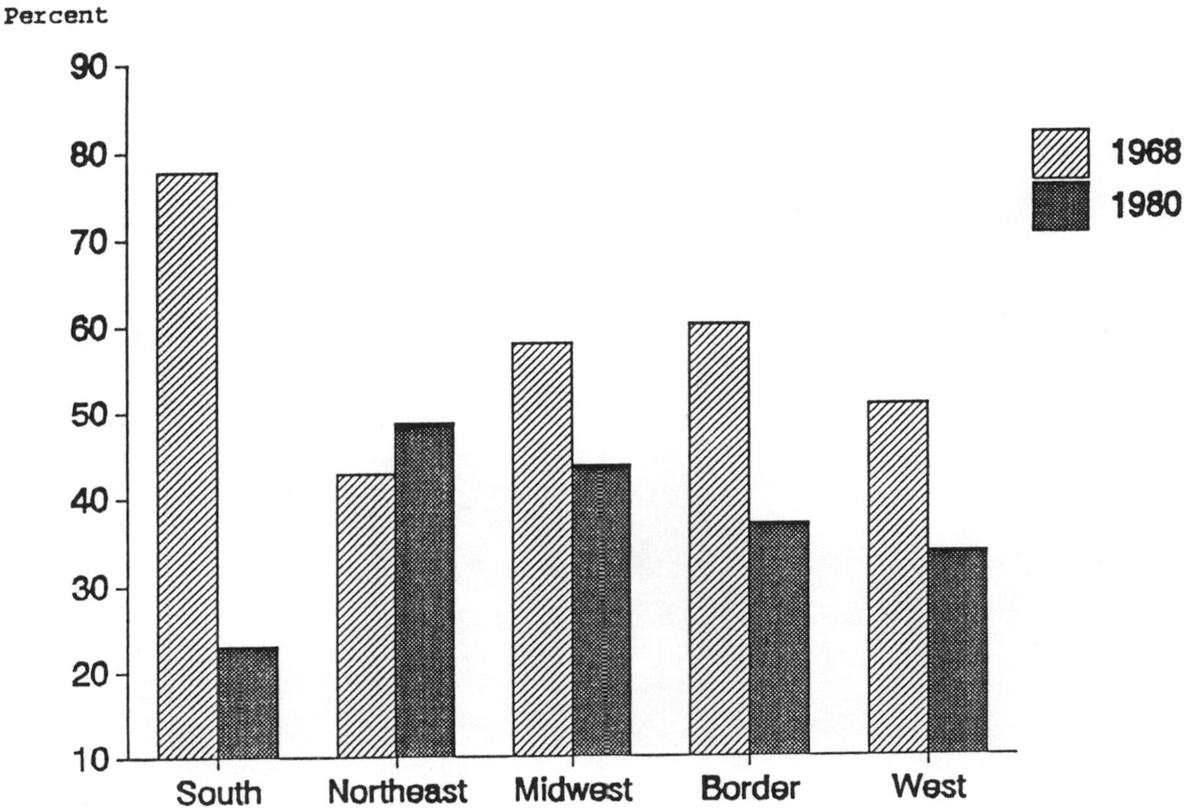

Percent

1968
1980

Source: U.S. Department of Education.

SUGGESTED READINGS

The modern civil rights movement has been a field of immense interest and output. Full citations for each of the documents are included in the text and these citations are intended to serve as a guide to some of the best firsthand accounts of the movement. Suggestions for further readings on a variety of subjects follows.

Background material can be found in: C. Vann Woodward, *The Strange Career of Jim Crow* (New York: Oxford, 1974); John Hope Franklin, *From Slavery to Freedom* (New York: Alfred Knopf, 1947); Harvard Sitkoff, *A New Deal for Blacks* (New York: Oxford, 1978); Donald McCoy and Richard T. Reuten, *Quest and Response: Minority Rights and the Truman Administration* (Lawrence: University of Kansas Press, 1973); and Aldon D. Morris, *The Origins of the Civil Rights Movement* (New York: Free Press, 1984). A plethora of works on the modern civil rights movement exist, from Anthony Lewis and The New York Times, *Portrait of a Decade* (New York: Random House, 1964) to Robert Weisbrot, *Freedom Bound* (New York: Norton, 1990). Two very well-written general studies are: Juan Williams, *Eyes on the Prize* (New York: Viking, 1987) and Harvard Sitkoff, *The Struggle for Black Equality* (New York: Hill & Wang, 1981). More analytical works are Manning Marable, *Race, Reform and Rebellion* (Jackson: University Press of Mississippi, 1984) and David R. Goldfield, *Black, White and Southern* (Baton Rouge: Louisiana State University Press, 1990). The best collection of essays is: Charles Eagles, ed., *The Civil Rights Movement in America* (Jackson: University Press of Mississippi, 1986). Two excellent oral histories are: Henry Hampton and Steve Fayer, eds., *Voices of Freedom* (New York: Bantam, 1990) and Howell Raines, *My Soul Is Rested* (New York: Penguin, 1983).

Scholars and independent journalists have written many fine biographies and institutional histories. Especially rewarding are: Taylor Branch, *Parting the Waters: America in the King Years, 1954-1963* (New York: Simon & Schuster, 1988); David J. Garrow, *Bearing the Cross: Martin Luther King, Jr. and the Southern Christian Leadership Conference* (New York: William Morrow, 1986); Clayborne Carson, *In Struggle: SNCC and the Black Awakening of the 1960s* (Cambridge: Harvard University Press, 1981); and August Meier and Elliot Rudwick, *CORE* (Urbana: University of Illinois Press, 1975). Also see: David L. Lewis, *King: A Critical Biography* (New York: Praeger, 1970); Peter Goldman, *The Death and Life of Malcolm X*, 2nd ed. (Urbana: University of Illinois Press, 1979); Howard Zinn, *SNCC: The New Abolitionists*, 2nd ed. (Boston: Beacon, 1965); Genna Rae McNeil, *Groundwork: Charles Hamilton Houston and the Struggle for Civil Rights* (Philadelphia: University of Pennsylvania Press, 1983); and Nancy J. Weiss, *Whitney M. Young, Jr. and the Struggle for Civil Rights* (Princeton: Princeton University Press, 1989).

Books that examine the relationship between the civil rights movement, the courts, or the presidency include: Carl M. Brauer, *John F. Kennedy and the Second Reconstruction* (New York: Columbia University Press, 1977); Robert F. Burk, *The Eisenhower Administration and Black Civil Rights* (Knoxville: University of Tennessee Press, 1984); Richard Kluger, *Simple Justice* (New York: Alfred Knopf, 1975); Raymond Wolters, *The Burden of Brown* (Knoxville: University of Tennessee Press, 1984); and Jack Bass, *Unlikely Heroes* (New York: Simon & Schuster, 1981). On the political gains of the civil rights movement and the process whereby new policies were developed, see: Charles Whalen and Barbara Whalen, *The Long Debate* (New York: Mentor, 1985); Hugh D. Graham, *The Civil Rights Era: Origins and Development of a National Policy, 1960-1965* (New York: Oxford, 1990); Pat Watters and Reese Cleghorn, *Climbing Jacob's Ladder: The Arrival of Negroes in Southern Politics* (New York: Harcourt, Brace, 1967); Stephen Lawson, *Black Ballots* (New York: Columbia University Press, 1976); Stephen Lawson, *Running for Freedom* (New York: McGraw-Hill, 1991); Frank Parker, *Black Votes Count: Political Empowerment in Mississippi after 1965* (Chapel Hill: University of North Carolina Press, 1990); Douglas McAdam, *Political Process and the Development of Black Insurgency, 1930-1970* (Chicago: University of Chicago Press, 1982); and Herbert Haines, *Black Radicals and the Civil Rights Mainstream, 1954-1970* (Knoxville: University of Tennessee Press, 1988).

Examinations of specific protests and communities range from, William Chafe, *Civilities and Civil Rights: Greensboro, North Carolina and the Black Struggle* (New York: Oxford, 1980) to David J. Garrow, *Protest at Selma* (New Haven: Yale University Press, 1978). On Mississippi see, James Silver, *Mississippi: The Closed Society* (New York: Harcourt Brace & World, 1968); Len Holt, *The Summer That Didn't End* (New York: William Morrow, 1965); William McCord, *Mississippi: The Long Hot Summer* (New York: Norton, 1965); and Doug McAdam, *Freedom Summer* (New York: Oxford, 1988). Two additional community studies are: Robert J. Norell, *Reaping the Whirlwind: The Civil Rights Movement in Tuskegee* (New York: Alfred Knopf, 1985) and David Colburn, *Racial Change and Community Crisis: St. Augustine, Florida, 1877-1980* (New York: Columbia University Press, 1985).

The civil rights movement encountered numerous forms of resistance, part of which is covered by Numan V. Bartley, *The Rise of Massive Resistance: Race & Politics in the South During the 1950s* (Baton Rouge: Louisiana State University Press, 1969) and by Neil R. McMillen, *The Citizens' Council* (Urbana: University of Illinois Press, 1971). On the FBI see, David J. Garrow, *The FBI and Martin Luther King Jr.* (New York: Norton, 1981) and Kenneth O'Reilly, *Racial Matters: The FBI's Secret File on Black America, 1960-1972* (New York: Free Press, 1972). Retrospective examinations of the urban disorders of the mid-1960s are still few in number. Two that have been written are: Sidney Fine, *Violence in the Model City: The Cavanaugh Administration, Race Relations and The Detroit Riot of 1967* (Ann Arbor: University of Michigan Press, 1989) and Tom Wicker, *A Time to Die* (New York: Quadrangle, 1975). On the relationship between the civil rights movement and the women's movement see, Sara Evans, *Personal Politics: The Roots of Women's Liberation in the Civil Rights Movement and the New Left* (New York: Alfred Knopf, 1979). On blacks and the Vietnam War see: Clyde Taylor, ed., *Vietnam and Black America* (Garden City, N.Y.: Doubleday, 1973).

Several comprehensive examinations of the status of blacks in recent America are: William Julius Wilson, *The Truly Disadvantaged* (Chicago: University of Chicago Press, 1987); Fred Harris and Roger Wilkins, *Quiet Riots: Race and Poverty in the U.S.: The Kerner Report Twenty Years Later* (New York: Pantheon, 1988); Gerald D. Jaynes and Robin M. Williams, eds., *Common Destiny: Blacks and American Society* (Washington, D.C.: National Academy Press, 1989); and Reynolds Farley and Walter R. Allen, *The Color Line and the Quality of Life in America* (New York: Oxford, 1987). In addition to this book, other collections of documents include: Joanne Grant, ed., *Black Protest* (New York: Fawcett, 1968); Albert Blaustein and Robert Zangrando, eds., *Civil Rights and Black America* (New York: Simon & Schuster, 1968); and August Meier, Elliot Rudwick, and Francis L. Broderick, *Black Protest in the Twentieth Century*, 2nd ed. (Indianapolis: Bobbs-Merrill, 1971).

INDEX

About the Editor

PETER B. LEVY is assistant professor of history at York College in Pennsylvania. He is the author of *The New Left and Labor in America, 1960-1972* (forth-
coming), and has written chapters in a number of journals.